D0204763

Praise for Dick Cave[tt]

"One of the best and wittiest conversationalists." —Groucho Marx

"A true sophisticate with daunting intellectual range." —Clive James

Praise for *Talk Show*

"For Cavett fans old, young, and yet-to-be, *Talk Show* is an inviting compilation . . . in his singularly exquisite and charming style. . . . Readers get a behind-the-scenes, on-the-sets, and inside-the-dressing-rooms view of the who's who of the past seventy-five years."
—*The Washington Times*

"Cavett's reflections recall a not-so-distant past when America still had a common cultural currency, and fame was something worth having, and worth cozying up to." —*The Boston Globe*

"Engrossing . . . [Many] felt when tuning in to his provocative programs as if a mind had entered in the wasteland. And a wit as well."
—*The Post and Courier* (Charleston, South Carolina)

"*Talk Show* chronicles [Cavett's] most memorable moments from his time as a host. And given that the man's interview history reads like a who's who of the most influential figures of the twentieth century (featuring Katherine Hepburn, Norman Mailer, Bobby Fischer, and John and Yoko, to name a few), it's no wonder he has some hilarious and insightful tales to tell." —*TV.com*

"Breezy, incisive, and amusing—nice to have you back, Dick."
—*Kirkus Reviews*

"In his beguiling profiles of celebrities . . . Cavett proves himself a solid writer as well as a talker." —*Publishers Weekly*

Also by Dick Cavett

Eye on Cavett
(with Christopher Porterfield)

Cavett
(with Christopher Porterfield)

TALK SHOW

CONFRONTATIONS, POINTED COMMENTARY, AND OFF-SCREEN SECRETS

DICK CAVETT

St. Martin's Griffin
New York

TALK SHOW. Copyright © 2010 by Richard A. Cavett. All rights reserved. Printed in the United States of America. For information, address St. Martin's Press, 175 Fifth Avenue, New York, N.Y. 10010.

www.stmartins.com

The essays in this book originally appeared, in slightly different form, on the Web site of *The New York Times,* which owns the copyright jointly with the author.

Designed by Meryl Sussman Levavi

The Library of Congress has cataloged the Henry Holt edition as follows:

Cavett, Dick.
    Talk show: confrontations, pointed commentary, and off-screen secrets / Dick Cavett.
        p. cm.
    Includes index.
    ISBN 978-0-8050-9195-3
    1. Cavett, Dick. 2. Entertainers—United States—Biography. 3. Television personalities—United States—Biography. I. Title.
PN2287.C38A35 2010
791.4502'8092—dc22
[B]

2010014289

ISBN 978-0-312-61052-4 (trade paperback)

Originally published in hardcover format by Times Books, an imprint of Henry Holt and Company

First St. Martin's Griffin Edition: November 2011

10 9 8 7 6 5 4 3 2 1

To M., who knows who she is

Contents

Introduction

*D*o you want to try it?
Always a provocative question, in any context. And one containing an implicit dare.

It was an inquiry from the *New York Times* about writing an opinion column, online. The phrase "penal servitude" leapt to mind, spoken by a friend who was driven just short of the madhouse by agreeing to turn out a punishing number of newspaper columns at painfully close intervals. Increasing insomnia and alcohol intake forced him to quit and take up gardening.

Given pause by his experience, I asked how often. Two a week. This sounded deceptively easy, having endured and survived the writing of five-days-a-week monologue material for Jack Paar, Johnny Carson, and Merv Griffin for years.

Not wishing to appear gutless (to myself), I decided to accept the challenge. And it was only for the month of February.

Most anybody, I should think, has at least eight interesting subjects inside him. Hadn't a famous writer—Graham Greene, perhaps—said anyone who has reached the age of twenty-five has material in him for at least four novels? I used to quote that when my book *Cavett* was published and I was asked by interviewers if age thirty-seven wasn't a little early for an autobiography.

The first few columns came easily. The fourth, harder. At five I sensed desperation, but managed to squeeze out the remaining three. I had done it and, in fact, found it surprisingly enjoyable.

Once they were completed, looking back on that first eight seemed like a piece of angel food cake, and I was glad to have added "journalist" to my image. Then the *Times* proposed that I sign on for a year. I began to sweat. A whole year.

The order, now, was down to one a week. In my dreams, the number 52 began to occur, made of concrete four stories high and marching toward me. A man I consider a real writer said, "I don't envy you. I tried thirty columns a year once and nearly perished." Was this going to kill me?

I couldn't think what the next column would be, let alone the required string of them, stretching far into the future. What else did I know? I felt written out.

Somehow, after three years, I'm still at it. Looking at that fact, like Shakespeare's Hermia, I am amazed and know not what to say.

Early on, I learned one thing. Writing lines to be spoken by famous comedians and writing for John (and Jane) Q. Public requires different sets of muscles.

Writing for Groucho Marx, or Johnny Carson, or Jack Benny, or any comic with a strong, familiar voice requires being able to turn them on in your head, so that what comes out is in their words and nobody else's. A misplaced or omitted *certainly* or *at any rate* or *y'know* will make the line wrong. For them. "You could have fooled me" is less Groucho than "Well, you certainly could have fooled me."

When Groucho guest-hosted *The Tonight Show* way back, the first laugh I got for him was an aside I wrote: "But enough of this bridled hilarity . . ." In Groucho's voice it got a laugh well out of proportion to its merits.

I found it relatively easy to write for others. It's not always easy to identify your own voice. It comes with time.

Before I ever sat down and tried to host a talk show, I had a call from Jack Paar. He had given me my first job as a comedy writer when I was still in my early twenties.

Jack was a hero of mine, more of an obsession really, and I rarely missed *The Tonight Show* when he was its host. When I got the job writing for Jack I thought that if there is a heaven, it will be an anticlimax. The fact that I was handsomely paid—think of it, $360 a week, and every week—barely occurred to me. I was there. On the inside of

The Tonight Show. I watched the show as it was taped every night and then watched it again at home.

I think Jack sensed my obsession. He called me aside one night after the show and said, "Kid, you shouldn't hang around here through the show. It'll ruin your life. Go home." After that I watched the show from a part of the studio where he couldn't see me.

Years passed and the chance for me to host a talk show came along. This had never, ever been my ambition. My highest goal in this regard was to some day, maybe, be a guest on talk shows. Hosting was not even a dream. That was for the giants of my time: Steve Allen, Jack, and Johnny.

When the non-dream came true and I was about to do my own show, a call came from Jack. It bore the single best piece of advice I or anyone doing such a show could get: "Kid, I've only got one piece of counseling for you. Don't do interviews."

What could Jack mean? To do the whole show myself? Show movies? Read to the viewers? That exciting, nervous, famous voice continued: "I mean don't just do interviews, pal. You know. 'Interview' smacks of Q-and-A and David Frost and his clipboard and 'What's your favorite color?' and crap like 'most embarrassing moments.' Don't do any of that. Make it a conversation."

In a way, it's the whole secret. Conversation is when people simply talk; not take a test on the air with Q-and-A. It's when something said spontaneously prompts a thought and a reply in someone else. When several people's talk moves around a subject, changes directions, and produces spontaneous and entertaining comments and unexpected insights, and takes surprising turns.

How right he was. You could do a whole good show without that tired old "Let me ask you this . . ."

Feel free to pass this on to anyone about to do a talk show.

A conversation does not have to be scintillating in order to be memorable. I once met a president of the United States, and his second sentence to me was about knees.

Back when I was still *persona grata* at the Nixon White House—a period of time that proved of short duration—I met Richard Nixon in a reception line. It so happened that on a recent trip to England, Nixon had been told that the greatest Hamlet yet was Nicol Williamson, currently playing the Dane on the London stage. But duty called in Washington, and Nixon had to return without seeing the play; so he invited Williamson for an evening of Shakespeare at the White House. Somehow, I was invited.

Tuxedoed, I moved along the reception line until I was nose-to-nose with the president.

NIXON: Who's doing your show tonight?
CAVETT: Joe Namath.
NIXON (*with a look of solemn concern*): How are his knees?

Part of the psychological makeup of Yorba Linda's most famous native son was his obsession with masculinity. *So-and-so was a real man,* he would say. And real men knew football.

It would not be long before I stopped receiving invitations to the White House. My lack of popularity with the Great Unindicted Co-conspirator came when I testified for John Lennon—after he and Yoko Ono had been twice on my ABC show—to support the case that John should not be deported by the Nixon administration. On one of the Nixon tapes, the president's henchman and lickspittle H. R. Haldeman can be heard educating his boss—who was minimally knowledgeable of popular culture—about Lennon's vast popularity, with the words "This guy could sway an election."

It was not long ago that I learned of another Nixon tape, on which the president can be heard saying to Haldeman, "Cavett—How can we screw him?" A little disconcerting to hear yourself thus discussed by the leader of the allegedly free world. (Doubters may yet find this on YouTube.)

It was not long thereafter that my entire staff was tax audited, all but ruinously for some of them. Nixon enjoyed using the IRS—illegally, of course—to punish those his paranoia perceived as enemies.

I wrote several columns on Nixon, and some readers didn't like my assertion that he was surely the most intelligent president we had among quite a few before and after him. When Nixon was still a practicing lawyer, a friend of mine saw him present arguments before the Supreme Court and said the range of his intellect was dazzling.

His authentic accomplishments—the opening to China, the War on Cancer, and more—have to be acknowledged. Had effective psychiatry, perhaps, gotten the Nixon demons under control before he became president, he might well have been remembered as a great one, rather than as a disgraceful criminal. A tragic waste?

But imperfect chief executives serve one purpose: they are manna to comedy writers. Jon Stewart's head writer on *The Daily Show* confessed on the Emmys that once George W. Bush left office, they really had nothing to say.

Our recently departed president provided great material for me in the early days of my column. One such instance was when we saw those clips of Bush doing a soft-shoe at the White House while the young Americans he had sent to die in Iraq continued to arrive in their coffins at Dover Air Force Base, where photography was forbidden by the White House. Once dead, our heroes were an embarrassment.

In my column about the little dance by the commander in chief, I referred to our leader as a capering loon. Many loved it.

Lots of readers commented on the *New York Times* Web site that they enjoyed my various efforts to say in written words what it felt like to sit next to certain iconic figures. It's the phenomenon known variously as charisma, star quality, and personal magnetism.

Being next to the chess master Bobby Fischer, I swear you could feel the force of an IQ flirting with 200.

Sitting next to Orson Welles, I could feel in my chair the vibrating majesty of that voice. And, of course, the monumental personality.

Other felt things: Katharine Hepburn's surging energy and intelligence; Richard Burton's poetic articulacy and glowing charisma; Bette Davis's stinging humor and unflappable poise.

Without peer in my book stands the sparkling genius of Groucho Marx. Sitting next to him, I was struck with the delightful fact that he heard his witty remarks and answers at the same time we did. I need to make this point clear. He didn't think of funny things first and then say them. They were reflexive, almost unconscious responses, and it was fun to see his surprised enjoyment of them at the same moment as ours.

Groucho was our major comic genius. That's just a fact, not an opinion.

An irritation lurks in the rereading of things you wrote some time ago. You find you originally chose the wrong word. Not entirely wrong, but one not as good as one you think of now.

Wrong-word fans will love reading my favorite essay on writing. Not by me but by Mark Twain. It can be found online and it's called "Fenimore Cooper's Literary Offenses." It's educational and hilarious, and I read it once a year. In one long paragraph, Mr. Clemens cites dozens of examples of how the author of *The Last of the Mohicans* almost invariably chose a clunker instead of the *mot juste*. It will make you laugh and improve your writing.

Nothing prepared me for the popularity of the very first piece I wrote for the *Times*, "It's Only Language." It's about the abuses of our mother tongue by all of us and particularly those in high places: Donald Rumsfeld's *mis-CHEEVY-us;* the creeping *anti-se-MET-ic; loathe* for *loath; flaunt* for *flout*—and of course a certain former president's inability to master perhaps the most important word in his limited vocabulary: *NUKE-you-lur,* for God's sake! And I've just about given up on *lay* for *lie* in even, um, the greatest newspapers. (Note plural.)

You will, I hope, get a kick or two out of these sweated-out pieces. Seeing them collected, I'm surprised at the wide range of subjects. Not just Nixon, but Bill Buckley, Paul Newman, John Cheever and John Updike on a show together, coincidences beyond belief, multiple Groucho, Johnny Carson, the art of a great magician (Slydini), and nostalgic childhood memories, pleasant and painful.

When you have completed your reading, compare and contrast with your other reading this term. And have your paper on my desk by Friday.

TALK SHOW

It's Only Language

Being the offspring of English teachers is a mixed blessing. When the film star says to you, on the air, "It was a perfect script for she and I," inside your head you hear, in the sarcastic voice of your late father, "Perfect for she, eh? And perfect for I, also?"

In these days of just about enough perils facing our nation, there is plenty of evidence around to conclude that our grip on our glorious language may be loosening. And the Bush administration, as in other matters, has not been among the good guys. Let's get everybody's favorite example out of the way. The leader of the free world's goofy inability to pronounce what is arguably the most important word in his vocabulary: "nuclear." What is so hard? A schoolkid botching it Bush's way—*NUKE-you-lur*—would have to stand in the corner. Fortunately, an oval office has no corners.

(Does Bush's atom have a *NUKE-you-luss*? Does it work in reverse? Is Bush's railway a *foo-NICK-lee-ur*? Let's bet.)

Andy Rooney tried to nail this matter on *60 Minutes*. Andy wondered as I do why the literate Laura doesn't do something. Every time the president commits this illiteracy, she must wince along with the rest of the world. Bush's "the French have no word for *entrepreneur*" is guaranteed immortality.

The French make fun of him, of course and, by extension, of us. I say let's irk them back by continuing with our clanging mispronunciations of their sacred tongue, such as *Vichy-SWA, coo-de-GRAH*, or *double enten-DRAY*—and best of all what we did to the French *chaise longue*, dyslexically turning *longue* (long) into "lounge" and *chaise* (chair) into "chase." A fox hunter's chair, perhaps? (Let Froggy puzzle it out.)

I think we're just stuck with the president's individualist English.

This is the man who gave us "I know how hard it is to put food on your family," and who told Brian Williams, regarding his alleged Camus studies, "I have an eckalectic reading list." Until he was nice enough to repeat it, I was sure he had said "epileptic," which at least would have been a word. I prefer the three-syllable version "eclectic," but then he *is* the Decider.

Donald Rumsfeld and about half of his military pals seem to feel that hidden weapons are found in a *cash-AY* (*cache*: from Fr., hiding place; pron. *kash*), provoking further giggles from our busy French detractors. The cashiered secretary of defense is equally hard on his own language, as with, "It wasn't wrong. It was just *mis-CHEEVY-us*." *MIS-chuh-vuss* is of course what he was after. Oh, and with all due respect, Mr. Erstwhile Secretary, a medal can be called a memento, but not a MO-mento. Princeton, class of what again?

Getting a little thing like words right, is it so important?

The right answer is: yes. As when poorly worded road signs cause fatalities. Sloppy language leads to sloppy thought, and sloppy thought to sloppy legislation. And why not a sloppy war? What if someone big, issuing an order of earthshaking potential, made the (tiny) error of confusing the last letters of Iraq and Iran?

Another whole category of language abuse is the stating of untruths which, when shown to be untrue, are repeated. As in Dick Cheney, the man who said to Wolf Blitzer, "We've had immense successes in Iraq," adding, "and we will have more immense successes." Blitzer looked, well, blitzed. Instead of lowering a large butterfly net over his guest, he got his breath and, charitably, did not request examples. And what of Condoleezza Rice? The same Condi who was willing to contribute "a mushroom cloud" to the Scare America campaign now insists that an escalation be called an "augmentation." What, in her new teatime vocabulary, would she call the WMD that caused the cloud? An "Instrument of Considerable Inconvenience"? What are the war dead in her sanitized lexicon? "The indisposed"? Or simply "those whose coffins may not be photographed"? Once dead, our brave soldiers are an embarrassment.

Incidentally, are Jews still Semites? Or are they suddenly "Semets"?

For years now the boo-boo *anti-se-MET-ic* has gained ground, even among rabbis, as well as TV talking heads, big-name news people, and the literati. Where did it come from? Listen for it. Try the Sunday morning shows for a likely catch.

And what about the various distortions of the easy word "heinous"? From lawyers especially you get *hayney-us*, *heeny-us*, and even *highness*. Look, guys and gals, it's easy. It rhymes with a well-known two-syllable word which some might consider not nice, but I guarantee will stick the correct pronunciation in your brain, especially if you compose a silly rhyming couplet. ("His behavior was heinous / And . . ." etcetera—which, by the way, is not pronounced *ECK-cetera*.)

And then there's the poor little *kudo*. It's a word *Variety* has used incorrectly—as in "De Niro received many kudos for his performance"—for enough decades that it is now forgotten that *kudos* (Greek for "praise") was already singular. There never was a *kudo*. Will *Variety* eventually take the word *pathos* and extract a *patho*? Stay tuned.

Last week during hearings, at least two of our star-spangled generals spoke of a *dim-you-nition* (diminution, perhaps?) of troops. Does ammunition then become *ama-nyoo-shun*? Let it pass.

It's gotten so bad for *lie* and *lay* that if a candidate got the votes of only those who don't know the difference, it would be a landslide. Upon hearing "He was outside laying on the lawn," I remember being glad my dad thought I was worldly enough to get it when he asked, "And who was the lucky lady underneath him?" Wouldn't anybody just know you wouldn't "lie it on the table"? Try playing it as it lies. It works just as well.

When the flight attendant would say, "We will be landing in Chicago momentarily," I used to enjoy replying, "Will there be time to get off?" But I see the forces of darkness have prevailed, and this and many wrong uses are now deemed acceptable by the alleged guardians of our language, the too quickly supine dictionary makers. Are they afraid of being judged "not with it"? What ever happened to "Everybody does it don't make it right"?

Certain misquotes are rooted in marble. It would take another act of Creation to restore "gild the lily" to Will Shakespeare's "paint the lily." ("To gild refinèd gold, to paint the lily.") There are hundreds of these. And there's "The senator *literally* exploded with laughter." Who cleaned up the mess?

Then there is that common ailment the tin ear, and its possessor's knack for rendering sublime quotations drab, often through insensitivity to the music of the words and their proper order. A good example is the great but frequently wounded quote of Mark Twain's on writing, a quote that causes, when done right, my forearms to horripilate.

Here it is: "The difference between the almost right word and the right word is the difference between the lightning bug . . . and the lightning."

Recently, an after-dinner speaker botched it. He got all the words in, but not in the master's order, ending with "the lightning and the lightning bug." I had to go out and walk around awhile. Word order is everything. Anyone who doesn't *hear* that it's imperative to end with the majestic word "lightning" would probably argue that nothing's wrong with *The Sierra Madre's Treasure*, Milton's *Lost Paradise*, *The Opera's Phantom*, *Music's Sound*, *The Sea and the Old Man*, and, who knows, *The Island of Gilligan*. (Have I beaten the point to death yet?)

(Let us note: the hapless speaker was at the DAY-us—dais—not the DYE-us.)

But let's be charitable. I soon learned it isn't necessary to correct. I quickly learned to bite my English teachers' boy's tongue and let a lady guest refer to an "elicit" affair. But if I ever find myself once again with the senator who spoke of his "incredulous" experiences, I shall pop him one.

I don't see the future as bright, language-wise. I see it as a glass half empty—and evaporating quickly. Almost daily irritants, like the dumb cluck's beloved "between you and I," will never be expunged, it seems. *Loathe* and *loath* will continue to change places, and *phenomena* and *phenomenon* will still be used interchangeably. But, finally, what the hell? It's only language. It's only what we live by.

A POSTSCRIPT: *Astute readers (two so far) subsequently informed me that President Bush's alleged "The French have no word for* entrepreneur" *is a bogus, made-up, fallacious invention. Although I still like it, I'm sorry if I victimized my readers with a fake artifact. And I owe Mr. Bush an apology, too, although hardly the size of the one he owes us.*

FEBRUARY 4, 2007

Ghost Stories

Why are people afraid of ghosts? "Ooh, no, I wouldn't want to see one! I'd be too scared"—accompanied by a tremolo of fear in the voice—is the common reaction. This puzzles me. I'd think anyone would welcome the opportunity. I've never heard of a ghost hurting anybody. In the main, ghosts are said to be forlorn and generally miserable, if not downright depressed. The jolly ghost is rare. In most reports they just sort of hang there in place, saying none of the things we would love to hear from them. And those who do speak have yet to say anything interesting.

This is a shame, since ghosts embody—pardon the expression—the main question facing us all: does something of us survive death? If they are in fact there, then the answer is yes.

I have never been converted to or even had much interest in spiritualism, occultism, Swedenborgianism, or any particular religion. And I never, except occasionally for a laugh, visit the quacks who call themselves psychics. (The chances of any psychic paying off are about equal to those of winning the lottery. Orson Welles told me how the alleged psychics have a collection of so-called cold reading dodges like "You have a scar on your knee." "Wow!" goes the sucker. But nearly everyone has one from childhood.)

I'm not an atheist exactly but remain what you might call "suggestible." (Is there a category of almost-atheist? A person who does not have the courage of his nonconvictions? I guess Woody Allen has, as so often, had the ultimate comic word on the subject. "You cannot prove the nonexistence of God; you just have to take it on faith.")

I can, with a little effort, like people who buy into screwy beliefs and cults, as long as no blood is involved. I confess I do have to remind myself almost daily that there are people on this earth capable of reading, writing, eating, and dressing themselves who believe their lives are ruled from billions of miles away, *by the stars*—and, of course, the planets. I don't scorn such people (exactly); it must be damned pleasant to think the wrong turns and heartbreaks in your life aren't entirely your own dumb fault but, partially at least, the doings of those great hulking clinkers, way up in the sky, which somehow take a personal interest in your doings. I can be tolerant.

Many years ago, Groucho Marx (Must I identify him for the young among us? I refuse. Look him up.) and his brothers (the real Fab Four) were playing a vaudeville house in Chicago. Groucho could always go unrecognized in public, thanks to the painted-on mustache he wore onstage. This allowed him to, as he put it, "go anywhere and mingle with the common man in all his dreariness." Back then, there was a prominent trance medium holding forth, and her devoted disciples (sometimes spelled s-u-c-k-e-r-s) solemnly offered to take the man born Julius Marx with them to a séance. Always intellectually curious, Groucho was glad to be asked along—though he told me he was "vaguely insulted" when his new friends solemnly cautioned him to show the proper reverence. "I'm not a clown twenty-four hours," he said. "I can also be serious."

The séance was held in the darkened parlor of some wealthy believer's apartment. Groucho reported a heavy air of sanctity about the place, "and not entirely from the incense." Lights were low and the faithful conversed in hushed tones. The medium began to chant unintelligibly, and then to emit a strange humming sound (I can't help seeing her as Margaret Dumont), eventually achieving her trance state. "I am in touch, I am in touch with the Other Side," she intoned. "Does anyone have a question?"

Groucho arose and asked, "What is the capital of North Dakota?"

He recalled being chased for several blocks, but escaped injury.

Trance mediums (surely not "media") flourished in this country well into the twentieth century, and there may be a straggling handful even today, socking away a sizable nest egg from the gullible before being escorted to the city limits.

The highly neurotic yet fearless Harry Houdini spent the latter part of his truncated life exposing prominent mediums and their use of magicians' artifices to convince clients they had pierced the veil. The great Houdini was a pathological mama's boy, and his motivation was mixed; he acted not only to ruthlessly expose frauds but also, friends said, in the forlorn and secret hope that he might unearth a genuine medium and thus resume relations with beloved Ma.

Believers in this field are not all dummies. Or at least not dummies in other areas. The great Sir Arthur Conan Doyle entreated his friend Harry repeatedly to confess that some of his magic—especially his astounding escapes—could be accomplished only with supernatural assistance, specifically by dematerialization. The vain and egotistical conjurer could not bear to reveal his secrets, and poor Conan Doyle hailed this as proof for his side. So ardent was the great author in his belief that he carried his conviction to the grave, if not farther. (Lady Doyle, it should be noted, was an "automatic writer," scrawling "words from beyond" while in trance.)

Hell, I just noticed that I have burst the bonds of my word limit just as I was about to say that I would love nothing more than to meet a ghost. I have three stories, each capable of producing that slight chill on the spine that is the *sine qua non* of a good ghost story. Can you wait?

FEBRUARY 7, 2007

Basil Rathbone's Mysterious Message

know, I know. I promised you several ghost stories. This curious tale requires a longer treatment than I expected. I shan't forget the others.

I have this story from none other than the great Basil Rathbone. (Sorry, youngsters. Google him or forget it.) I hope it doesn't sound too strange to confess that, even as a kid, I had a sort of crush on Rathbone. I can't detect any erotic element in it; I just wanted to look, talk, and act as he did. I was in high school, and back then I knew him only as Sherlock Holmes, but that was plenty. I was sorry to learn that he disdained those fifteen or so Holmes pictures as "my bread and butter films," preferring to be remembered as Romeo, Karenin et al. Where else would a kid my age meet Basil Rathbone but in Lincoln, Nebraska?

He was there to narrate a huge concert-drama event at the University of Nebraska, and he'd agreed to meet informally with the drama students there. I played hooky and went, of course, thinking that surely Lincoln High School would understand. (It failed to.) The event took place in the small "experimental" theater. I bulldozed my way backstage, and there he stood—not on the screen but feet from me. I sidled up to where he was chatting before going onstage. There was the inimitable voice (no impressionist has ever done him), and the first words I heard him speak were, "Of course I only made the one picture with Greta."

I can almost feel the chill now. I thought to myself, "Toto, we're not in Nebraska anymore." (But we were.) A moment later I caught, "So Norma Shearer walked by and I said, 'Norma' . . ." I don't think I knew the phrase "name-dropping," a thing I did plenty of after meeting Basil. It struck me that Basil couldn't be a name-dropper; these were the people he knew and worked with. It was his world. And oh, God, how I wanted to be part of it.

I checked out how he used his hands, when both talking and hanging them at his sides, index fingers almost pointed, the rest curled. (The London Academy of Music and Dramatic Art?) You don't want to hear about my sessions at a full-length mirror, practicing these cherished physical niceties. I treasured every overheard utterance—as in "I seem unable to conquer my fear of flying. I'm nervous as a kitten on an aeroplane." Holmes, scared? I mused.

(Is this getting to be too much for anybody? Just in case, let's get to our promised subject, the story Rathbone told me some years later, when we were both in New York.)

Rathbone was entertaining a friend one night at his home in the Hollywood Hills. Both men were keenly interested in dogs and their breeding. His friend had brought with him two handsome specimens. As it got late, the two friends had a parting drink and called it a night. The friend and the canines got into the car and drove away. But, sadly, not very far.

As Rathbone turned to go back inside, he heard the screech of brakes and the sickening sounds of a ghastly car crash. His friend and the dogs were killed instantly. In deep shock, and with the thought "He was just standing here" pounding in his aching head, he briefly viewed the nightmare crash scene. Afterward, he recalled, "I staggered back to the house in a trance, only vaguely aware of a ringing telephone." Mechanically he picked it up and heard the voice of the MGM studio's night switchboard operator. "Sorry, Mr. Rathbone, but I have a woman on the line who simply *must* talk to you. She says it's desperately, desperately important." *Probably some smitten fan*, he thought as the operator said, "Sir, I've never heard anyone be so urgent. She hopes you'll know what a certain message means."

Rathbone, impatient and in a daze, snapped, "For Christ's sake, put her on and be done with it!"

The woman was calling from her home, located way to hell and gone on the far side of Los Angeles. She had a low and cultivated speaking voice and identified herself as a trance medium and clairvoyant. At that time the movie colony was going through one of its periodic infatuations with psychics, astrologers, table-tipping séances,

Ouija boards, and such. Rathbone scorned all such claptrap but, he said, "the woman's voice was so compelling."

"I have for you, sir, what we term 'a calling of urgency,'" she said. "It came to me with such impact that, although not knowing its meaning, I simply had to find you. The message is brief. Here it is in its entirety: 'Traveling very fast. No time to say good-bye.' And then, 'There are no dogs here.'"

The next time I saw Rathbone (FYI, he lived at 135 Central Park West), more years had gone by, and he was in the act of receiving a summons for letting his dog Ginger off the leash in Central Park. I thought he might have decided, looking back, that it had all been some sort of bizarre coincidence or a highly improbable prank. But how? He said, "At the time, of course, I was quite shaken by it." And now? "I am still shaken by it."

FEBRUARY 13, 2007

Luck in the Afternoon

Groucho stories, even if you've heard them, are still good. Like the well-known story of his daughter and the restricted country club pool. Groucho: "But my daughter's only *half*-Jewish. Can she go in up to her waist?"

I have a particular fondness for the one I'm about to tell you, partly because I got it directly from Groucho. I may have told it in the 1982 documentary *The Marx Brothers in a Nutshell*.

The setting is vaudeville. The young Marx brothers had barely heard of movies and were rollicking around the country as big stage stars and enjoying the fruits of fame, one being its proven effectiveness as an aphrodisiac. "You know my brother's name is often mispronounced," Groucho would say. "My uncle [Al Shean] who named us all pronounced it 'Chicko' because of my brother's monumental success with 'chicks.' He was catnip to all women. And we were opposites in other ways, too."

They were playing somewhere in Iowa. One night while they were removing their makeup, there was a knock at the dressing room door and a middle-aged Jewish couple came in. After effusive compliments on the boys' act, the husband said, "We know you boys are Jewish, and we thought you might like to come to our house on Friday night for a traditional Jewish dinner." The invitation was accepted.

On Wednesday, Groucho and Chico were out strolling, and Chico, with his genius for numbers (and lack of it for gambling), noticed a house address. He said, "Isn't that the number of those nice people's house?" It was, and it was the house. They decided to pay a call.

They rang the bell and an attractive girl appeared. As luck (or something) would have it, there were the couple's two pretty daughters. The parents were out.

Groucho: "Thanks to Chico's skills in this area, in two shakes of a lamb's tail we were out of our clothes and in bed with the two daughters. Balancing Chico's great luck in getting us there, his ill luck dealt the next card. The bedroom door opened and there were the parents.

"Chico was more accustomed to this sort of predicament than I was, so I followed his example—which was grabbing up our clothes and hightailing it out the window. Fortunately, we were on the ground floor. In any case, the penultimate thing the parents saw were our two buck-naked rear ends disappearing over the windowsill. The *ultimate* thing they saw was Chico's head reappearing momentarily, saying, 'I hope this doesn't affect Friday night.'"

FEBRUARY 15, 2007

Jet-lagged in the South China Sea

Don't expect much here today. I am somewhere in the South China Sea, bound for Hong Kong, and am suffering from a case of jet lag that would kill an ordinary man. Thanks to New York's recent ice storm, my flight to Sydney was canceled. For no good reason, I then had to get to Australia by way of Hong Kong in order to board a ship that was bound for—you guessed it—Hong Kong. I am now the possessor of the sour fruits of a twenty-three-hour air journey and the mental consequences thereof. I am a mess.

The air journey to Australia was killing enough. Adding six more hours to it should happen only to an unrepentant surviving member of the Third Reich. Pseudosleep—for two consecutive nights—in the reputed comfort of reclining airline seats is a bummer. (Japan Airlines has the best ones. You float as if on a cloud.) Upon landing after so many hours in the air, you feel your IQ drop a good forty points. Looking for your watch on the wrong wrist is just one of the kinds of dumbness that plague the jet lag victim.

Jet lag offers those who have been spared classic depression a taste of it. You're dazed and unfocused and indifferent to all life's pleasures. And your judgment is off. Errors swarm, as just now when I looked back a line, trying to figure out if the typed word "indifferent" looks right with three *e*'s in it.

Jet lag seems to liberate my usually controllable nasty temper—the one that struck on the air on a notorious show of mine when Norman Mailer got testy and snapped, "Why don't you just read the next question off the question sheet?" Incensed, not wishing to be confused with David Frost, who did just that (I like to think of myself as a conversationalist), I replied in as gentlemanly a way as I could, "Why don't you fold it five ways and put it where the moon don't shine?" (This was often misquoted as "stick it," which would be vulgar.)

I'm sure that the toxic combination of temper and jet lag was responsible for what happened next.

Wandering in the bowels of the ship, somewhat crudely attired, I was confronted by two members of the crew who clearly disapproved of my old Levi's shirt. The large man asked in an unpleasant manner, "What are you doing down here?" "Yeah," added the large female accompanying him. (And now let's move to scriptlike dialogue, if you don't mind.)

DC (*instantly spoiling for a fight*): Doing? Until you got in my way I was walking.

HIM: Are you a passenger?

DC: I'm not a stowaway.

HIM: What are you?

DC: I'm crew. (*We entertainers on the cruise are, in fact, defined as "crew."*)

HIM: Just what do you do on the ship?

DC: You first.

HIM (*chest puffed out a little over voluminous gut*): I happen to be the chief engineer.

DC: Gee, I don't meet many celebrities.

HER: Why don't you have one of these? (*She points to her ID badge, situated on her ample* poitrine, *allowing my next unforgivable remark.*)

DC: Men don't have those.

HIM (*simmering*): Just tell us what you do.

DC: I'm an entertainer.

GRIM-VISAGED HELGA: Oh, yeah? What kind?

DC: I'm a jester, a coxcomb, a pantaloon, if you will. And now, I have wearied of our horrid little trio and shall take my leave.

I thank whatever gods may be that I refrained from saying to the voluminous chief engineer the Bard's "Dress'd in a little brief authority" or, in another style, something like "Tell me, Chief, when you step on a scale, does a card come out saying, 'Please, one at a time'?"

As I walked away, I fully expected to be cut down from behind by a well-aimed boomerang. But no, somehow I exited with my salients intact. I might add that my being an American did nothing to enhance their opinion of me; this phenomenon, I'm told, is encountered virtually everywhere. I thought of referring, while abroad, to "my uncle, Dick Cheney." (The man who sees "successes" and "good progress" in bloody disaster. Cheney would have sent General Custer a congratulatory telegram.)

Do you mind if I knock off now? Just mentioning that name has added to my desire to lie down. Did I mention trying to put on a T-shirt the way you put on trousers?

FEBRUARY 21, 2007

What My Uncle Knew About War

I was never a soldier, but God knows I wanted to be. Not in later years when my draft number came up for real, but back in my Nebraska grade-school days when Jimmy McConnell and Dickie Cavett watched John Wayne in *Sands of Iwo Jima* at least five times, one of us sneaking the other in free through the alley exit. Then we went home, got our weapons (high-caliber cap pistols), and took turns being John Wayne. The alley was Iwo Jima.

Years later I met Big John. It couldn't have been better. He was in full cowboy drag on an old Western (studio) street and mounted on his great horse Dollar. He looked exactly as he did in *She Wore a Yellow Ribbon*, and it took my breath away. I didn't just like him, I loved him. I sorta wished I hadn't liked him quite as much, so I could have asked him, "Duke, how come not you nor any of your four strapping sons ever spent one day in the armed services?" ("I'm merely asking," I might have added to lighten the tone. Or delay the concussion.)

I didn't dodge the draft, and unlike Dick Cheney I didn't have "a different agenda." I didn't have to. I had mononucleosis (imagine how the *NUKE-you-lur* president would injure *that* word in pronunciation) and, my draft board said, they had way too many guys and nothing was happening, war-wise. Sound preposterous? And yet there was such a time.

I have a statement: anybody who *gives* his life in war is an idiot.

I guess I left off the quotation marks to let the words have their full effect. They aren't mine, but I'm related to them. They're my Uncle Bill's words, and his credentials for uttering the remark are a shade better than mine.

He may well have been the sole marine to survive driving landing barges on three bloody invasions in the South Pacific. I asked an old marine vet once how rare Bill's survival was. He was gifted of speech: "I'd say survivors of what your uncle did could probably hold their reunion in a phone booth and still have room for most of Kate Smith." (We'll pause while youngsters Google.) "My guess is that your uncle is unique."

Bill said that aside from knowing that any minute was likely to be your last, the worst part of the job was having to drop the landing barge's front door so the guys could swarm out onto the beach. Despite the hail of bullets against that door, he had to drop it, knowing that the front five or six guys would be killed instantly.

The phrase Bill hated most was "gave his life." That phrase is a favorite of our windbag politicians; especially, it seems, the dimmer ones who say "Eye-rack."

"Your life isn't given," I remember him saying, "it's brutally ripped away from you. You're no good to your buddies dead, and when the bullets start pouring in you don't give a goddamn about God, country, Yale, your loved ones, the last full measure of devotion, or any other of that Legionnaire patriotic crapola. You just want you and your buddies to see at least one more sunrise."

Bill also served on land and experienced something so god-awful that he thought he would go mad: "Tom [his best friend] and I were trotting along, firing our rifles, and I turned to say something to Tom and his head was gone." (Bill had great difficulty telling this. I guess I felt honored that he had not been able to speak of it for years.) He said the worst part was that while still holding the rifle, the body, now a fountain, continued for four or five steps before falling. He hated to close his eyes at night because that ghastly horror was his dependable nightly visitor for years—like Macbeth, murdering sleep.

By sheer chance I was out on the sidewalk in front of Bill's house (we lived next door) when he arrived home from the war. I wasn't even sure it was Bill at first, he looked so much older.

I blurted, "Hey, Bill, welcome home." He was two feet from me but neither saw nor heard me. I knew the phrase current then. Bill was "shell-shocked." Not the now current "post-traumatic stress disorder" or whatever the PC-sounding phrase is today. For the first six months he was home, he slept in the yard.

You will think less of me for this, but my friend Jim and I, noticing how poor Bill jumped at sudden sounds, thought a firecracker might be in order. Bill's training kicked in by reflex. He hit the ground so fast it looked like film with frames removed. And, lacking the standard-issue shovel, he started digging with his hands. He never knew who did it. As for Jim and me, I trust that this will be deducted from our shares in paradise.

Isn't it the excellent combat chronicler Paul Fussell who gets credit for the phrase "the thousand-mile stare"? It described the look of the haggard soldiers coming back from their first battle as the eager, fresh-faced kids—which they had been a few days earlier—filed past them on their way "in." By definition, both groups were the same age, but there were no young faces in the returning group. They looked more like fathers than sons.

The other word Bill hated was "sacrifice." Sacrifice is something you give up in order to get something in return. What good are we getting from the war in Iraq? Cooked up as it was by that infamous group of neocons (accent on last syllable) who, draft-averse themselves, were willing to inflict on the (largely unprivileged) youth of this country their crack-brained scheme for causing democracy to take root and spread like kudzu throughout that bizarre and ill-understood part of the world, the Middle East.

What *service* is this great country getting out of all this tragedy, other than the certainty that historians will ask in disbelief, "Was there no one to stand up to this overweening president?"

I cringe at the icky, sentimental way the president talks about what we owe to the people of plucky little Iraq. You'd think we all grew up ending our "Now I lay me down to sleep" with "and please, Lord, be good to Iraq." They detest us now, along with just about everybody else. Personally, I don't give a damn what happens to Iraq, and don't think it's worth a single American life. Or any other kind. Haven't philosophers taught us the immorality of destroying something of infinite value—like a human life—in order to achieve a *possible* good? I guess not.

For weeks the word "cause" has rolled around in my head, attached to an elusive quote. I found it. It's from Shakespeare's *Henry V* (as distinct, I suppose, from Paris Hilton's *Henry V*), and it's the part where the king, in disguise and unrecognized, sits at a fire listening to some of his men discuss the next day's battle and what it means to be fighting in a good cause. One says, "But if the cause be not good, the king himself hath a heavy reckoning to make, when all those legs and arms and heads, chopped off in a battle, shall join together at the latter day and cry all, 'We died at such a place,' . . . their wives left poor behind . . . their children rawly left. I am afeard there are few die well that die in a battle. . . . Now, if these men do not die well, it will be a black matter for the king that led them to it."

FEBRUARY 28, 2007

An Innocent Misunderstanding

Like me, you may not get much fun out of learning that all your life you've misunderstood something important. I think you can have some fun with this. Wanna play?

Cast your mind back about a dozen years to Tonya Harding. For the newly born, she was the young skater who hired a goon acquaintance to lurch out of the shadows and whack rival skater Nancy Kerrigan in the leg. The attack effectively put Nancy out of commission and delivered to sportsmanship a black eye the size of Cleveland.

Despite all this, gritty Tonya's fanatical admirers remained loyal. On the TV news one of these ardent supporters—in this case an adenoidal female teen—gushed into a newslady's mike something like, "It's rilly awful. The papers and like everybody are rilly forgetteen about like Tonya's constitutional right to be presumed innocent until proved guilty. It's the, like, cornerstone of our democracy." (I have omitted a few "likes.")

In New York's most recent case of law officers pumping a half gross of lead into an unarmed citizen, a prosecutor, of all people who should know better, urged press and public to remind themselves of the presumption of innocence "that governs us all."

In the Enron case, a top-flight and expensively suited lawyer, a goodly, portly fellow looking a bit puffed from having walked a few yards, expressed his anger on the eleven o'clock news about a columnist who wrote something unfavorable about his client. He snorted something like, "Whatever became of the presumption of innocence?"

What do all these good folks have in common? All of them—Tonya's strident fan, the district attorney, and his tubby eminence the attorney—are all, to put it less strongly than one might, dead wrong.

The presumption of innocence has nothing to do with any of the above.

For some years I've had a kind of mini-hobby of asking lawyers and others in the legal profession where the famous "presumption of innocence" comes from. The answers are richly varied: "Hmmm, good question," "the Constitution," "the Bible," "It's a rule of law," "the Bill of Rights," "the Magna Carta," "the Kama Sutra." (He had been drinking.) All these responders were male, by the way. The two lady lawyers I asked got it right.

The frequent answer that presumption of innocence resides in the Constitution is curious. I have searched and searched for it. Assuming that my copy of the Constitution is not a Reader's Digest version, it just ain't there.

If you take up this game, you'll get a lot of "It comes from old English law," spoken with great certainty. I submit for your consideration this from a scholarly article about presumptions in law:

> Probably the most famous presumption is the presumption
> of innocence though, despite universal reverence for it, the
> maxim cannot be found in the Magna Carta, the English
> Bill of Rights of 1689, in the works of the great English
> jurists, Bracton, Coke, or Blackstone or any English case
> law prior to c.1800.

I wouldn't blame you for being annoyed at this point, wondering what, if anything, it does mean. It's been called the most misunderstood phrase in our language.

It was rife during the O. J. Simpson catastrophe. Wouldn't it be fun to know if some of the jurors who freed O.J. actually thought he *was* innocent? (I've decided that if I chance to meet the Juice at a party, I will chat amiably and then say, "If you'll excuse me, I feel the need to talk to someone who *hasn't* murdered anybody.")

Anyway, have I teased you long enough? The P. of I. has nothing whatever to do with you and me. We can talk, write, broadcast, and even put up a billboard (if so foolish) stating that the accused is the one who did it. It has to do with our system. If you find yourself accused of a crime, you do not have to prove your innocence. The burden is on the other side. The prosecution has to prove your guilt. That's about it. And it is not even a rule of law. It is a rule of *evidence*, relevant only to the judge and the jury.

I once heard an exasperated Dan Abrams, the MSNBC legal correspondent, state it simply and best: "I've had to say it before and I say it again. The presumption of innocence has no relevance outside the courtroom."

Why do you suppose so many of us have had it so wrong for so long? See if your lawyer answers correctly. If the answer is wrong, be magnanimous. Lawyers work hard and, like us, they're human, many of them. Should you feel you're losing the argument, toss in, "How come the jails are full of people awaiting trial if they're presumed innocent?"

Anyway, if you've read this far and found this interesting, go ahead and have some fun with it. Presume guilt.

MARCH 28, 2007

What Was He Thinking?

s it just me, or has the time come to get out the fool's cap, dust it off, and place it smartly on the head of John McCain?

What has happened to that man? He makes a nitwit public remark about the newly "safe" Baghdad in which General David H. Petraeus, commander of the American forces in Iraq, saunters about without a helmet. When it is learned that the general, being of sound mind, goes out with a small army of Humvees and fully armed bodyguards, McCain is embarrassed.

He backtracks and rephrases weakly, insisting that he didn't mean to say "without protection." He should have left it at that and it would now be quite forgotten. Where were his advisers?

Instead, he hops a plane to Baghdad and proceeds to stage (the operative word) what must be one of the strangest travesties in modern political history.

We at home are treated to the sight of a gregarious McCain, shopping and giggling in the marketplace—and wearing no helmet. He is, however, clad in a flak jacket. What's wrong with this picture? A man in a flak jacket selling safety?

Unseen, we learn, are a surrounding force of more than one hundred soldiers armed for action, a small fleet of Humvees, strategically placed sharpshooters, and streets blocked off for the theatrical occasion. Above are a Black Hawk and two combat helicopters. Did he think we would not find out the extent of this stunt, endangering not only the troops requisitioned for the performance but also the shopkeepers seen with him, marking them as America-friendly with the usual attendant results?

I pictured McCain as a furious movie director, chewing out his cameraman: "You goddamn idiot, you weren't supposed to show the flak jacket, the soldiers, the armed might. . . . Now I look like a consummate ass!"

Right.

What will daredevil McCain's next stunt be? Driving in a NASCAR race without a seat belt?

I've tried to think of the appropriate caption for the shot of the bare head of the smiling McCain, there in blood-soaked Baghdad. How about "What, me worry?"

(We later learn that there just happened to be an attack an uncomfortably short time later on the very spot that Knievel John and his troupe of conscripted extras just vacated.)

May we return for a moment to the absent helmet? Makes our soldiers look a little sissy, doesn't it, feeling the need of this apparently dispensable piece of equipment? (Raises another question: could a helmetless head in a combat zone contain anything worth protecting?)

As background to this mindless event, we learn that before, during, and after it, a hefty number of our soldiers have been killed, along with the usual boxcarload of civilians.

You hate to say it, but it's hard to imagine even the "Bushies" coming up with such a silly and dangerous jape. It makes Karl Rove & Co. look like statesmen. What politically does McCain hope to gain these days? What will the voters think? Mightn't a presidential candidate so ardently cheerleading for the extension of this war fall equally in love with a future one?

At a press conference a day or two earlier, the current president trotted out his oft-repeated remark about being "tired of the people in Congress who think they know more about war than the generals on the ground." I wish a gutsy reporter would offer, "Mr. President, we are into our fifth year of this bloody war. Is it sacrilege to ask just what's been so hot about the performance of our generals on the ground?"

And then there's "If we announce a departure date, the enemy will just hunker down until we leave." Isn't that what most of Iraq's "army" also will do? (They're referred to by our troops as the "Keystone Kops." Except the Kops showed up for work.)

Doesn't never announcing a date allow them to return to their hammocks and let G.I. Joe continue to absorb the bullets?

And finally, above the smoke and the blood and the flying body parts looms the figure of our elected leader, mouthing once again his favorite three-word phrase, "making good progress."

Sir, what in the name of the sweet baby Jesus would *bad* progress look like?

APRIL 5, 2007

Imus in the Hornets' Nest

Don Imus must feel as if he has been run over by a cement truck, which then reversed and backed over him.

It's probably true that the women on the Rutgers basketball team are not Imus fans and, as he says, they probably didn't know who he is. It would be interesting to know exactly how the ladies got the bad news. Did someone say, for example, "A broadcaster announced on the air that you have undesirable ethnic hairdos and that you are prostitutes"?

Imus claims he doesn't know how this happened and brought the ceiling down on him. As one who has had many opportunities to misspeak and to offend—and has taken them—I know how he feels. Much of the show's appeal has to do with the entertaining danger in watching Imus and his colleagues dance on "the line" and sometimes on either side of it. This time he stepped off the starboard side onto a hornets' nest, to mix metaphors.

Is there not a sort of conundrum in everyone's agreeing that the words are horrible, and not fit to be broadcast or heard—and then hearing them re-aired every twenty minutes on most TV channels? Not even euphemizing the H-word. Some of the seeming astonishment expressed about how well-spoken, attractive, articulate, and self-possessed the basketball players are—all true—at times bordered a bit uncomfortably on Obama's being called (surprisingly?) "articulate" and "clean."

Would a white team be surprisingly articulate?

I don't know all the questions to be asked about this. Some of them would be: Who said the words? What was the context? How damaging were the words meant to be, and how damaging were they in fact? What is known of the speaker? Is he a racist? Does he discriminate against black people? Has he ever done anything good for them?

It has reminded me of a hilarious old black comic I saw once at the Apollo Theater—the best house for comedy. In style, he affected lack of education and worked in dialect. "White folks sometimes seem amazed to see us folks can stand up on our hind legs." (Audience giggles.) "And *speak*." (Big laugh.) "Sometimes I think they gonna offer me a dog biscuit." (Pandemonium.)

At such times as this, the camera-shy reverend Al Sharpton can be counted on to pop up, this time in Draconian mode. He wants Imus out, gone, the show canceled, and Imus dead, professionally at least.

Hold on a minute, Your Amplitude.

Millions like this show. All kinds of people, from college professors to firemen to actors, writers, and—I'm told even G.I.s in beds who have survived both Iraq and Walter Reed Army Medical Center.

Nobody in his right mind defends what Imus said. Certainly not Imus. For decades, he has been an equal-opportunity offender. For many, the combination of this style plus his contrasting high-quality guest list add up to the program's quirky appeal. But it was inevitable that one day, as just happened, a land mine would be stepped on by the risk-taking host. It shouldn't be confused with Hiroshima.

Imus retooled his show and himself from an earlier persona, making it a program that welcomes a who's who of guests. This very upgrading makes the blunder stand out in starker contrast than it would if his show were solely goofball, escapist entertainment.

I've noticed over the years that the hate-mail, get-'em-off-the-air crowd always tries to constitute itself as a pressure group that will "write to all your sponsors." They want to not just get you off the air but also—to savor the full enjoyment—bring you to your knees financially. In rare cases where they have succeeded, the health of their target has been destroyed. This is what that old bag Lillian Hellman did to Mary McCarthy.

But Imus, I'm sure, has a shekel or two stashed away in case he were bounced or just decided to chuck it. He is a reader and would not be at a loss to fill his new free hours.

What is Donald Imus really like? I appear on his show sometimes, but I don't pretend to know what all is concealed by the mask he works behind as an entertainer. He appears to be white, gentile, and a family man. He's a skilled conversationalist, an experienced broadcaster, a wry humorist, and, lest we forget, an authentic philanthropist.

In addition, he belongs to a few minorities himself. He is a blond, a genuine cowboy, a recognized bugler, and one of three people in the media who pronounce both *c*'s in "arctic."

The final irony of all this is that when the suffering is past, good is likely to come of it. But if you change, Donald, don't throw away all of the old Imus. We don't want you to come back as Pat Boone.

APRIL 11, 2007

When That Guy Died on My Show

"Hey, Dick, I'll never forget the look on your face when that guy died on your show."

I'd say I still get this about twenty times a year, a high number considering that the event referred to happened in 1971.

I'm never sure exactly how to answer. Let's call the speaker Don. Usually it goes on:

DON: I'll never forget that.

DC: Ah, you were in the audience?

DON: No, I saw it.

DC (*uneasy*): Well, you see, that show never aired.

DON: C'mon, you're kiddin' me.

DC: It's true. And you're just one of a lot of people who are so sure that they saw it that they could pass a polygraph test.

DON: How did I see it then?

DC: I hate to spoil your fun, but the only way you might have seen it is if you knew a couple of ABC engineers who ran off a copy that night to take home to spook their wives and girlfriends.

DON (*with an expression that says "Why are you pretending I didn't see it?"*): But I just know I saw it.

DC (*now trying to comfort poor Don, who has had a cherished memory threatened*): Maybe I described it so vividly the next night that you thought you actually saw it . . . and it was in all the papers and on the late news shows.

DON (*baffled*): Geez, I swear . . .

DC: See, Don, we taped so close to airtime that they had to quickly put on a rerun. The family hadn't been notified or anything.

DON (*noticeably crestfallen, not seeing*): I see.

As I bid Don good-bye, it's clear that he is convinced I'm crazy. I mentally recite my favorite two-line rhyme:

> A man convinced against his will
> Is of the same opinion still.

When I'm doing an appearance somewhere and taking questions from the audience, I can always count on "Tell about the guy who died on your show!" I generally say, "I will, and I promise you that in a few moments you will be laughing." (That gets a laugh.) I go on: "First, who would be the logical person to drop dead on a television show? A health expert." (Laugh.) I go on to explain that he was Jerome I. Rodale, the publisher of (among other things) *Today's Health* magazine. (Laugh.) The irony gets thicker.

He'd been on the cover of the *New York Times Magazine* that Sunday, and we needed one more guest. He was a slight man, and looked like Leon Trotsky with the little goatee.

He was extremely funny for half an hour, talking about health foods, and as a friendly gesture he offered me some of his special asparagus, boiled in urine. I think I said, "Anybody's we know?" while making a mental note to have him back.

I brought out the next guest, Pete Hamill, whose column ran in the *New York Post*. Rodale moved "down one" to the couch. As Pete and I began to chat, Mr. Rodale suddenly made a snoring sound, which got a laugh.

Comics would sometimes do that for a laugh while another comic was talking, pretending boredom. His head tilted to the side as Pete, in close-up as it happened, whispered audibly, "This looks bad."

The audience laughed at that. I didn't, because I knew Rodale was dead.

To this day, I don't know how I knew. I thought, "Good God, I'm in charge here. What do I do?" Next thing I knew I was holding his wrist, thinking, *I don't know anything about what a wrist is supposed to feel like.*

Next, in what felt like a quick film cut, I was standing at the edge of the stage, saying, "Is there a doctor in the . . . (*pause*) . . . audience?"

Two medical interns scrambled onto the stage. The next "shot" that I recall was of Rodale flat on the floor. The interns had loosened his shirt and his pants and were working on him. He was the ghastly pale of a plumber's candle.

Other memories that seem to come in stop-frame sequence:

- Two stewardesses in the front row who'd been winking and joking with me during the commercial breaks were now crying. I guess from their training and having seen emergencies, they knew the score.
- Watching the awareness that this might just be real start to roll backward through the audience. Their reluctant awareness that this was *not* part of the show.
- A cameraman standing on his tiptoes, his camera pointing almost straight down on Rodale and the "action."
- Someone running onstage with a small tank of oxygen with a crucial part missing.
- The bizarre feeling of denial that this *must* be part of the show. After all, we were in makeup and there were stage lights and a band and an audience that had been laughing and clapping only moments earlier.
- Pete Hamill amidst the turmoil, as an ambulance crew arrived, calmly and professionally making notes in his reporter's notebook. (He got a memorable column for the next day.)
- Finding myself in a fog in my dressing room, discovering a few strange objects in my pocket that someone must have handed me. A ChapStick, a watch, and some keys, clearly from the dead man's pockets.
- A voice in the alley as I got in the car: "Hey, Dick, was that for real?"

I went home and looked up Robert Frost's poem "Out, Out—," which ends with the words "And they, since they / Were not the one dead, turned to their affairs."

The next morning, I called my mentor and former boss Johnny Carson. The story was all over the news. I asked Johnny how I could ever do another show. "It's like Kennedy's death, isn't it, Richard?" he said. "You wondered how anybody could ever do another show. This won't sound very profound, but you just go out and do it. And you'll get a couple of surprises."

That night I told the whole story in the (comedy) monologue spot. No laughs then. I dreaded coming back from commercial.

No one referred to the tragic happening, and everything meant to be funny got what seemed clearly to be larger-than-usual laughs. This, it turned out, was the main surprise Johnny knew was in store for me. Everyone was eager to get back to laughs.

This is the topper. Upon warily deciding to view the sorry event a few weeks later, along with my staff, we noticed three things that, incredibly, no one had recalled Rodale's saying: "I'm in such good health [he was seventy-two] that I fell down a long flight of stairs yesterday and I laughed all the way." "I've decided to live to be a hundred." And the inevitable "I never felt better in my life!" (The gods and their sense of humor.)

Recently, someone claimed that when he first snored I said, "Are we boring you, Mr. Rodale?"—which I emphatically don't recall.

Months later, Katharine Hepburn asked me to stop by her house in Manhattan to talk about her possibly coming on my show. As I settled myself in her cozy living room, admiring the charcoal sketch of Spencer Tracy, in she came, plopping herself down on the Persian carpet, the white slacks on her legs forming a long V as if she were a girl playing jacks. Her first words were not "Hello" but "Tell me everything about the man who died." Her dad was a doctor and she loved, and pretty much practiced on her fellow actors, medicine.

When I got to the part about asking for a doctor, I said, "Why did I take that awkward pause after saying 'Is there a doctor . . .'?"

"Because you knew," she said, "'Is there a doctor in the house?' would get a laugh."

She was right. As always.

MAY 3, 2007

Back On with the Show

Pardon my modest blush while I do something here that may appear uncomfortably self-serving. A recurrent theme in your replies to these columns has been how much people miss my old show(s) and how they wish they could see them now. A recent commenter confessed to a lifelong "crush" on Katharine Hepburn and just learned that I did two full shows with her on my ABC late-night show. Another writer, Hepburn-smitten, would "give anything" to see them. You, sir (as I recall), can give considerably less than that. And you could probably see them today. Another writer suggested that DVDs of the shows would be a good idea. I don't know which of us should be embarrassed, but DVDs are already out here.

The company that put them out made wonderful collections of some of my best shows. Their existence is a partially kept secret, owing to someone's apparent idea that it would be either poor taste or bad business to advertise them.

I made a splendid infomercial with mouthwatering excerpts from the shows, but I have yet to see it or hear of anyone who has. (I assume it was made to be seen in America.) I hate to think that DVD makers have taken as their model the shoddy work of book publishers. Both minor and major publishing houses long ago perfected the art of unselling an author's work. That excellent writer Calvin Trillin has threatened repeatedly to do a book titled *An Anthology of Authors' Atrocity Stories About Publishers*. I think the most likely reason he hasn't yet produced this tome is that no one would be able to lift it. (Could he be having trouble finding a publisher?)

The *Dick Cavett Show* DVDs come in collections and, to my surprise, the entire shows are there, not just excerpts. *Rock Icons* has just about everybody. One whole disc (of three) is of Janis Joplin—talking, laughing, singing, and displaying her wonderfully winning personality. I miss her a lot.

"Extraordinary" might be the word for my verbal exchange ("conversation" would be too strong a term) with the immortal Sly Stone. I liked Sly well enough, but what passed in the air between us was more a selection of sounds, really, than discernible words, let alone sentences. There are those who opined that Sly just might have contained, that night, at least traces of various elements of the pharmacopoeia, including some that act upon the speech centers of the neocortex, basal ganglia, and cerebellum. Watching this segment after all these years, I want to yell at the screen; I keep hoping I'll say something like "It's been nice talking to you, Sly, if that's what we've been doing." But you have to hand it to him. He is, I am happy to say, still with us, unlike others of his colleagues on these DVDs. Janis and Jimi Hendrix departed within about a week of each other.

The other sets are Ray Charles (great talk between his numbers); John and Yoko (so nervous during the first two segments of the first two shows that they consume half a pack of Viceroys between them); *Comic Legends* with Jack Benny, Bob Hope, Woody Allen, George Burns, Lucille Ball, Carol Burnett, and a knockout Groucho Marx. (Bonus: He sings "Lydia, the Tattooed Lady.") The Groucho alone is worth a year's tuition at Harvard. The fifth set is called *Hollywood Greats* and contains both complete Hepburn shows with a bonus of twenty-five minutes of Kate never seen before. Also the complete shows with a great Bette Davis and Robert Mitchum, Mel Brooks, Kirk Douglas, Fred Astaire, Orson Welles, Alfred Hitchcock, John Huston, Frank Capra, and . . . what's his name? the boy from Omaha . . . ah, yes, Marlon Brando. Whatever that set costs, it's a bargain.

The Bette Davis is the one in which she had just made a lovely statement about how comfortable she felt talking with me as her host. My reply was the obvious thing anyone would have said at that moment: "So how'd you lose your virginity, Bette?" When the laugh eventually ended, being Bette Davis, she topped my question with "I'll tell you!"—getting an even bigger laugh. As a woman of her word, she delivered. (I don't want to spoil it for you.)

On another show with Miss Davis—irked at how celebrities always (when on television) managed to say something nice about people I knew they loathed—I tested Bette. I said, "Bette, who's the worst pig you ever worked with?""Miriam Hopkins!" (Proofreader: I intentionally omitted the space between the question and the reply, hoping to convey how instantly the answer came. I'm not sure it didn't actually overlap my final word.) Such a relief from the usual gush, "All people in our business are wonderful, really."

"Bob" Mitchum (he said it was okay) was a delightful surprise to lots of people. A faultless actor, he was also a brilliant man. You couldn't name anything he hadn't read. He was a genius at accents. David Lean told me that when they made *Ryan's Daughter*, Mitchum offered him seven regional Irish accents to choose from. I had to pry to get him to admit he wrote poetry and music.

Idiots in bars liked to pick fights with him . . . once. He told me he was sitting alone on a bar stool in Hollywood, minding his business, when a total stranger approached from the side and delivered a hard closed-fist right to the Mitchum cheekbone. Everyone froze. With characteristic avoidance of the obvious, Mitchum turned, looked at the man through those heavy-lidded eyes, and said, "I hope that isn't your best punch." He got a round of applause.

I could go on and on but, as I said above, I'm just a bit uncomfortable selling myself. And I feel silly guaranteeing that the product is worth it. But it is. That's merely a fact, not an opinion. (And it's nice being craved.) Thus I shall not apologize for what to some may seem crass plugola.

I've checked on these DVDs in stores from time to time. Part of the fun is trying to find them and hearing clerks say, "We don't have those," while I'm gazing at a set of them on the shelf two feet away. Oh, and as a tip, somehow they're not always on the right shelf. So far, I've found them shelved under "Movies," "Jazz," "Sports," "Religion," and "Dr. Phil." Amazon has them at bargain prices. Tell them I sent you. (See where it gets you.)

MAY 9, 2007

An Author's Nightmare

"You should sue your publisher."

Those attention-getting words were uttered by a man who was invariably referred to as "the grand old man of Chicago book dealers." That, rather than "Hello," was his greeting when my coauthor and I once entered his shop.

His place had the familiar scent of a real old-fashioned bookstore for book lovers, enhanced by carpeting and the traditional brass bell that tinkled as you opened the door.

"I ordered fifty copies of *Cavett,* HBJ sent me nine copies, and I sold them all that morning," he said. He was referring to Harcourt Brace Jovanovich, our publisher. "It's three weeks now that I can't get any more copies out of your publisher. People come in for it every day. Do you have a good lawyer?"

How could this be? How could they not send the books?

It was Christmas buying time, the book had made the *New York Times* bestseller list, and Chris Porterfield and I were in Chicago doing a media blitz. We did the *Donahue* show (then in Chicago), and Irv Kupcinet's show and Studs Terkel's and made numerous other Chicago radio and TV appearances. How could the book not be in a popular bookstore? Any comfort from thinking maybe this was an isolated case quickly dissolved. "And the Kroch-Brentano chain of stores," he said, emphasizing the word "chain," "can't get it either."

He told us where to find one of those stores, and we went there. "Nice to see you," said the department clerk. "It'd be even nicer to see your book. People are driving us crazy."

(If this were a forties movie, the picture would start to undulate, and the music would tell us we're going back in time.)

Authors telling me similar stories began to play back in my head, but not having been an author when I'd heard them, I'd paid scant attention. Some had been famous people, but some not so famous. The typical author might have been a guy who spent three years writing a book in his humble apartment while his wife taught night school to make ends, if not meet, come into closer proximity. Then suddenly, delight: the book got good reviews. But the publisher did the typical poor job of distributing it, and still another potential bestseller was strangled in its cradle by the incompetence of the publishing house. People with such stories often said, "Nobody knew my name, of course. This wouldn't happen to you." (Ha!)

(Screen becomes wavy again and we are back at the *Cavett*-free book counter.)

I felt the vein at the left of my forehead begin to pulsate—a sign my staff would watch for during taping of a show. It was an infallible indication that I was getting irritated by a guest.

"May I use your phone?" I asked the nice clerk. I called HBJ and asked to speak to Mr. Jovanovich, the tall, erudite, handsome head of the company who had urged and encouraged and wined and dined me, ultimately seducing me into doing a book. The seduction included long, pleasant, chatty lunches with him at Lutèce, an elegant (*et très cher*) French eating joint. Lunch included fine wines selected knowledgeably by my host. Mostly we dined alone, but once we were favored by the presence of the elegant, witty, and still knockout-beautiful Paulette Goddard. All boded well for the book.

"Hello, Harcourt Brace Jovanovich."

"Bill Jovanovich, please."

"Mr. Jovanovich isn't in."

(Temple throb increases.) "Where is he?"

"He's in Europe, I'm afraid."

"Don't be afraid. Where in Europe?"

"I'm afr . . . I believe he's traveling right now."

"Who's running the store while he's gone?"

"The president of HBJ."

"Let me have him."

"He's at the Yale Club right now."

"Are you equipped to reach him there and put him on the line with me?"

"Is this an emergency?"

"I'll say."

(*Our camera cuts to the Yale Club locker room. Men in and out of towels parading about.*)

Attendant: "Locker room."

"Mr. [I cannot recall his name], please."

"He's in the steam room."

"Get him out."

"Yes sir!"

(*A suspenseful pause.*)

(*The president of HBJ, presumably holding his towel in place with his free hand*): "Hello, who's this?"

"Dick Cavett. In Chicago. I'm in a Kroch-Brentano store. They've all been out of *Cavett* for weeks. What the hell is the excuse for this? Are you not allegedly a professional enterprise?"

At that moment, a nice lady came to the book counter and asked for . . . you guessed it . . . *Cavett,* and registered disappointment. I put her on the phone, saying, "Tell this man your problem."

She: "I haven't been able to find Mr. Cavett's book anywhere in Chicago. I'm going to have to buy Lawrence Welk's book instead."

Me (*taking the phone*): "How fast can you get the books here?"

(I forget what he said, but it was unsatisfactory.)

"What about overnight air express?"

"Yes, *Dick* [the pointed way of saying one's name by the annoyed]. That would be expensive."

As expensive as not selling the book for three weeks?

"Before you return to the comforts of the steam room, I'll make this easy for you. If the books aren't here by tomorrow morning, I'll cancel *The Dinah Shore Show,* the Carson show, the *Today* show, and all the rest of this so-called selling tour and come home. Your hapless company has one book on the bestseller list and you can't manage to distribute the goddamn thing. You must be very proud."

(I hung up, as loudly as possible this side of breakage.)

The books winged their way to the Windy City the next morning, worth their weight in air express fees. I did the other shows, the book sold pretty well despite HBJ's best efforts, and life resumed.

It was in telling this tale to Calvin Trillin that I learned of his ongoing project, *An Anthology of Authors' Atrocity Stories About Publishers*. Even if he got a publisher and the book came in at under sixty pounds, they'd fail to get it to the stores. That practice, I've been told ever since my battle of Chicago, continues, like Bush's war, to this day.

My friend and prolific writer of books Roger Welsch, who made overalls chic on *CBS Sunday Morning* over the years with his "Postcard from Nebraska" (which Johnny Carson told me was the only "must see" on his personal televiewing list), recently was asked to do a book signing—a semi-pleasant aspect of book promoting. The author sits in a bookstore framed by stacks of his work and signs them for chatty purchasers. Roger said he got slicked up and drove a good distance to Grand Island, Nebraska. He entered the bookstore and became a bit uneasy, because nothing resembling a crowd was in evidence. In fact, nothing resembling even a person was there, except for the lady who ran the place. "How nice of you to come!" she effused and went and got the store's copy of his book from the window for him to sign. He drove home.

When asked to sign now, he asks politely if "book" is plural.

MAY 16, 2007

A Life in Rim Shots

What does it take to be a comedy writer? Some people ask because they want to be one and some (the more fortunate ones) because they merely want to know.

Woody Allen has pronounced it to be a mystifying gift, not susceptible to rational explanation. As a kid he was able to roll out jokes on a daily basis for columnists, and for comics, while others his age were perfecting their sandlot baseball. (Which he also did quite well, by the way.) Neither of us has ever been able to figure out why one person, upon hearing a news item, has jokes about it occur to him, while another doesn't. And couldn't if his life depended on it.

Mine did, which it does when you're a daily gag-writer for, in my case, Jack Paar, Merv Griffin, and Johnny Carson. And two glorious weeks with Groucho (see below).

It started when I thrust myself into the life and career of Jack Paar while making sixty dollars a week as a copyboy at *Time*. By sheer luck and some calculated timing I contrived to get a monologue into Paar's hands as he returned from the men's room at NBC. (Jack, always one to improve a story, claimed I had importuned him *in* the men's room.)

I found I had entered a daredevil profession. I had committed myself to the challenge issued by a huge star, a giant of the TV medium. It was, "I dare you to come up with funny stuff of a high professional level not just now and then but five days a week, year-round." And, in Jack's chilling phrase, with which he sometimes froze a new comic waiting to go on, "Better be funny, pal."

It took Bob Hope's longtime head writer, Mort Lachman, to put into words a thing I had only sensed. "Comedy writing can be a fairly easy life," he said, "and you'll make absurd amounts of money if you have two things: a sense of humor *and the ability to turn on the comic you're writing for in your head.*"

A light went on. I realized, when I wrote for Jack, and later Johnny and others, the absolute importance of this. In music, the inability to do it would be called "having no ear." I saw writers who failed to get renewed at the end of those fateful thirteen weeks of trial because they sensed no difference in having their comic say "doubtless" as opposed to "indubitably" or just "sure." Perfectly good jokes weren't recognized as such by a, shall we say, "working class" comic because the word "perspicacity" turned him off, where "smarts" would have saved the writer's gag. And job.

I wrote for Groucho Marx when he hosted *The Tonight Show* for two weeks, and he adjusted my wording of a joke by a single word. As written, it ended with, "Well, you could have fooled me." Its rhythm didn't sound right to him. "It needs a *certainly*," he said. "Make it, 'Well, you *certainly* could have fooled me.'" Groucho's East Side New York accent made "certainly" come out as "sightny," as distinct from the Brooklyn "soitny." He was, needless to say, right. To the faultless Marx ear, without those few added syllables the line didn't quite scan.

The brain process that results in a joke materializing where no joke was before remains a mystery. I'm not aware of any scholarly, scientific, or neurological studies on the subject. The crux of the mystery is when exactly the ad-lib artist becomes aware of the spontaneous joke he has just spouted. In the case of a comic genius like Groucho, I'm convinced that the process in the speaker's head that results in funny words spoken is somehow preconscious. Sitting next to him, I saw him be both delighted and . . . this is important . . . surprised by what he had just heard himself say. He was as much the audience to the joke as the rest of us who heard it.

Once Groucho and I were in Lindy's for lunch and a columnist notorious for messing up quotes and anecdotes approached us. "Say something funny, Groucho," he unforgivably mouthed. A moment later he had something and went away, scribbling contentedly. "He'll screw it up, you know," I said. Groucho: "I know. The only way to get him to print a joke right is to tell it to him wrong."

Was there ever another such a man?

In my own case, without seeming to put myself in Groucho's category (*ça va sans dire*), it has happened enough to deepen the mystery. One night in *The Rocky Horror Show*, in which I appeared on Broadway, I was doing both prepared material and ad-lib stuff. While talking, I put my hand in my pants pocket looking for a note I wanted to read. Not finding it, I did the same with the other hand, prompting a galoot in the crowd to yell, "Hey, Dick, you playin' wit yerself?" Instantly I said, "I've got people who do that for me." The roaring laugh almost knocked me backward and I thought, "That's good. But where did it come from?" Because I didn't think it and then say it. I heard it. When they did. Would someone please explain?

All I could think of was that we had only one more performance before closing and that if it had happened a year earlier I would gladly have paid the guy to come back every night.

I wonder how it would have appeared on his income tax.

MAY 23, 2007

No Gagging the Gags

Talking about comedy writing last time, I omitted an interesting phenomenon thereto: the fact that the gag-writer's brain often works independently of his conscious mind. Sometimes alarmingly so. Because the topical joke-writer's livelihood depends on his ability to crank out—if the show is on daily—good, current stuff, fast and for immediate use. And after a great deal of this, there's something that develops and takes on a life of its own.

The late Steve Allen noted that the more comedy you write, the more you *can* write. It happened to me. Thrown instantly into the front lines, as I was, of daily writing for Jack Paar on *The Tonight Show*—a task nothing at Yale prepares you for—it seemed that each day of the week got a bit easier. Monday hardest, Friday a breeze. Friday's jokes seemed to write themselves. Rust set in on the weekend and, again, Monday wasn't easy.

This might be a nice time to throw in my favorite fact about myself: I was a gold medal pommel horse state gymnastics champion in Nebraska. There, it's out. (Since you ask, I clinched the title with my triple rear dismount.) And, shamefully perhaps, this means more to me than "three-time Emmy winner." And it's always left out of my introductions, possibly because it is not believed. It was not only the hardest thing I've ever done in my life—nothing else comes close— but it paralleled gag-writing in the sense that what you lost over the weekend was astonishing. A remarkable insight into the difference between being in shape and *really* being in shape. Dancers know this, too.

The weirdness that I'm getting at is most likely to happen to the experienced professional comedy writer who, thanks to punishing practice, is in splendid condition. It's a bit scary and it strikes on those unfortunate occasions that that arch Chinese proverb calls "interesting times."

If there's a catastrophe—plane crash, miners trapped, kidnapping, ghastly murder—writer-brain kicks in by itself and makes jokes about it. The machinery starts without you; you hear it in your head and you feel ashamed.

When John F. Kennedy was assassinated, I was in California and was friendly with one of Bob Hope's top writers. As soon as the nightmare news came from Dallas, he automatically got in the car and drove to Hope's house. I asked him some time afterward how "Rapid Robert" took the news. He replied that it was the only time in his life that he'd seen Hope, who was mainly Republican, speechless and in tears.

The writer said, "I was the same. But the awful thing was, I couldn't stop my brain from coming up with jokes about the tragedy. It happened to the other four writers, too."

"Jokes like what?"

"Oh, God, I don't know. Stuff like 'From now on Texas will be called "Baja Oklahoma."' A bright and tightly constructed Bob Hope–style one-liner. A good, solid joke. But, alas, the context."

Did it keep happening, I wondered. Did the well-trained mechanism keep churning 'em out?

"Relentlessly," the writer admitted. "There I was, stunned, driving to Bob's house in Toluca Lake as usual, but with tears running down my face, and those unbidden jokes kept vomiting out of me. My joke-writing muscles were in tip-top shape and, to mix a metaphor, I couldn't halt the machinery."

I wondered aloud what psychiatry would say. Could it be a well-intended protective mechanism of the mind, trying to sweeten the shock and horror of the day?

"I've wondered about that," he said. "If it was well intended it failed. It just added a grotesque element to the painful haze of that day and made it even worse. And they were what we called 'strongies.' Well-made laugh-getters that I would have been proud to hand in if not for . . ." Here he trailed off, still affected by the strange memory.

"Could you write them out now, if you were to do a book about it all?"

"Mercifully, I've repressed them. By the dozen. Funny, isn't it? They were so vivid. I can only remember the one I mentioned earlier and one other one."

Naturally, I asked what it was.

"The Dallas police have threatened Lyndon Johnson with protection."

MAY 30, 2007

Sopranos Grief

welcome any advice anyone has about a certain problem: how is a person supposed to live without *The Sopranos*?

Last Sunday's penultimate episode gave me a vivid nightmare. A woman I know was unable to sleep at all after watching it. God knows what watching the ultimate one will do this weekend, on what we the devoted think of as Black Sunday.

The great David Chase, who created it all, decided to pull the plug on his stately craft while her sails are still billowing, an action as rare in the world of television as a sincere compliment. Or a program as good as *The Sopranos*.

I'm glad it's only a rumor that he has had to increase security for himself against armed fans unable to accept the reality of the long-dreaded terminus. How can we fan(atic)s of the show express our boundless gratitude to Mr. Chase? Maybe we could all sign one huge "thank you" to him—a Hallmark card the size of New Jersey. Were this Japan, Chase-san would have long since been declared a Living National Treasure.

Accusations of name-dropping are bred of envy, and I felt it strongly toward anyone who met or claimed to have met actors from the show—until, that is, I met actors from the show. I came bounding home some years ago to announce to my wife (the late Carrie Nye, an actress) that we could go to a party where there would be members of the cast. She declined: "They're such fine actors, but I don't want to know that they're actors. I want them to remain those people."

Please resist envy, then, when I say that I have gotten to know and hang out with the sinfully talented Michael Imperioli ("Christopher," Tony's problem nephew, as well as the author of numerous episodes). Having dinner with him (and his wife) had no effect whatever of the kind my wife refused to risk. There he was, a day later, on the show: Christopher again. Moving, scary, and certainly no one I had ever met. The magic of acting.

This year, Michael got me onto the set and I was in hog heaven. Getting to rub shoulders with cast members and lucky souls like wardrobe people and best boys who got to be there every day, and magic names I knew from the screen credits like Brad Grey—all of it a most heady experience. I stayed long and late and left feeling like a kid coming back from the circus, with nothing to look forward to but home and school.

I don't know how to relate, nor what to say, to people who gave the show a pass because they "didn't want to see another crime show." I suppose it's possible to lead a full life without ever having known what is meant by "Bada Bing" or "Big Pussy" or "Uncle Junior" or "Dr. Melfi," but I'm not sure. I doubt that such willfully self-deprived souls would welcome my sympathy. But, my God, what they missed. If I were artistic commissar it would have been required viewing.

(I feel much sorrier for those who sampled it and found nothing to admire. They are beyond hope.)

I gave DVDs of the show's first season to a very intelligent, well-educated couple I know. They are high-toned people. They scorn television. To shut me up, they agreed to watch at least part of the first show late one afternoon. They tolerated, with a snicker, my suggestion that as in the potato chip commercial, they couldn't watch just one episode. They later confessed that they barely moved as both dinner and bedtime came and went before they could make themselves shut it off.

A special Emmy should be awarded for the casting. There was not a dud in the carload. And no one was ever just a type. They were whole, intricately complex people and we got to peer into their lives and personalities to a degree I've never seen achieved before.

I don't know enough about camera technique or cutting and editing skills to be able to explain why the violence was, strange to say, better violence than you get elsewhere. It was cruelly and sometimes repellently real. You got a solid, visceral punch. Where else would a man, having stomped and kicked the head of his victim, look down later during his therapy session and remove a bloody tooth with some clinging gum tissue from his cuff? You wouldn't say it was funny, but it was handled in such a way that it was not entirely unfunny.

Maybe the show's trickiest accomplishment was the way it made characters clearly deserving of hate be so sympathetic. You could not only find yourself liking an evil character but having fun feeling guilty about it. How could you not feel a tug at your heart when a tough and disreputable gangster, Paulie Walnuts (Tony Sirico), confesses to having sought professional help? ("Right now we're working on my coping skills.")

I found it rewarding to watch each episode a second time. Subtleties of both dialogue and acting were often missed on a single viewing.

I'm afraid, by the way, that I have no patience with pressure groups of the kind that have arisen from time to time wanting *The Sopranos* killed because it gave a bad name to Italian Americans; implying, they felt, that all folks from Italy are gangsters. It doesn't, of course, and couldn't. But it reminds me of when the same problem came up with the highly popular *The Untouchables*. Why, it was demanded, must all the crooks have Italian names? Since the show dealt with real figures, it would have been a bit silly to change Al Capone's name to, say, Al Hollinshed. (A great comedy writer, the late Jack Douglas, offered a solution. When asked about this, he said, "Why not get the gangsters to change their names?")

The fact that James Gandolfini wasn't necessarily the first or only choice for the role of Tony is scary. And Edie Falco has confessed that she almost didn't get the part of Carmela; not because she wasn't good enough but because she almost didn't go to the casting appointment: "I'd been four other places that day and I was tired and it sounded like a show about singers and . . ." As she admits, what she got was, simply, "the part of a lifetime."

Gandolfini and Falco. These two gifted actors created a classic dramatic couple. I see them as no less than the Lunt and Fontanne of their particular artistic world. (I can hear the uninitiated saying, "Get hold of yourself, Cavett." Let 'em.)

Well, it's nearly closing time in the gardens of New Jersey. The

Sopranos Web site is full of speculation by fans. Will Tony die in the final episode? (If the show ends but he doesn't, where does that leave him? And us?) Will David Chase ever reveal the formula for such a smashing success? And could it be as simple as: perfect writing, casting, acting, directing, costuming, lighting, and editing? And makeup?

Having to make do without any new episodes of what, in the fullness of time, will be judged to be the Mount Everest of television achievement is a chilling prospect.

If only there were a rehab place to deal with us, the addicted ones. Or, maybe, some kind of *Sopranos* Nicorettes?

POSTSCRIPT: It's nice for me to think that someday a trivia test may contain an extra-points-for-difficulty question: in what episode of The Sopranos *was Dick Cavett seen?*

The jackpot answer is: May 13, 2007. Tony and Carmela are in bed, anguishing over their problems and unable to sleep. She asks if it's okay to turn on the TV. And there I am: Little Dickie Cavett from Nebraska being watched by two of his idols. (I blush to confess that I sort of hoped one of them would utter a favorable comment.) It's a clip from my Katharine Hepburn shows.

This so gladdened my heart that I think—now, at least—it's my favorite résumé item. (Do you think Miss H. would be similarly thrilled?)

JUNE 6, 2007

Virginity, Lost

Do you suppose it's possible today, somewhere in America, to graduate from high school with one's virginity intact? Everything would seem to point away from the possibility.

It was not so in my day. In spades.

Even in the allegedly innocent 1950s, there were always rumors in junior high and high school of this or that pair who had visited the promised land, but even rumors were few. In general you had little reason to think that your contemporaries were quaffing sweet nectars that you were not. And then, the first thunderbolt.

Eighth grade, Irving Junior High School, Lincoln, Nebraska. A tall, rugged, and handsome "German-Rooshen" lad transferred to our school from western Nebraska. The girls swooned. He seemed bigger and older than the rest of us. We never got to know Terry very well. After only a month he had to backtrack to his native Scottsbluff to tidy up some unfinished business. And I had learned a new term: shotgun wedding.

My God, we all thought. *That meant that Terry had . . . that he had . . .* The mind would not accommodate the envious thought. We felt shriveled, insignificant, and deprived.

My guess is that virginity was epidemic in my high school class. There was the inevitable handful of luckless souls whose suspected plight was borne out by the passage of time. A few in a class of hundreds. We could live with that.

The word "virginity" has gone through considerable alteration in my lifetime. It once meant innocent. Pure. Unsullied. Today, we are told, our young folks mean by it the self-mastery to stop short. This leaves a repertoire of things I doubt my older relatives ever dreamed of. Richnesses of erotomania are okay, as long as you manage to eschew what the stolid Brits still call "a bit of the old slap and tickle." What a gargantuan change from my sweet 1950s.

Should my Welsh Baptist preacher grandfather have known the keyword, he would have died on the spot and met his Maker upon reading news accounts from today like the recent REPORT FELLATIO ON JUNIOR HIGH SCHOOL BUS.

In the same sense that we are mercifully unable to fully recall how great pain and sickness felt, once they are past, the intensity of the blinding horniness of our earliest years is similarly muted by time.

What a shock it is. Hardly anyone I know recalls puberty as a gradual thing, but rather something as sudden and as without warning as a land mine. The busy, active, ball-playing, model-plane-constructing innocent seventh-grade lad (in my case) is suddenly no longer alone. He is now accompanied in life by a most miraculous organ.

A bunch of us at my last class reunion were being shown the new section of our old alma mater, L.H.S. The hip, smart new male principal said, "You might need a little warning for this next room."

What I saw angered me. Clearly they had let a toy store open a large showroom on school premises. It was in the form of a playroom with all kinds of climbables and rideables and playthings for the small fry set. I don't think any of us got it immediately.

"This is so a goodly number of our girls can continue to attend classes."

Our collective jaw fell. Poor dumb old innocent us. It was the most remembered item of the reunion.

I have more on these matters, but may I beg off for now?

I'm taking an antibiotic (having nothing to do, mercifully, with the subjects at hand) and it's doing its dirty work, sluggishness-wise . . .

So let's leave our poor hero for the moment at this point in his story. Leaving him, in Shakespeare's haunting phrase, "yet unknown to woman."

JUNE 21, 2007

Cinema Days

How clearly I recall hearing a friend who was a World War II vet say, probably in the late fifties, "I wouldn't be surprised if one of these days we'll see two people actually goin' at it on the screen." He died not long after that, and so failed to see his seeds of suspicion blossom into an overripe orchard.

Some cinéaste will have to tell me when the first on-screen coitus was simulated, but what was all but unthinkable back then is all but unavoidable now.

When I was a kid attending movies, love scenes (old style, where kissing was the high point) were cues to groan, get up, and go back to the lobby to buy Milk Duds and ice cream sandwiches and Turkish Chewing Taffy and those wax bottles of a cloying sugar liquid, and numerous other causes of massive dentistry at an early age. By the time you returned, the odious love scene usually had passed. In this age of celluloid full frontal, are today's kids so jaded that they get up and—muttering, "Icky love stuff"—go back to get their molar-destroying goodies during today's more vivid on-screen trysts?

I can't imagine what the effect of witnessing full nudity would have been on us in the horny adolescence of those sheltered days, when you gazed at a nude in a photography magazine and tried to imagine, if her leg moved a little. . . . Let alone today, when film sex is not always simulated. (See *The Brown Bunny* et al.) The mind boggles and falls in a faint.

My purportedly better than average IQ failed for years to help me figure out what to me were two puzzling movie non sequiturs: the censor-evading symbolism of a passionate kissing scene that dissolved into fireworks exploding in the night sky, and its companion the less subtle train entering a tunnel. (See, for example, Cary Grant and Eva

Marie Saint in Hitchcock's *North by Northwest*. In that one, the lovers were at least on a train, but I still didn't get it. An older friend enlightened me. I undoubtedly said, "I knew that.")

Nor was I a party to the other guys' lickerishly described activities in the last row at the movies (traditionally the last row, but not always, I was to learn) with the pliable girls who were part of those guys' world but, alas, not mine. Where did they get them? What did they say to them?

It was no damn fun, knowing that Tom and Lyle—and even Eldon!—were somewhere in our local Moorish cinema palace in the dark paying scant attention to the feature while, as Groucho phrased it, "getting their hat blocked." All while I sat alone in my room licking stamp hinges.

Has anyone done a study, I wonder, of how much abstinence bred of fright may have been caused in those days because of a singular convention faithfully observed in movies of the time: it was a fact of nature that a single roll in the hay was invariably accompanied by ruinous conception, regardless of the calendar. It was the sole reason that when Dorothy got tumbled in the garage-size entrance to a storm sewer in Antelope Park in ninth grade by a guy we all knew, and the rumor swept the school, one day after the event I—the would-be class wit—yelled across the street at her, to tickle my grubby friends Tom and Phil, "Hey, Dorothy, what are you gonna name it?" To my ignorant surprise, "it" never appeared. (Nor until now did full awareness of the crappiness of my remark.)

We know that Herr Dr. S. Freud was nearly keelhauled on dry land in Vienna for his explosive revelation that children are profoundly sexual beings. Which brings us to what must, perhaps stretching a point, be called my own loss of unsullied innocence. Out of the blue, my unspotted past acquired a spot.

It happened in a movie theater. The setting: a Saturday matinee in the Grand Theatre, Grand Island, Nebraska. (It still stands; barely, I think.) The cast and the props in our little unsavory playlet were myself and the old sod who slithered unnoticed into the seat beside me, his folded raincoat covering his lap. (This was not last summer; I was in second grade.)

Nothing about what happened meant sex to me at the time, partly because I didn't know either the fact or the word. Being a quick lad, it took but moments to figure out approximately what was going on. I seemed to partially recollect some vaguely understood parental warning once that might apply here, having to do with "some men." Mainly I was annoyed and embarrassed and overly aware that I had been made to unwillingly encounter another person's—in John Cleese's classic phrase—"naughty bits."

And annoyed because it caused me to lose the thread of the plot of the Hopalong Cassidy movie I'd been enjoying in my unsuspecting solitude. There was no fear, for some reason, but simply the imminent humiliation and concern at the thought, "What happens when the lights go on?"

At probably the first frame of THE END, I shot up the aisle with my assertive neighbor in pursuit. I was too fast and agile for him. Looking back, I got my last view of the old goat, keeping track of me while he frantically bought candy. His mistake. I ducked into the Farmers' Market, out the back door into the Christian church's lilac hedge, and thence home.

I was certainly not stupid enough to tell my parents. My usual Saturday movie companion, Mary, was sick that day, hence my solo attendance, but I knew neither of us would get to go unchaperoned again if I related even a moderated version of my sordid tale.

Decades later, an old friend to whom I had told the story found himself sitting by chance right beside me in a New York theater. I hadn't seen him. As the lights went down he leaned his head next to mine and gurgled, "Give me your hand, little boy," producing an uncanny similarity to the tone of my long-ago, gender-bent lothario. I might have struck him if I weren't laughing so hard.

Well, now. What can we learn from this, boys and girls?

I'm not aware of permanent damage from that far-off misadventure in the dark. But in later years, exposure to too much reading in certain schools of psychiatry almost convinced me that not only must I be scarred by it but that I probably caused it. I was surely guilty of having contributed to the happening according to the theory of one "head candler" (S. J. Perelman). People who had such experiences were not innocent at all, but in fact complicit in the same way that women invite rape and that the Jews, in the popular anti-Semite's phrase, "brought it on themselves." Such silliness.

I have wondered how rare or how common my experience was. Do you, for example, have anything similar to report?

I see I have run off at the mouth, or the keyboard, again. In the interest of some sort of thematic balance, if nothing else, I probably ought to round out the whole business with at least the circumstances of the loss of what might be awkwardly called my "other virginity." But I do have at least some regard for your sensibilities, dear reader, and no one should have to endure two squalid confessions; at least not at one sitting.

Agreed?

JUNE 27, 2007

Is Bigger Really Better?

It was only a few years ago that I first noticed an obese person in a commercial. Then there were more. Now, like obesity itself, it has gotten out of hand.

This disturbs me in ways I haven't fully figured out, and in a few that I have. The obese man on the orange bench, the fat pharmacist in the drugstore commercial, and all of the other heavily larded folks being used to sell products distress me. Mostly because the message in all this is that it's okay to be fat.

As we know, it isn't.

It isn't, mainly, because of the attendant health issues. The risk of several cancers, crippling damage to joints, heart attack, stroke, diabetes, and sleep apnea—a much underpublicized life threatener—defies sense.

So why is it so prevalent in our culture and in the media? Could it be that the ad agencies—always with our best interests at heart, of course—are making use of the appalling fact that obesity in the United States has doubled and rapidly redoubled to the point where one-third of the population is imperiled by gross poundage? Fat people, the commercial makers may feel, are entitled to representation. What's wrong with that?

Everything.

Anything seen on TV is, in a subtle and sinister sense, thereby endorsed. I've done shows with Ku Klux Klansmen, Mafiosi, and Nazis (both domestic and Third Reich). Despite my being not overly cordial to them, always a nagging little voice in me wondered if there wasn't something wrong with having them on at all. Was it somehow a tacit endorsement, just putting them on television? After all, there's that sign in the variety store that sits atop the pyramid of schlocky

plastic vegetable slicers: AS SEEN ON TV! Just being seen on the tube . . .
it's gotta be good.

Commercials are not the only exposure that obesity gets on TV. It
is by no means a rarity on the wonderful Judge Judy's show when both
plaintiff and accused all but literally fill the screen. I guess a nice person would not point out that Jerry Springer's guests and audience
frequently bring to mind (particularly for those of us from western
states) a herd of heifers. But there it is. I'll try to be nicer.

Television comedy, in particular, has become an equal opportunity employer of the gigantic. It seems as if nearly every sitcom has a
requisite fat, sassy black lady (or man) or a fat, avuncular white Uncle
Jim large enough to absorb the scripted fat jokes. I have yet to see one
of those Comedy Central shows with multiple stand-up comics that
doesn't include someone the size of the Hindenburg. Frequently the
comic is black or Hispanic—the two groups, according to many studies, currently bearing the brunt of the obesity plague.

These comics' routines invariably center on their weight vs. their
erotic life—the abundance of former and lack of the latter. When
being huge is a jokester's bread and butter, remaining so becomes a
professional necessity as well as an encouragement to overinflated
young would-be performers eager to emulate them. They see that fat
is funny. And funny is money.

When I was a kid in Nebraska and the eagerly anticipated (and
wildly politically incorrect) freak show came to town, it starred such
favorites as the Cone-Headed Savages; He Has Two Noses; Alzora, the
Turtle Girl (if you're still out there, Alzora, please write to me!); the
Pig Man; and, for an extra quarter and behind curtains, something
called Is It a Man or a Woman?

And, of course, the ever-popular Fat Lady. Dora, in this case. The
idea that Dora's rotundity would be a novelty rare enough that one
paid to look at it is sad. (Today, in a two-block walk, I can safely pre-
dict seeing at least one woman who could put Dora out of business.)

In the playground, did you, too, have the nasty little ditty beginning, "Fatty, Fatty, two by four"? In Nebraska, we had the song—but no
one to torment with it. No one was fat. Sounds incredible now, doesn't
it, in the midst of our current tragedy.

More recently I found myself in Tiananmen Square, and a Chinese guide pointed to a bus unloading what seemed to be half a mile away.

Americans, he said.

How can you tell from here? I naïvely asked.

Fannies, he said, making the wide gesture with both hands.

Every summer Irish girls come to Montauk, Long Island, to work. Some years ago, when obesity was getting into surge mode, I asked two of them if they noticed any difference in America from year to year. They sort of giggled and conferred, not sure if they should say it, but then they did: "You are so huge!"

But it's no longer true that Europe and Asia can point to America and smugly sing, "Fatty, Fatty." We've exported our revolution with our fast-food chains. Japan now has obese children for the first time in its thousand-year history. Mad for anything American, young Japanese have made McDonald's (charmingly: *ma-ca-do-naru-doz*) their second—if not first—home, partaking there more than once a day.

But fear not: we still have the lead. And in a future column, perhaps, we can explore just why an ever growing portion of America's population treats the body as if it were a Strasbourg goose.

JULY 25, 2007

Him, to Kick Around Again

GENTLE READER: *Who knew that the subject of obesity would strike such a nerve? The whopping number of replies must have set some sort of record for both clarity and intelligence. I greatly enjoyed reading them, ranging as they do from virtual scholarly essays to "Good-bye, Mr. Cavett."*

And speaking of good-bye, I am not gone but merely at the end of a somewhat lengthy summer layoff. But now you will, I hope, enjoy reading about a happening that involves one of the "big names" of the twentieth century. It can only be described as bizarre.

A blast from the past."

Do you know where this phrase comes from? So far, Google has not produced a firm answer, other than that it's frequently used by disc jockeys, but no one is confident of who specifically gets credit for its birth.

When trying to place a quote, we are advised to always guess Shakespeare first. (Without checking, I'm fairly certain that King Lear's "blasted heath" is not "from the past.")

I gather that the phrase is generally used for something positive; a pleasant reunion with or reminder of something good, like a favorite song. Recently I've had a rather startling BFTP, but pleasant is not, shall we say, the first adjective that leaps to mind in describing it.

Here's what happened. I was called to Hollywood to be part of an event honoring "Pioneers of Television." The previous year's honorees had included Sid Caesar, whom I had avidly watched and worshipped in my teens while still in Nebraska. If he was a pioneer, was I—who came to TV a quarter century after Sid—really one also? And if so, what did that make Pinky Lee, Jerry Lester and Dagmar, and Kukla and Ollie's Fran? Aborigines? Stone Agers?

And what, then, was the man whose name I knew but had never seen until the coaxial cable finally stretched as far as Nebraska? I mean, of course, the then king of the new medium, Milton Berle. About whom the great Fred Allen once said, "Milton . . . is the moron's messiah."

This year, Betty White, Ed McMahon, Tony Orlando, and the hilarious Tim Conway were my fellow "pioneers." Impertinently, I asked whether we would be making our entrance in a covered wagon.

But let's get to the blast.

I arrive at LAX, and a nicely groomed and dressed young man approaches, puts out his hand, and says, "My name is Trinklein."

"Not your first name, I hope," I reply, proving that one should not try to be funny with jet lag.

He is good-naturedly aware that the name is unusual. What remains of my German allows me to translate it mentally into "little drink." Or even "drinklet." Graciously, he concurs with my translations.

Leading me to the obligatory black limo, he says, "I have something in the car that I'm pretty certain will interest you." Something about all this begins to resemble the harmless-seeming opening of a spy novel.

In lower levels of showbiz, the surprise in the limo is sometimes a cutie, sporting merely shoes and a baseball cap. I'm told. But Trinklein is clearly too classy for that. As we glide into the river of traffic, he produces a laptop and inserts a DVD, saying that a woman friend of his who has access to such things has gotten this for him. In the sense of the phrase "Are you ready for this?" I was not.

The screen is filled by a black-and-white photo of two men, seated facing each other across a vast desk. The background décor includes various national flags on flagstands. The two men are instantly recognizable; or they are, at least, to everyone above a certain age.

One—the one whose office it was—is the Great Unindicted Co-conspirator himself. Yes, the admirably earnest but unskilled former member of the Whittier College football team. From Yorba Linda. (Anyone who hasn't guessed his identity by now must move to the back of the class.)

The other gent's visual trademark is his tough-guy crew cut: it is the notorious loyal henchman and lickspittle H. R. Haldeman.

Up comes a sign: NIXON WANTS REVENGE ON TALK SHOW HOST CAVETT. And my blood runs, well, if not cold, at least chilly.

As the chunk of dialogue you are about to read plays out audibly, the still of the two men remains on-screen, creating the illusion that you are seeing them speak the words now being heard in their actual voices.

When the scene begins, it seems my name has just been uttered.

NIXON: So what is Cavett?

HALDEMAN: He's . . . Oh, Christ, he's . . . God, he's . . .

NIXON: He's terrible?

HALDEMAN: He's impossible. He loads every program . . . automatically he'll . . .

NIXON: Nothing you can do about it, obviously?

HALDEMAN: We've complained bitterly about the Cavett shows.

NIXON: Well, is there any way we can screw him? That's what I mean. There must be ways.

HALDEMAN: We've been trying to.

CUT.

A blast from the past indeed. My jet-fogged head didn't know quite what to make of it. Oddly, I thought, "Is this real?" But Trinklein was clearly not a computer-nerd prankster.

I promise you that, even this long after the fact, there is something unsettling when it's your name being abused by the chief executive of the United States. And isn't there something nauseating about the spectacle of the most powerful man in the world scheming to "screw" a late-night chat show host that he apparently sees as part of a widespread conspiracy to bring him down? Were there no more important international issues, perhaps, to be worrying about?

I was told that many people think the Nixon tapes have all been heard by now and, like the LBJ tapes, can even be listened to recreationally at home or at the beach.

Not so. It is only recently that the vast body of them were wrested from wherever they were being withheld and are now the property of the National Archives.

I've been told that I'm on other tapes, too, embedded along with who knows how rich a lode of still undiscovered Nixonian utterances of anti-Semitism, homophobia, and his somewhat alarming preoccupation with being "a real man."

Has history ever known so prominent a figure to be at once so frighteningly bizarre and so greatly gifted? Nixon's rise and fall is almost classical. I'd be surprised if no theater director has yet staged a modern-dress, slightly updated *Richard III* with the lead actor got up as our Tricky Dick: "Plots I have laid, inductions dangerous, by drunken [!] prophecies, libels and dreams to set [those on my enemies list] in deadly hate the one against the other . . ." etc. And certainly both had winters of discontent.

There's more to tell in this strange Tale of Two Richards, but I must draw the curtain of discretion for now.

But don't let me forget to tell you how John Lennon figures in all this.

SEPTEMBER 18, 2007

Witness for the . . . Who, Exactly?

I was too young to understand what everyone was so excited about on a seemingly ordinary Sunday afternoon one December when my mother came out to collar my (only) friend Mary and me where we had been playing "Indians"—and marched us inside to hear the radio.

"I want you to hear this because it will mean something to you when you get older. The Japs have gotten us into the war."

I was at a total loss. I didn't know who "the Japs" were and I didn't know what or where "the war" was, and there was a woman next door whose name was Pearl Evans. I liked her, and you simply have to take this on faith, but I was glad she wasn't the Pearl who had gotten attacked.

What, I hear you cry, could this have to do with what I promised last time: more about R. M. Nixon? The somewhat strained connection is that it was the first time something thrillingly dramatic came into my life via a broadcast medium. That phrase was still singular way back then. There were to be four more such instances (the best was Watergate).

The very day my dad brought home our first television set, the Army-McCarthy hearings began—and were riveting. One met the great Joseph Welch and, at the other end of the human scale, the sparsely lamented lawyer Roy Cohn. So reptilian was Cohn in appearance—and in fact—that you expected him, at any moment, to shed his skin.

If you, dear reader, would rather hear more about Groucho than about Dicko (RMN), I agree with you. But for the moment, the Yorba Linda Wonder must remain center stage, at least until I've therapeutically exorcised his ghost on your time, so to say.

John and Yoko came on my show in 1971. And came on again. Their appearances have been preserved on my *Dick Cavett Show: John and Yoko* DVD. (I insert this for historical reference purposes only. Certainly not as an egregious commercial plug. And it just hit me that there are people out there who may wonder, "John and Yoko who?")

A bit later, certain things began to entangle John. He very nicely asked if I would be willing to do him a favor. Recklessly, perhaps, I said I would. Of course. Especially considering what he and his wife had done for my Nielsen numbers. Would I help him resist the Nixon White House's plan to have him deported?

Deported, for God's sake!

Sure! I said. (*Ominous chord*)

How did this lowdown scheme by the famously klutzy golfer get spawned? I didn't learn until years later that on one of the infamous tapes out of which Nixon wove his own noose, the wily H. R. Haldeman can be heard inveighing against the top Beatle. Having presumably educated his boss as to who John Lennon was, Haldeman deftly stimulates the Nixon venom sacs with these fateful words: "This guy could sway an election."

The Justice Department was enlisted, and the only deportation proceeding against a musical artist that I know of began. (Think of it! A politicized Justice Department!)

Nervously approaching for the first time those lofty, majestic buildings with the grand pillars scared this still somewhat innocent lad from the Great Plains. I knew the main court building, with those long steps, from multiple viewings of Sidney Lumet's classic *Twelve Angry Men*. With my heart at least halfway to my mouth, I entered what looked like the courtroom on *Law & Order,* although both it and Sam Waterston were still in my future.

And there, down an echoing marble corridor, stood John Lennon, dwarfed by the high-ceilinged architecture of this Temple of the Law. He was solemnly clad in a respectful black suit, pants tightly pegged, and those awful round glasses.

I was not a brilliant witness. I trusted my usual facility for ad-libbing to carry me through, and it evaded me. Every few words were accompanied by unaccustomed internal self-criticism. As in:

"Mr. Cavett, what is good about John Lennon, in your view?"

(*Gulp*) "He's a force for . . . (*Dry mouth stops me for a moment as I wonder what in hell the rest of that sentence is going to be. What am I going to say?*) . . . um . . . for good," I managed to squeeze out. Haltingly, I bore on: ". . . for young people."

"How, Mr. Cavett, for young people?"

"Well, as an example for young people who want to do . . . (*Do just what, Dickie? Think of something!*) "Who want to do something good with their lives." (*Jesus, Dick, that's pitiful!*)

I couldn't look down from the stand at John, figuring he was thinking he might have done better inviting Sly Stone than me.

I got a chance to wince again at my alleged testimony when it was quoted in the *New Yorker* the following week. Somehow I can't imagine I played a major role in the fact that John's side won. But his victory supplied the administration with yet another self-inflicted wound to lick.

I'm sure that even the dullest reader can see how my aligning myself with John Lennon in court could well have narrowed my chances of, say, being invited to Tricia's wedding.

And, reading your comments, I see that a perceptive reader has asked whether I had any other evidence of additional darts winged my way from Pennsylvania Avenue.

Yes. Years later I was stunned to learn that, post-Lennon, my entire staff was audited by the IRS, right down to the lowest secretary. (In rank, I mean. Nothing personal.)

I had nearly forgotten how "screwing" enemies real and imagined by illegally wielding the IRS as a weapon—sometimes ruining lives—was one of the paranoid-in-chief's favorite amusements. Of course there is the possibility that more than a dozen people's IRS audits—in defiance of the laws of probability—just *happened* to come up simultaneously, by coincidence. If so, I'll just have to live somehow with the thought that I have done a posthumous injustice to an innocent man.

To those who feel I am too hard on Mr. Nixon, yes, I willingly acknowledge his many gifts, his intellect, and his great accomplishments.

Of course I have not forgotten his remarkable feat of "opening up" China.

Without him, what would we have done for poisoned toys?

SEPTEMBER 26, 2007

Hey, Listen! This One'll Kill Ya!

I have a disturbing problem with losing things. My vulnerability to loss-distress could properly be labeled not only inordinate but neurotic.

I don't mean the major losses like losing a friend or a family member or a limb. With me it's almost as bad losing small stuff. I once re-drove 140 miles of that awful dismal part of Wyoming to retrieve a glove. I drove almost that far in Nebraska to recover a T-shirt from a motel. It wasn't even an I SAW GRACELAND or ORGY VOLUNTEER T-shirt, just a plain Fruit of the Loom. But it was mine and I loved it. It was part of the stuff that is me. And part of me had been amputated.

Clearly fodder for a few sessions with one's shrink.

It was in this spirit that, one beautiful spring day a good many years ago, I found myself returning to Gosman's great seafood restaurant in Montauk Harbor. I had eaten there the previous night and my fervent hope was that a waiter had found my battered but beloved Tilley hat, and that it and I would be reunited.

This was, by the bye, my second Tilley hat. The first had suffered an unusual fate. It was admired by Miss Katharine Hepburn (you know, the famous actress), who asked, in front of her house on East Forty-ninth Street, "Where'd you get that hat?" "It's a Tilley hat," I said. She snatched it off my head, put it on, looked great in it, and kept it. I considered wrestling her to the ground for it, but there were witnesses. And I'm not sure I'd have won.

The second hat—successfully recovered from Gosman's—reminds me of an experience that I would have *gladly* missed for the world. It has, after many years, not yet lost the power to make me wince. It happened during the Ford administration.

Doubtless there is a precise and economical phrase in German meaning "the unfortunate telling of a story that one realizes too late is ill suited to the occasion." (My considerably rusted college German suggests *"Die zu späte und ungeeignete Realisierung von der Unge-hörigkeit von eine Geschichte erzählt,"* but I may be wrong.)

It was late morning, and the waiters were busy setting up for the lunch crowd. Roberta Gosman, of the Gosman's Gosmans, asked whether I had noticed their star diner. She pointed to a couple at a nearby table right on the water, a spot where cheeky gulls have snatched succulent clams and oysters from the forks of startled diners.

The pair: an older man and a nice-looking younger dark-haired woman. He was hatless and somewhat eccentrically—considering the clear and golden weather—enveloped in a black raincoat. He resembled an old seabird of the kind one finds wounded on a beach, peering out at the horizon and awaiting life's terminus.

I shall not protract the suspense. It was the deposed Richard M. Nixon. With him was Julie, the more Cordelia-like daughter who had stood by her luckless dad to the bitter end.

And beyond.

Finding my hat had elevated my mood to a giddy level, encroaching just a bit, perhaps, on hypomania.

I guess it was out of some dumb desire to amuse the waiters that I grabbed up two menus. Approaching the famous seated pair from behind, I piped, "Our specials today include the Yorba Linda soufflé, the Whittier College clam chowder . . ." I invented a few more fictional Nixon-related specials; you get the idea. At least I self-censored any Checkers or Watergate references.

With me now standing at his elbow, the former president looked up at me and, with the familiar Nixon gravity of tone, uttered, "Oh, yes. I thought that was you." I wondered how, since I had been behind them, but then sometimes it's my voice.

A word about Nixon in the flesh.

Upon finding themselves vis-à-vis the gentleman for the first time, most people have reported the same thing: you couldn't take your eyes off his nose. There's a famous photo of Nixon and Bob Hope comparing ski noses, but that's profile—the thing that struck you most was its appalling width. As wide as your first two fingers held together. What would normally be seen as the caricaturist's exaggeration was, in the case of the Nixon proboscis, factual reporting.

Any modicum of humor in my waiter charade had by now evaporated. And there I awkwardly stood, with nothing to say.

Something like "Nice to see you, won't disturb" followed by "Good-bye" would have done fine. However, exhibiting some sort of self-destructive tendency, dwarfed of course by my listener's own, I unwisely pushed on.

"I guess the last time I saw you was when you were nice enough to invite my wife and me to that wonderful evening of Shakespeare at the White House with the great actor Nicol Williamson," I rattled on. He appeared to recall the event, if not my attendance thereat. Need I insert here that this event had been well before my later . . . um . . . troubled relations with the Nixon White House as reported previously in this space.

Despite increasing evidence that my alleged social and conversational skills were apparently on the fritz, I pressed on.

My canoe was edging ever closer to the falls.

I said to the president, "Mr. Nixon, in the reception line that night you asked me, 'Who's hosting your show for you tonight?' and I told you Joe Namath."

I did not add that upon hearing this that night, my tuxedoed president had knitted his brow in the manner of an untalented actor trying awkwardly to combine small talk with deep concern and asked, "How are his knees?"

Memory has buried how long I may have stood there like a stopped clock. I can think of any number of funny or serious answers to the unlikely question now, but not then. I think I may have managed something like, "Yes, well, better we hope . . . I guess . . . eh?" as I quickly moved along. (Since I composed the previous sentence and this one, I've learned that poor knee-afflicted Broadway Joe was on the official Nixon enemies list.) I gratefully slid along the reception line to Mrs. Nixon. Seeing her, what popped into my head was Mort Sahl's hilarious onstage description of the infamous Checkers speech: "And Pat sitting in the corner behind him—knitting a flag."

"I thought you might enjoy this particular evening," she said cordially. I have always liked Pat Nixon and felt hellishly sorry for her. If "in sickness and in health" ever meant anything, that woman fulfilled the vow well beyond the call of duty. God knows if she had written a full-disclosure memoir of her life with him it would have gotten—and deserved—the biggest advance in the annals of publishing. Shelved, I should think, under Abnormal Psychology. There was always that almost Mona Lisa face she put on when having to stand or sit behind him in public view, raising the right corner of her mouth ever so slightly to a degree that suggested a prelude to a smile and also, to me anyway, a hint of pain.

To me she earned sainthood as much as Mother Teresa did, the difference being that Mother T. wanted the life she got. It would be hard to say that of Mrs. Nixon.

But let us return to our awkward little trio on the dock in Montauk.

Standing there feeling as I often have on the air when a guest is less than voluble, I tried talking myself in hopes that the guest, in a competitive sense, would tire of my taking up his airtime and chime in. But the technique that worked on the air fizzled at Gosman's.

Then I half thought of something, with emphasis on the word "half." I glimpsed a possibility. "Oh, I just remembered that a funny thing happened that night. You may recall that just as we all sat watching the last minutes of Williamson's show, a smell like paper burning wafted into the room."

Nixon and his daughter clearly didn't recall, and even I was still not quite sure I remembered exactly what the funny thing was and how the story ended.

I told how it smelled sort of like a small fire in a wastepaper basket and that there were a few looks of alarm but then it went away and the show ended. I went on—since no one else was talking—to say that coming up the aisle I found myself beside the great British critic and wit Kenneth Tynan, who was doing a profile of Williamson for the *New Yorker*.

At that very moment I remembered how this story ended. And I would have preferred dying to going on but hadn't the choice.

"I asked Tynan what he made of the smell of smoke," I said with half a voice.

"And what did he say?" the former president probed, sounding a bit like a cross-examiner. I gulped and said in a thin voice, "He said, 'They've let Agnew into the library.'"

There is a specially constructed booth or chamber in a lab at Harvard that is designed to be the most silent place on earth, so acoustically muffled that the occupant is often spooked by the sound of his own blood circulating.

That day, at that moment, I knew how that occupant might have felt. The quiet was crushing. Not only was there neither laughter nor smiles from my two-person audience, but the gulls seemed to have fallen silent.

In defiance of the rule that women are generally adept at saying just the right thing at an awkward moment, Julie said, "I hope your nightclub act was funnier than that."

While I wondered how she knew I'd had a nightclub act, her infamous parent said, with a breathtakingly straight face, "Oh, I see. Book burning."

The three of us must have said some form of adieu.

And like a concussed fighter with no memory of being carried from the ring, I got home somehow.

OCTOBER 17, 2007

Hail, the Conquered Hero

"You take my life when you do take the means whereby I live."
—Shylock

The "Imus incident" burned so brightly way back when, knocking big stories from front pages. It seems so long ago.

How absolutely silly it looks from this distance.

A widely popular entertainer and broadcaster made an offhand and—as became instantly clear—ill-advised joke about a basketball team made up largely (but not entirely, I was surprised to learn, given the attention the story was getting) of black women.

The joke hit the fan and Yeats's "the worst" filled themselves with passionate intensity. A senator held up a picture of the team and righteously intoned, "How could he say those awful things about these lovely girls?"

And no one hit the senator with a pie.

A lot of people did not come off well.

Experts at exploitation and manipulation seized on the event and flew into action. Overreactors outdid themselves. Alleged friends of the unlucky man in question measured their comments a bit too cautiously, perhaps, for their current comfort.

Wee embers were fanned into an inferno by skilled flame fanners and the professionally offended. Demands were high-handedly demanded. All sorts of people piled on the wounded body. It began to resemble the way certain birds and beasts pile on the ailing pack member and peck or chew it to pieces.

Among the erstwhile Imus program's virtues was that it provided a welcome relief from political correctness. (The vocal group Blind Boys of Alabama were not presented as the Visually Challenged

Boys . . .) The Imus show had long been an eccentric mix of news, music, sports talk, and—thanks to its well-read host—first-rate conversation. The booking of significant guests was a constant. There were authors, "personalities," notable achievers, politicians, and pundits of every stripe. (And, pleasantly, a host who stood apart from at least half of his colleagues by not pronouncing "pundit" as "pundint.") At the risk of seeming class-conscious, whenever I've appeared with Imus, the folks who mentioned seeing me were certainly . . . well . . . is there a nice way of saying "well above average"?

The component of the show that caused the furor was that treacherous quicksand, humor.

Imus and his supporting cast were remarkably up on the latest slang, rap talk, and inside argot of the music world, the sports world, the street, and all minorities. They knew everybody's trash talk. Hearing it helped the listener feel hip, too. Or at least hep.

But there lay the snare that entangled Imus.

There's no getting around what he said, of course, but it's worth asking under what circumstances would a man ever be justified in calling a bunch of women—of any color—by the volatile term "hos"? The first requirement, really, would be that he would have to know them. How can an insult be personal if the person delivering it and the person(s) receiving it don't know each other? Imus would have had to meet the ladies and determine to his satisfaction that they were, um . . . how to say? . . . ladies of light virtue. And then he would have to decide to broadcast the authenticated fact. And what on earth would have to be in his mind were he to do that?

But it's as if that's what actually happened. He didn't know the women later seen on television and in the dopey senator's photo. He threw in a bit of slang as he might have about laundry if it had been a Chinese team, or garlic or Mafia if Italian, or the *turistas* if they had been from south of the border, or Nazis if from Argentina. Not everybody's favorite kind of humor, but easily tolerated—although clearly not by some—for all the good stuff in the other 239 minutes of the show.

What force needed to enter the picture to fan the flames into a California fire? Who but that ofttimes amusing rogue—except when he was Tawana Brawley's patron—Al Sharpton, the very reverend. (And, to a lesser extent, Jesse Jackson—the same Jesse Jackson who brought the phrase "Hymie Town" to a wider audience.)

I seem to recall a history of cordial relations between Sharpton and Imus. I often wish an unwell part of my brain didn't notice such distractions as the fact that the letters in "Al Sharpton" rearrange to spell "trash no pal." But let that pass. I've always liked both Sharpton and Jackson when they're at their best.

Christian forgiveness, with so many reverends around, seems in short supply. Some weeks back an all-black panel convened by one of the cable news shows—after word came (since confirmed) that the host would likely be back by the end of the year—gave Imus a vigorous going-over. A lady sociology professor, seething with disdain, weighed in wondering how anyone could even think of allowing back on the air "this merchant of hate."

Hey, prof, get some guy wires on that wrath.

And some perspective. Do you not encourage, in your students, keeping distinctions clear? And the ability to spot ludicrous comparisons? Would you assign an essay on the topic "Four Merchants of Hate: Joseph Goebbels, Charles Manson, Osama bin Laden, and Donald Imus of Central Park West?"

A particularly painful sight has been the performance of members of the National Association of Black Journalists, clubbing and pounding the radio/television host as if he were a Grand Kleagle. They, too, want him to remain exiled to Elba.

Seeing journalists, black or white, so ardently on the wrong side of an abridgment of free speech and censorship matter is upsetting.

I watched a fellow from the NABJ triumphantly announce recently on Chris Matthews's show (I think) that not one of the team members' hair was, in fact, the "nappy" style at all. So Imus's sin was . . . inaccuracy?

This journalist also looks forward, if Imus returns, to "seeing the network keeping a good sharp eye on him." How—particularly in your profession, my friend—do you develop such a crush on censorship?

Barbara Ciara, president of the NABJ, claimed not long ago that Americans black and white "still have the sting of that insult ringing in their ears." Leaving aside the mixed metaphor (stings don't ring), we must move in different circles.

(Note: Since writing the last few paragraphs, I've learned that there's been a little "give" in some of the critics' attitude. Surely not because they might want to appear on what is certain to be a popular program.)

Will the returning Imus be a different Imus? A meek, caponlike replica of his former astringent self? Comics today are doing Mormon jokes all over the place. Would the "new" Imus not dare do one, for fear of bringing the entire Tabernacle Choir down on his head?

There is really no getting away from the injustice that's been done. A program enjoyed (and missed) by millions was trashed for the sake of the few. No one who contributed to the denouement of the Imus show and the mindless abuse heaped on him has anything to be proud of.

Although of rather less significance than, say, a failed foreign war, the whole episode seems nonetheless to take its place among those aberrations in our society that cause foreigners to shake their heads in disbelief.

A black minister said, "This incident, I feel, will be merely the beginning of great strides and an age of greater understanding between all the peoples of our country." A nice sentiment and certainly a welcome change of tone from the "hate merchant" crowd.

But it pains me to say that I fear this good and optimistic man of the cloth is in for some disappointment. Such profound, more-than-skin-deep matters don't get resolved so easily. The incident will not have one iota of effect on our stinking racism.

NOVEMBER 2, 2007

In This Corner, Norman Mailer

It was at a vividly bad time in Norman Mailer's life that I met him, and a sort of water-treading time in mine. He had stabbed his wife, and I was a copyboy at *Time* magazine.

Time had just done a rough piece on Mailer, even publishing a ghastly, wild-eyed picture of him being arraigned at the station house. The magazine's treatment of Mailer had been much protested, as I knew from working at the copy desk and seeing the mail.

One night after work, I emerged wearily from the subway on Central Park West. There was Mailer. My pulse accelerated. He was with three tough-looking guys and he, too, was tough looking. But I was a big fan and I just had to be able to say to the guys back at the copy desk, "Guess who I met last night."

"Hi, Mr. Mailer. I'd just like to say hello. I can't very well apologize for *Time* magazine, where I work, but . . ."

He came toward me, exuding the well-known Mailer menace, hands held pugilistically.

"What do they pay you there?" he said, still coming.

"Sixty dollars a week. I'm only a copyboy! But I'm a big fan of yours!"

I'm sure I overstated how bad I really felt about what they had "done" to him. He looked at me with a stare like a drill, said "Get a more respectable job," shook my hand, and walked away.

I was to see the Mailer pugilist walk once more in my life, about a decade later and in a then unimaginable setting: my late-night show on ABC. It was in 1971, and it was without doubt the damnedest show I ever did. Or ever heard of.

I thought the guest list looked quite respectable. Three literary figures, and by no means boring ones. All colorful personalities. I thought it would be a nice, pleasant evening. So much for my instincts.

It was not a show to appeal to Joe Six-pack, perhaps, although had he watched it he would have liked it for the action. There were those who later said we should have known what was coming, but, perhaps a bit stupidly, we thought it would be a good show with a mix of fascinating people. That proved to be the least of it.

It all began nicely enough. My monologue went so well that I was able to enjoy the feeling the host gets when he scores: the knowledge that your illustrious guests are watching you on the monitor in the green room, seeing you succeed. (This joy is balanced by its opposite, when you bomb: not only is the audience out front watching, seeing you fail, but so are the illustrious guests backstage.)

Gore Vidal came out first and was his usual articulate and witty and trenchant self, always giving a sort of lesson in the elegant use of language. He told about surprising Eleanor Roosevelt standing at her toilet with her back to him. (She was arranging gladioluses in it.)

Janet Flanner, who had written the *New Yorker*'s "Letter from Paris" for as long as anyone could remember, under the pen name Genêt, came on second and won over the audience instantly by telling of her annoyance at finding Ernest Hemingway in her bathtub in Paris, "using all my hot water." (Bathrooms seemed to be the developing theme.)

Mailer's entrance was the tip-off. He came on from stage left doing that pugilist walk: his hands were fists and carried high, and he had the tousled look of having visited a favorite bar or two en route. His suit was disheveled, his bow to Miss Flanner courtly, and his refusal to shake Vidal's extended hand caused a murmuring in the audience.

When I said I couldn't help noticing what had just happened, I was told by Mailer that he did not approve of Vidal and found him intellectually shameless. Seeming to sense quickly that Flanner might well be on Vidal's side if discord ensued, Mailer then quoted himself on something he had written about Vidal in *The Prisoner of Sex*:

MAILER: I said that the need of the magazine reader for a remark he could repeat at dinner was best satisfied by writers with names like Gore Vidal.

FLANNER: All those writers called Gore Vidal.

VIDAL: I know. There are thousands of them, yeah.

MAILER: There are two or three.

CAVETT: Who are some of the others?

MAILER (*with a dark look*): I don't know.

CAVETT: Who wants to host the rest of this show?

Mailer, years later, told me that it was at this point that "in the face of the Cavett wit and Flanner's deft interruption"—adored by the audience—and in consideration of his alcohol content, he realized he was not being skillful at mounting a sustained argument. About here, the crowd started to disapprove audibly of some of Mailer's offerings. When he maintained that Vidal's writing was "no more interesting than the contents of the stomach of an intellectual cow," they booed heartily.

Mailer's mission, it became rapidly clear, was to eviscerate Vidal for what Vidal had written about him in the *New York Review of Books*. (In brief, he'd said that Henry Miller, Norman Mailer, and Charles Manson—"3M for short"—represented "a continuum in the brutal and violent treatment of women.")

This was tossed about a bit and Mailer told Vidal that if he—Vidal—could teach him something about writing, then he would look up to him. When Vidal denied being the Famous Writers School, he got a laugh, displeasing Mailer thereby.

MAILER: Why don't you try to talk just once, Gore, without yuks? Why not just talk to me instead of talking to the audience?

VIDAL: Well, by a curious thing we have not found ourselves in a friendly neighborhood bar, but both, by election, are sitting here with an audience, so therefore it would be dishonest of us to pretend otherwise. (*Applause.*)

I wasn't sure whether it was the stately grace of Vidal's sentence or the applause that made Mailer look even madder. He had passed me the review to hand to Vidal and was now trying to get him to "read what you wrote," when he noticed Janet Flanner whispering to Vidal.

MAILER: Hey, Miss Flanner, are you workin' as the referee or as Mr. Vidal's manager? (*Laughter.*) I'm perfectly willing to accept you in either role ... my mind is fragile, and I find it very hard to think, and if you're muttering in the background, it's difficult.

FLANNER: I made only the slightest mutter. (*Laughter.*) You must be very easily put off center.

MAILER: It's true, you made only the slightest mutter.

FLANNER: A tiny mutter.

MAILER: Yes, yes, but I listen to you spellbound.

FLANNER: I won't bother you anymore. (*Laughter.*)

Mailer reported later that it was at this point that he began to wonder whether anything he did was going to work, and that he made a small vow never to drink again before going on TV.

It was here that Vidal made some nice remarks about Mailer's writing and how like the Phoenix he is reborn in ever fresh manifestations.

What happened next should play out for you uninterrupted.

MAILER: You seem to have figured out that the next reincarnation for me is going to be Charles Manson.

VIDAL: Well, you left yourself—

MAILER: Why don't you read what you wrote?

VIDAL: You let yourself in for it, and I will tell you—I'll give you a little background here—that Mailer has—

MAILER: We all know that I stabbed my wife years ago, we do know that, Gore. You were playing on that.

VIDAL: Let's just forget about it.

MAILER: You don't want to forget about it. You're a liar and a hypocrite. You were playing on it.

VIDAL: But that wasn't a lie or a hypocrisy.

MAILER: People who read the *New York Review of Books* know perfectly well—they know all about it, and it's your subtle little way of doing it—

VIDAL: Oh, I'm beginning to see what bothers you now. I'm getting the point.

MAILER: Are you ready to apologize?

VIDAL: I would apologize if—if it hurts your feelings, of course I would.

MAILER: No, it hurts my sense of intellectual pollution.

VIDAL: Well, I must say as an expert, you should know about such things. (*Laughter.*)

MAILER: Yes, well, I've had to smell your works from time to time, and that has helped me to become an expert on intellectual pollution, yes.

VIDAL: Yeah, well . . . I was going to say, I—

FLANNER: Not only do you insult each other, not only in public, but as if you were in private. That's the odd way—

MAILER: It's the art of television, isn't it?

FLANNER: It's very odd that you act so—you act as if you were the only people here.

MAILER: Aren't we?

FLANNER: They're here, he's here, I'm here . . . and I'm growing very, very bored. (*Throws kiss to Mailer with her white-gloved hand, getting a big laugh.*)

MAILER: You still haven't told me whether you're Gore's manager or the referee.

CAVETT: If you make history here by punching a lady. (*Laughter.*)

FLANNER: I won't have it! I won't have it!

MAILER: Now, look, you see the sort of thing that goes on. Now you say I make history by punching a lady. You know perfectly well . . . you know perfectly well that I'm the gentlest of the four people here. (*Laughter.*)

CAVETT: I just hope it lasts through the next whatever we have left.

MAILER: I guarantee you I wouldn't hit any of the people here, because they're smaller.

CAVETT (*beginning to steam*): In what ways smaller?

MAILER: Intellectually smaller.

CAVETT: Let me turn my chair and join these people. (*I do.*) Perhaps you'd like two more chairs to contain your giant intellect. (*Applause.*)

MAILER: I'll take the two chairs if you will all accept finger bowls.

(Mailer wrote later about this moment: "This remark was sufficiently gnomic for Cavett to chew and get to no witty place.")

CAVETT (*mystified*): Who wants to grab this on our team? (*Pause.*) I nearly have it. It means something to me. Finger bowls. Things you dip your fingers in after you've gotten them filthy from eating. Am I on the right track? Am I warm?

MAILER: Why don't you look at your question sheet and ask a question?

CAVETT: Why don't you fold it five ways and put it where the moon don't shine?

(*Following this exchange, wild, sustained laughter. Mailer, eager to reply, can only stab the air with his finger until it subsides.*)

MAILER: Mr. Cavett, on your word of honor, did you just make that up, or have you had it canned for years, and you were waiting for the best moment to use it?

CAVETT: I have to tell you a quote from Tolstoy?

(*Mailer turns his chair away from us and to the audience.*)

MAILER: Are you all really, truly idiots or is it me?

(*A chorus replies, "You!" Then, applause.*)

CAVETT: Oh, that was the easy answer.

(*Bobby Rosengarden's band plays us off into the commercial break with the Gillette fight song, "To look sharp . . ."*)

I think we all agreed without ever saying so that, of our little quartet of alleged luminaries, Janet Flanner came off best.

TV critics writing about the show—and it seemed like every single one did—mostly agreed with Mailer's appraisal of himself as "a lout and a slob." A much smaller number felt sorry for him. "Pitting Norman in a battle of wits, particularly these three wits—Vidal, Flanner, and Cavett—was like putting him in a boxing ring with Ali and adding Frazier and Foreman for good measure," wrote one. (I still want to know which of the three boxers I was.)

All of us still spoke, and both men were—singly—on later shows of mine. Not together, but on. Vidal said his relationship with Mailer finally resolved itself into pretty much what it had been for decades: "We pass, and like two old whores on the street, say 'Still at it, Norm?' 'Yep. Still at it, Gore?'"

What with Norman dead, in going over that transcript I feel twinges of guilt about not having treated him nicer, but what the hell? He wasn't dead then. And he certainly asked for it and gave as good as he got.

My affection for him has never faded, and I saw him many times after that. And God knows, the man who could write a book called *Advertisements for Myself* got huge delight out of the evening's notoriety. He claimed that after that show he got more mail than in the rest of his career put together, adding, laughingly, "and some of it was even on my side."

I know someone who sure as hell hates being dead.

NOVEMBER 14, 2007

When They Told Me Norman
Wrote a Book . . .

I'm mightily impressed by the literacy, enthusiasm, and high quality of your comments on my previous column, on Norman Mailer.

And I appreciate the naysayers as well. (At least as much, I'm sure, as recent presidents "appreciate" their critics.)

Since then, a curious thing has happened.

Much ink was spilled at the time of that notorious show. But I had no idea how much until just now. I Googled "Mailer Vidal Cavett Show." And I won't be hurt if you do so yourself to verify the startling results. It says: "Results: 1–10 of about 30,000 for Mailer Vidal Cavett Show." (Just for fun I typed "The Dick Cavett Show" and was hit with the words "about 387,000." That's more than Nielsen said were watching my first show. Would someone please read all the entries for me? And have your report on my desk by Friday.)

If you somehow don't have time for them all, you might enjoy checking out "Charlie Rose / Dick Cavett." I was on Charlie's show a few years ago, and his producers plucked out and rebroadcast the most notorious segment from the Mailer-Vidal skirmish—the "fold it five ways" section—so you can see it with your own eyes in all its rich and flaring glory. (It's about a third of the way into *Charlie Rose*. Note especially the body English.) Sorry for this ego-related detour. Back to our story.

And now for a surprise. To both you and me. "You know, Norman wrote a whole book about that show," someone said to me a few years after it aired. "It's called . . . something about dots." I probably nodded politely, knowing full well that were this true I, or someone, would have heard about it.

But here's the spooky part. Three days ago, wandering for no particular reason to my wall of bookshelves (and books), my eye fell upon a group of four volumes about the same size. Only three of the titles were legible. Idly removing the dim one, donning glasses and holding it to the light, I experienced near syncope. I all but swooned. (Cue eerie theremin music on soundtrack.)

On the spine, in faded gold against deep brown, there it was: "Of a Small and Modest Malignancy, Wicked and Bristling with Dots." By Norman Mailer.

In disbelief—and intrigued by the catchy title—I eased the cover open. There, in a nice handwriting, appeared:

> *To Dick,*
> *My remembrance of a*
> *couple of things that passed.*
> *Cheers,*
> *Norman*
> *April '82*

In the popular cliché, my pulse quickened. It's a small treasure of a book, 120 pages of Norman's ruminations about—and experiences on—TV. It's a great read, and fully the latter half is about "our show." I could pass a polygraph test that I know not when or whence it came into my possession. I must have brought it home years ago from the office in a bag of books and, without looking at them, shelved them.

But for Mailer/Vidal devotees, it's a bit of a heartbreaker. A page at the very back tells us: "This first edition of 'Of a Small and Modest Malignancy, Wicked and Bristling with Dots' is limited to three hundred numbered copies on Mohawk Superfine and a deluxe edition of 100 copies on Curtis Rag bound in leather, all of which have been signed by the author. Printed at The Castle Press for the Lord John Press."

(I didn't get a leather one, alas, and I have yet to find its number; but who cares? It's mine and I love it.)

It deserves a wide audience of Mailer and Vidal fans. I wish I could lend it to you, but as you know, lending books is a fiction. You *give* them. Nobody returns the damn things.

Instead I'll make some disjointed highlight selections for you— some of what they like to call "insider stuff."

The following bit went unreported. It took place in the green room, where guests sit and watch the show before going on. (I only learned about this afterward from Vidal.)

In his familiar third-person manner, Norman writes of himself:

> When he arrived at the studio, they rushed him to makeup. Vidal had been supposed to go on first, but hadn't arrived. Would Mailer object to taking his place? He had hardly given his assent before he was informed that Vidal had arrived, after all. Would he now mind if Mr. Vidal went on as originally planned? Since Mailer had formed the little vice when appearing on Cavett of comporting himself as the star, he would not pretend to happiness at finding himself on the shuttle. Still, he kept his mouth shut. He did not wish to jostle his liquor.
>
> At this moment, alone in the green room, he felt a tender and caressing hand on the back of his neck. It was Gore. Vidal had never touched him before, but now had the tender smile of a man who would claim, "It doesn't matter, old sport, what we say about each other—it's just pleasant to see an old friend."
>
> Mailer answered with an openhanded tap across the cheek. It was not a slap; neither was it a punch. Just a stiff tap.
>
> To his amazement, Vidal gave him a stiff tap back.
>
> Norman smiled. He leaned forward and looked pleasantly at Gore. He put his hand to the back of Gore's neck. Then he butted him in the head.
>
> "Are you crazy?" asked Vidal.
>
> "Shut up," said Mailer.
>
> "You're absolutely mad. You *are* violent," said Vidal.
>
> "I'll see you on the show."
>
> He was, after Vidal left (and that was quickly enough), obliged to pace about. Other people came into the green room, saw him, and went away. It was obvious: he did not feel like speaking.
>
> The show began. Cavett did his monologue, and it was

a good one. Cavett had the only smile that came through
the valves of video looking wicked and angelic at once.

Then follows the action described in the preceding column. But
here are a few more choice exchanges I'd left out, random bits Mailer
included in his book.

After Norman has complained that Gore had attacked him in the
magazine article "as part of his particularly dirty little literary game,"
we get:

> VIDAL: Well, I'll begin to answer Norman's charge about what a bad
> person I am. The attack on him. Really if you want to know,
> Norman, is simply what I detest in you—and I like many things
> in you, as you know, I'm a constant friend despite this—but
> your violence, and your love of murder, your celebration of
> rage, of hate. Your "American Dream"—what was the dream? A
> man murders his wife and then buggers this woman afterwards
> to celebrate an American man's dream. This violence, this
> knocking people down, this carrying on, is a terrible thing.
> Now, it may make you a great artist—an interesting artist, I
> don't say that, but to the extent that one is interested in the way
> the society is going, there is quite enough of this violence with-
> out your celebrations of it. (*Vigorous applause.*)

Gore began to speak again, when suddenly Norman heaved up
out of his chair and lurched toward him, a bit shakily. The audience
gasped. Gore, an old army man too, raised one arm to deflect what
looked about to be a right hook. I thought I was going to be in a real
fight before the cameras, wondering just what part of Norman's anatomy I would go after, and thinking, *Do I take my jacket off?* But
Mailer merely snatched the offensive article from Gore's hands and
wobbled back to his seat, pleased with the shock he had delivered.

More from our forest of oddities that night. You will recall from last
time that Mailer had at one point asked the audience, "Are you all

really, truly idiots or is it me?" And that a chorus of "You!"s was roared back. The laugh I then got with, "Oh, that was the easy answer," served to deepen the Mailer scowl. This was followed by some far-from-average audience participation:

> CAVETT: I'm sorry, Norman, I interrupted you. You were talking to the assembled audience.
>
> MAILER: Yes, I was going to ask the audience what I was doing that was making them cheer every time the other side connected with a pass.
>
> MAN IN AUDIENCE: You're rude.
>
> WOMAN IN AUDIENCE: You're a snot.
>
> MAILER: That's fair. Someone said I'm rude and someone said I'm being a snot.
>
> WOMAN IN AUDIENCE: You're a pig. Why do you have to argue so negatively and insultingly to your guests?
>
> MAILER: They're not my guests any more than they're your guests.
>
> CAVETT: It seems it's your show now.
>
> WOMAN IN AUDIENCE: Why do you have to answer them with insults and nasty statements, and they're answering you maturely and with dignity? (*Applause.*)
>
> MAILER: That's because they're mature and full of dignity and they'd cut my throat in any alley, and I answer crudely because I'm crude and a lout and a clod, that's why.
>
> (*No one argued with this.*)

And as we neared the end of this warm and peculiar happening, a brief disquisition on murder:

> VIDAL: I made my case very carefully in the article [about Norman's propensity for violence] but I will say, giving you a few minutes more on the program, you will prove my point. . . . I come back to what I said. I detest this violence in you. You have actually written that "murder is never nonsexual."
>
> MAILER: Well, is it ever nonsexual?

VIDAL: Well, I'm—

MAILER: Don't you know, Gore?

VIDAL: Not having murdered anybody lately, no, I don't know. . . .
I'm going to give you a line that Degas said to Whistler—two
celebrated painters—and Whistler was a great performer like
Norman, and Degas said, "You know, Whistler, you act as if
you had no talent." You, Norman, represent yourself as if you
really had no talent at all, and of course you are one of our
best writers.

(*Norman "exposes" the fact that he, too, saw that quote in a recent
article by Edmund Wilson and "thought it was marvelous."*)

VIDAL: Good. I'm glad that we both agree that the sentiment is
correct.

As it must to all good things, the end was coming when Norman
insisted on clarifying the incident of the murdered woman in his
novel *An American Dream*. The one Gore had attacked for its ghastly
violence. Note how the less than totally savory moment is so expertly
seasoned by the great Janet Flanner:

MAILER: . . . in fact, he did not simply bugger a woman, he entered
her another way as well, and . . .

FLANNER: Oh, goodness' sake. (*Laughter.*)

MAILER: I know you've lived in France for many years, but believe
me, Janet, it's possible to enter a woman another way as well.

FLANNER: So I've heard. (*Laughter.*)

CAVETT: On that classy note . . .

FLANNER: I don't think it's restricted to French information, dear.
(*Laughter.*) Practically international. (*More laughter.*)

MAILER (*subdued*): Are we quitting on that classy note?

(*We had to, returning for less than a minute.*)

CAVETT: Well, it's been an interesting evening around the old
table. Miss Flanner, I'm glad to see you got those cookies [from
a commercial] that you wanted.

FLANNER: It's the only solace. (*Laughter.*)

CAVETT: Could you all come back New Year's Eve? (*Laughter.*) Let us know who you think won and we'll see you next time we're on the air. If.

Of the years of shows I've done, this was the only one where I consciously thought, in the middle of it, *I wish I could be sitting out front watching this.*

Mailer's version, in his book, of the last seconds: "The good-byes were short. Mailer turned around, and Vidal was gone."

And mine: In the long shot, as credits rolled, you saw three of us still seated, with Norman walking off slowly. Alone. Like an old fighter who has absorbed a goodly number of body blows.

NOVEMBER 25, 2007

With Readers Like Y'all . . .

Y ou might not guess that at least half the fun of doing this column is getting to read your "comments," as they are called on the Web site.

But it's true.

I don't even mind reading things like "Enough with the heavy stuff. Let's get back to Groucho." (I am trying to remember one I recently heard. By the time we finish here, I might come up with it. Isn't memory annoying when you get past forty?)

In a moment I'll glance back at mail about earlier columns, but I stand particularly amazed all over again at the high quality of so very many of the recent Mailer-Vidal reactions.

They're literate, funny, well composed, and, in many cases, what I would call "publishable." (With, of course, a real dumbo here and there for contrast.) I especially liked hearing from people who, as one man put it, were "delighted to get the inside view of that remarkable show."

Lots of people were sorry that Norman came off so badly—sorry, as someone wrote, that so great a talent "could act like such a lout." Some related how kind Norman could be, based on personal encounters. "The nicest, politest, sweetest man I ever met," wrote one lady.

Among the replies to the first Mailer column was a moving letter from Stephan Morrow, who had directed and acted in Norman's work and knew him from the Actors Studio. Mailer had called to thank Morrow for his work on a film version of Mailer's *The Deer Park*. Thrilled by the call, Morrow in turn thanked Mailer "for his kind words," but the author, Morrow writes, "quickly countered with, 'I don't want you to confuse this with kindness. I'm not being kind here, I just liked what you did with my play. I've seen it done badly too many times.'" (I can't wait until the next time I commend someone and they say I'm being kind.)

Maybe I should have included one or two of my own such "positive" Mailer experiences. (For instance: he was on an earlier show of mine, during which he said to Muhammad Ali, "I came to sit at your feet." Ali was amused.)

Here's another. One night, after a heavily fueled party brimming with literati at George Plimpton's salon/apartment, Norman said to me, "Let's walk." (This was well before *that* show.) Mailer was smartly clad in a belted Burberry. It was past midnight and a misty ground fog gave the few lighted windows and street lamps—and our aimless strolling—a sort of imitation-London aura. As we wandered among East Side brownstones and town houses, chatting civilly, ever and anon Norman would pop into a phone booth only to soon emerge looking displeased.

"I know a couple of places we might be offered a drink," he would explain, putting his little number book back in his pocket. We resumed our walk. Glad that he kept failing to score another drink that neither of us needed, and aware that drink had loosened my tongue, I launched into a now forgotten and very long narration about something or other. Maybe it was a sudden realization that I was with a master wordsmith who hadn't spoken for several blocks that made me offer: "Norman, shall I drop the rest of this lengthy tale?" "No, no," he said convincingly, brows tightly knitted in concentration, "I'm learning how to tell a story."

Only the gods know if what I had just received was a memorable compliment or a tolerable hint of wicked Maileroid humor. Whichever, I was seeing what good company he could be.

As for the less benign mail, well, after many years of getting (euphemistically) "mixed reactions" from the public, you can even find pleasure in, for example, "Mailer should be given a talk show and Cavett sent back to the mailroom." The writer seems unaware that Mailer is dead and that I never worked in a mailroom, but that doesn't spoil it for me.

As Richard Nixon liked to say when under assault, "You have a right to your opinion." (I always wished I could be there to say, "Really, sir? Who would have guessed? I must jot that down.")

Brando—you know, the famous actor—advised me once, "You either learn to develop a callus in this business or you go home."

(Maybe that's what allows me to get a kick out of even the sincerest attacks. As when, years ago, having just had someone like, say, Jane Fonda on my late-night show, I received the following masterpiece from Waco, Texas, crayoned in block letters on a Western Union telegram blank: "Dear Dick Cavett: YOU LITTLE SAWED OFF FAGGOT COMMUNIST SHRIMP!" I wrote back, "I am not sawed off!" I wonder if they got it.)

The column on obesity certainly struck a nerve. It appears also to have cost me some admirers. Replies ranged from "Thank God! Someone had to say this!" to "How could you?"

For the record, it was not meant to be an attack on anyone but rather a lament over the size (sorry) of the problem and the lethal nature of the disease. I recall one that went, "O.K., Dick Cavett; so you hate me because I'm fat. Well, I hate short men who try to be intellectuals." (The word "short" came as a relief. For a moment, I thought she'd meant me.)

A goodly number of you out there have written varied versions of "Why don't you come back on TV?" I'm not sure. It does help if you're asked.

For a long time I have fended off occasional longings to be "back on." As a maimed veteran of cancellations and of the horrors of starting up all over again, one gets weary of once again being dragged through the journalists' apparently required questions.

The most irksome one, asked with bright enthusiasm and pencils poised, is the mindless, "How's the new show going to be new and different?" I was always torn between answering "The guests will stand" and replying "It's not going to be either new or different. Is there anything wrong with the old tried-and-true format?"

Once, in a writers' meeting, a not very helpful network figure said, "Dick, I'm sure you don't mean to say the show will be just like other talk shows." A witty employee of mine—the writer Marshall Brickman—responded, "As in, 'Oh, no! Another square painting?'"

But I think the recurrent comments lamenting the fact that I'm not on are beginning to get to me. I'm developing an itch. I do still have a large number of my faculties. So if you hear of a talk show that isn't being used, let me know.

I enjoy seeing a long-lost friend pop up in the comments, like Peter Kelley, an agent and fellow ingester of sushi in our mutual olden days. And what a kick to see the name Frances de la Tour among the recent comments. Her vivid and witty performance in Alan Bennett's *The History Boys* is stamped on my memory, and possibly my soul. (I must be tired . . . I almost added "if you will," and I loathe that stupid phrase.) The good feeling you get when hearing from someone you've admired like that reminds me of Jack Benny's asking me if I knew of "that brilliant new young comedian, Woody Allen?" "I know him," I said, "and he's a big fan and admirer of your work." The great man beamed, and his reply was almost childlike in its sweetness: "Gee, it's nice, isn't it, kid, when somebody you like likes you?"

Finally . . . do I owe you a laugh or two? I'll try for two.

A reader of this column accosted me, pleasantly, behind the Metropolitan Museum of Art, in Central Park. He was a rabid explorer of the Internet. *Go home, Cavett,* he said (more or less), *and go to YouTube.* (I was innocent of the fact until quite recently that there's what seems like half my career, and everyone else's, on YouTube.) He said, "Once you're at YouTube, type in 'Dick Cavett Eddie Murphy' and see what you get." Thinking accurately that maybe his directions were beyond my skills, he added: "Or just Google 'Dick Cavett Eddie Murphy.'"

What I got thrilled me.

It was an all but forgotten (by me, at least) segment of David Letterman's NBC late-night show. Dave plays it perfectly, finding himself (comically) aghast at certain—how to say—revelations about the Cavett/Murphy relationship. Best leave it at that. I don't want to add here, but I will, that a columnist back then called it "the funniest segment on a talk show this year." I hesitate to quote that for two reasons. One, someone might do some research and discover the fact that the year was only three weeks old when he said it. Also, a thing can be killed with excessive praise. But you will laugh at least once, I'm sure. And let's keep quiet about it around the Right (sometimes) Rev. Al Sharpton. And please don't be offended by some rather questionable matters regarding a portion of the . . . um . . . anatomy of Diana Ross. (Have I teased you sufficiently?)

And now, as sort of promised, a morsel of lagniappe for the ever hungry Grouchophile. (I remembered it!) My guess is that it might be new to you.

Groucho was lunching with the late John Guedel, whose name you've seen as producer on the credits of *You Bet Your Life.* A couple approached their table and the man said, "Groucho, we just adore you. Say something insulting to my wife." Groucho looked her over and said to the husband, "With a wife like that you should be able to think of your own insults."

I dearly love that. Such a blessed antidote to the oppressive goodwill of this allegedly festive season with its annual soar in the suicide rate.

DECEMBER 29, 2007

A Potpourri of Pols

I can't figure out what it is that keeps me watching the current star search for our next president.

It's not *all that* compelling or entertaining. Or at any rate it certainly doesn't rank anywhere near the three riveting television events of my lifetime: the Army-McCarthy hearings, Watergate, and the O. J. Simpson trial. Things that, day after day, held you enthralled, afraid to look away for more than a moment for fear of missing the next bombshell.

And yet I dutifully watch Keith and Chris and Wolf and those Sunday morning talk shows Calvin Trillin has labeled the "Sabbath Gasbags."

Admittedly, it's all important stuff. But what is missing? We can surely agree there are damn few laughs (see Twain, below). Even inadvertent nastiness (when it is inadvert) gets quickly apologized for. (Of course, by the time you read this there may have been out-of-control carnage.) Perhaps it's that inexcusable thing I said in an acting class years ago, after a slight teenage girl had done a speech of King Lear's: "For me, it lacked majesty." The laugh it got still pains me.

Maybe it's just that it is not indubitably and overwhelmingly obvious that a large number of the candidates, arrayed across the stage in bas-relief, are qualified to fill the Hardest Job in the World.

In a much earlier column about John McCain in this space I posed the question: "What has happened to that man?" McCain had just participated in that ludicrous look-how-safe-Baghdad-has-become charade, sashaying around a seemingly unguarded open market. It was impressive and seemed to make its point—right up until it was revealed that just off camera our intrepid John was being protected by a throng of fully armed troops—fore and aft and hovering overhead. One of the shopkeepers seen on camera told a newsman, "Now I am a target."

Despite that bruise to his integrity, McCain looks to be himself again. I do worry that near the end of the day he appears to be what the British call "puffed." But so do they all. Isn't it time some more humane way of campaigning was devised that didn't nearly wreck the participants, what with the rushed meals and bad sleep and vocal strain (if not injury), and the stuffed-down local kitchen specialties and obligatory ethnic snacks and fatiguing killer schedules? Mightn't the country miss out on fine, qualified potential presidents unwilling or unable to endure an ordeal that would tax a triathlete? I half-expect McCain to drolly observe that the Hanoi Hilton was at times restful compared to this.

It has to be awful on all of them, with the exception of Fred Thompson, who seems to be campaigning from a Barcalounger.

I find McCain—apart from his unwillingness to detach himself from his "victory in Iraq" mirage—greatly appealing. And, of the flock, he seems to be the one with a genuine sense of humor. He deserves the Best Comic Ad-lib trophy for his remark to Romney during a debate. Referring to Mitt's so readily adjustable convictions, McCain said, "We agree—you are the candidate of *change*."

Romney's response was the predictably clunky one about getting personal, which has become the habitual retort of the lackwit.

As a kid, I sent off for a book for performing magicians like myself called *Heckler Stoppers: Snappy Retorts for All Occasions*. Sadly, the wittiest of them were on the level of "Your mother wears army shoes." But maybe some genuine wit could get rich putting one out for politicos lame in the quick-comeback department. If all those so impaired bought one, it would be an instant bestseller.

Political comic relief is not a trivial subject. All candidates should bear in mind Mark Twain's edict, "Against the assault of laughter nothing can stand."

John of Arizona seems like a man you wouldn't be afraid to trust with a preposterously difficult job like the one he is after. Though Dennis

Kucinich is an interesting case. Whenever I've seen him answer a question he has done so thoughtfully, intelligently, manfully, forcefully, and articulately. Yet he's treated as no more electable than you or I. Is it merely his size and appearance? Where is it written that a candidate bearing a greater resemblance to a garden gnome than to Mr. America can't be president? Had Dennis been born into Mitt Romney's body, might this campaign be a whole different story?

And what of the current occupant of Romney's body? He fascinates me. He's intelligent, knowledgeable-seeming, handsome, well dressed and groomed, pleasant, and mature in manner. So why does something emanating from him seem to whisper the word "bogus"?

Part of it could be his hair. To my eye it just might be an expert colorist job—an indicative lapse in that alleged *sine qua non* authenticity—with those artful white flecks here and there and the Paulie Walnuts temple patches. I may be doing him a disservice. It may be a case of nature and not artifice, in which case I should be forced to apologize in this space and to down a bottle of Shinola Black in public.

There is one question I have not seen Romney asked. It's the one a friend dared me to put to John Wayne when he appeared on a show of mine: *Sir, how is it that neither you nor any of your multiple strapping sons have ever served a day in the armed forces?*

(I confess that I didn't ask Mr. Wayne because I so wanted the Duke to like me. I sure liked him.)

If Hillary Clinton's so-called cry was planned, she is, along with her other talents, one hell of an actress. But for my money, her greatest moment was that niftily executed and funny response to the boorish query about how she felt about being lacking in the "likability" department. If it was meant to put her off, it backfired. Her "Well, that hurts my feelings" and "But I'll try to go on" could hardly have been delivered better by Meryl Streep. Or Elaine May.

Barack Obama seems a sort of miracle. He has frightened me only once, when he seemed to have fallen into the royal "we." The one favored by monarchs and also by athletes, usually in conjunction with their expressed gratitude to God for choosing their side to win. To borrow from Mark T. again, somewhere he said that "only presidents, editors, and people with tapeworm have the right to use the editorial 'we.'"

This campaign seems unusually free of inside dirt and nasty rumors. There have been some touchy moments and less than pure remarks and tactics, but certainly nothing shattering nor comparable to the tactics of the lowbrow thugs who gave us Swiftboats. Fortunately there's plenty of time left for all that. My only possible offering in that regard is from a distinguished friend who worked alongside Rudolph Giuliani on some New York City project. His take? "That is a bad man."

I irresponsibly throw that in for what it's worth.

Would anyone be upset if I knocked off at this point? Meanwhile, let's all remember that there is one blessing that all of the candidates can revel in and enjoy: they needn't have any fears about being inferior to the incumbent.

JANUARY 18, 2008

Was It Only a Game?

Among this year's worst news, for me, was the death of Bobby Fischer.

Telling a friend this, I got, "Are you out of your bloody mind? He was a Nazi-praising raving lunatic and anti-Semite. Death is too good for him."

He did, indeed, become all that. But none of it describes the man I knew.

Towering genius, riches, international fame, and a far from normal childhood might be too heady a mix for anyone to handle. For him they proved fatal.

I'm still sad about his death. In our three encounters on my late-night show, I became quite fond of him.

Viewing the tapes of those memorable appearances, a licensed professional in the field of psychiatry might see foreshadowings of the savage illness that eventually engulfed him. I didn't.

Some years back, the writer Rene Chun was working on a book about Fischer and confessed to being unprepared for the maddening—and maddened—thing that the poor man had become.

Getting low on advance money, and having learned that Fischer had been on my show several times, Chun asked if there were any way he could see these "invaluable documents—short of unaffordable fees." I sent them to him.

He had written me about a still picture he'd found:

> Thought you might like to see this photo. When I came across it recently, I was struck by the warmth it transmits to the viewer. Both of you look like you are having a fabulous time. Studying the photo it's obvious that these two

men genuinely like each other. Fischer is clearly comfortable with you.

If you screen Fischer's *Tonight Show* appearance, which aired shortly after his '72 victory, the enigmatic chess champ comes off well, but doesn't look nearly as comfortable or spontaneous during the course of 15 minutes as he does here in a single frame. Of course, this is just an isolated image. One would have to see the entire show to make a judgment. But I suspect that the Fischer in your interviews is a Fischer we haven't seen before. The famous *60 Minutes* piece that aired just before the '72 match depicts a totally different Fischer—anxious, guarded, serious as hell. . . .

You were lucky enough to be the only media person that Fischer seemed to be completely at ease with. Taping not one, but several interviews with you speaks volumes about your character and integrity. [*I'll be the judge of that.—D.C.*]

Fischer could smell a show biz phony in an instant. . . .

It must seem strange to people too young to remember that there was once a chess champion—of all things—who became arguably the most famous celebrity on earth. And that his long-anticipated match against the reigning Russian champion, Boris Spassky, was broadcast and watched worldwide as if it were the Super Bowl, except that chess drew a much bigger audience.

There was another element that added to the drama. With Fischer the American and Spassky the Russkie, the monumental match was seen as a Cold War battle.

The Russian chess champions considered themselves the undoubted best. Time out of mind the Soviet chess dynasty had reigned supreme, viewing themselves as a rightful symbol of Soviet superiority in all fields.

PBS broadcast the drama in sports fashion, complete with play-by-play commentary by Shelby Lyman, who himself became a household name. People stayed home from work, glued to their sets, and PBS got its highest ratings ever. The country and the world became chess crazy. And Fischer crazy. Chess sets, dusty on the shelves, suddenly sold in the millions.

We ordinary mortals can only try to imagine what it might feel like to be both young and so greatly gifted at a complex art. And to be better at it than any other living being, *past or present*. There are plenty of geniuses and lots of famous people, but few are both. Is anyone really capable of surviving such a double burden?

We assume that geniuses are blessed creatures who don't have to work hard to achieve their goals. Hard for us, easy for them. But Bobby as a kid—IQ pushing 200—put in ten to fifteen hours a day of brain power and heavy concentration that would kill an ordinary person. (Or at least me.)

The chess world was already well aware of this kid prodigy. But they were unprepared for him to suddenly go up against the acknowledged top player of the day in the United States Chess Championship. And win—at the age of *thirteen*. When asked what happened, he said, "I got better."

What does the spectacle of such dedication to seemingly unreachable goals—until he reached them—do to our image of our own accomplishments? Even those of the so-called overachievers among us? Touchingly, when he returned to my show after having disposed of Spassky, triumphant in the eyes of the world, he opined that he might be wise to try developing some of the rest of himself. He had begun to see that a life of nothing but chess was "kind of limited." (He went to dinner in Reykjavík with friends. "Bobby couldn't follow the conversation," one said. "He sort of backed into the corner, got out his little pocket chess set and played with himself.") He announced on my show that he was now "reading a lot of magazines, trying to keep up with what's going on in the world." He was still in his twenties.

Until the advent of Bobby Fischer, my image of a young chess genius was not flattering. I pictured a sort of wizened and unpopular youth, small of frame, reclusive, short, with messy hair, untended acne, thick glasses, and shirt sticking out in back. And also perhaps, as the great V. Nabokov wrote in describing somewhat genderless piano prodigies with eye trouble and obscure ailments, "something vaguely misshapen about their eunuchoid hindquarters."

* * *

Getting Fischer on my show that first time, before the big match, was considered a major catch at the time. If anyone in the audience shared my image of what a chess genius probably looked like, Bobby's entrance erased it.

Here was no Nabokovian homunculus. There appeared, somewhat disconcerted, a tall and handsome lad with football-player shoulders, impeccably suited, a little awkward of carriage and unsure how to negotiate the unfamiliarity of the set, the bright lights, the wearing of makeup, the band music, the hand shaking and the thundering ovation—all at the same time. I had hoped to avoid the cliché "gangling," but Bobby gangled. He sort of lurched into his chair.

Once seated, he was something to behold. Six foot two (tall in those days), athletic in build, perfect in grooming, and with striking features. The face radiated intelligence. You couldn't confuse him with anyone you'd ever seen.

And there were the eyes.

Cameras fail to convey the effect of his eyes when they were looking at you. A bit of Svengali perhaps, but vulnerable. And only the slightest hint of a sort of theatrical menace, the menace that so disconcerted his opponents.

Looking out over the audience, I could clearly see entranced women gazing at him as if willing to offer their hearts—and perhaps more—to the hunky chess master.

When I asked him about such matters, he said that the awful demands of his life—the global travel; the constant study, sometimes until dawn, followed by play; the punishing five-hour sessions at full concentration, day after day—all this made it "pretty hard to . . . (*hesitates*) . . . build up a relationship." He seemed quite surprised with himself, as did friends watching, that he had allowed so revealing a moment. (That old Cavett magic, no doubt.)

One thing he said in that first appearance became famous. At one point I asked him what, in terms of thrills, the chess equivalent might be of, say, hitting a home run. His answer: "I like the moment when I break a man's ego." There was a trace of a chill in his laughter.

For me, watching the Fischer shows after all this time contained quite a few surprises. For example, I winced watching the first one when I heard myself use the word "paranoid." That awful word that in the later, bad years became almost part of Bobby's name. But back then it passed unnoticed.

On the post-Spassky show it was Bobby himself who uttered the P-word. I re-winced. He claimed that Harold C. Schonberg, then the *New York Times*'s music and chess critic, "said I was paranoid." Somehow the joker in me came up with, "No he didn't. You're imagining it."

Happily he got the joke—a beat before the audience did—and laughed heartily. (People who knew him were in disbelief that he could actually laugh and be funny on the show.)

He didn't know it, but I had spotted him earlier that day. We were walking to my studio at the same time, but from opposite directions. He towered over passersby who would stop in their tracks and gaze worshipfully. From a distance, you could see the consonants in his name on their lips: *B, F.* He seemed unaware of them, with his ever-present little transistor radio clapped to his ear like a teenager.

He had come to like soul music, he said.

That night Tony Randall was on, which Bobby enjoyed, and both of us inquired about his reported loutish behavior in Reykjavík that nearly prevented the Great Match from happening, what with his incessant demands and threats to walk out and accusing the Russians of cheating and demanding to have the swimming pool to himself. (They had actually promised him that in their eagerness to get him.) Bobby, looking thoughtful, surprised lots of people with, "I'm afraid that a lot of what I did was . . . not too bright." (*Friendly laughter.*)

Crazy as it sounds, the paranoia was not all on one side in Reykjavík. The Russians demanded that Bobby's chair be taken apart, so they could look for a hidden device that Spassky thought might be causing him to feel hypnotized. Bobby loved it.

Randall had vastly amused the audience when he told a story about a piece of hate mail that came to him not at his own show but, of all places, at the old *Opera Quiz* weekend radio show with its presumably cultured and genteel limited audience. Tony was a sometime panelist. The nasty letter began, "The only thing more disgusting than watching a faggot like you on television is when you go on Dick Cavett's and having to watch you two faggots sit there together, yakking like two faggots," etc. The audience was hysterical.

Fischer, having watched this from backstage, came out to a long ovation. Wanting to dispel the myth that he and Spassky were non-speaking enemies, he insisted that despite all the gossipy press to the contrary, he and Boris were truly quite good friends, and went bowling together. "Really buddy-buddy," he said, adding, "not like you two, of course." (*Booming laughter.*)

Tony asked him if he'd like to be on *The Odd Couple*. Bobby's "maybe" fetched a healthy laugh.

With a little pressing about could he imagine another life for himself, he confessed to having given some thought to becoming an actor. If he had been able to use all that was in him, he might have proved a forerunner of the genius actor Javier Bardem. Fine actors can use a touch of madness. (Geo. C. Scott, with several touches, comes to mind.) Bobby had acquitted himself stylishly as a guest on *The Bob Hope Show*. Strange to think that at that time Bobby was known to even more people than his world-famous host. I couldn't help wondering if Bobby F. knew who Bob H. was until then. "He's a funny guy," Bobby allowed.

Our mental health advisers, shrinks, and friends advise us to avoid guilt at all costs. But they don't tell you how. There seems to be an unlimited number of guilts available to us. When someone we know—or are related to—comes apart and deteriorates physically and mentally and commits suicide, don't most of us think, "Maybe I'd have been the one who could have made the difference; done or said this or that and saved the poor soul?" How much of such thinking is charitable and how much egotistical? For a time I was pained by that thought that I might have been Bobby's salvation. But then we comfort ourselves, concluding that of course it would have been too late. And then, alas, comes, *But would it have been?*

I like to think I would have gladly boarded a plane and tracked

Bobby down—in whichever of his far-flung refuges around the globe he was holing up in—and tried to be of help. But how would he have, as they say, received me? Would I still be one of the few (some said only) people Bobby ever really liked? Might pathology have erased memory? Would I have been utterly forgotten? Or a Jew bastard, sent to further hurt him? (Bobby's mother was Jewish, as was his biological father, who left when Bobby was two.)

The thought that he might have been delighted to see me and that I might have brought him even brief pleasure—parted the clouds for him for a while—is hard to think about. Because it means I should have done it. This is going to always haunt me.

Somewhere on the Internet I ran across a picture of the later, ailing Bobby. I don't know where it was and don't want to see it again.

It's a color head shot. It's not pleasant to see how the magnificent edifice had crumbled. He looks ancient, he's balding and that great face that shone with intelligence is all but hidden by a massive growth of white beard. It could be an actor playing King Lear. He is facing the camera but the eyes are cut sharply to one side. They look both suspicious and frightened. Those great Fischer eyes of old have been replaced. They're not these.

I'm surprised in writing this how much emotion there still is in the subject for me. There's no story like it: genius kid, precocious, plunged into triumphant victory, money, and world fame—no one under thirty should be subjected to fame—then gradual decline into raving lunatic. "Those whom the gods would destroy, they first make mad."

You'd think, with all the hells Bobby descended through in his allotted sixty-four years, that those gods could have spared him the agony of kidney disease—a notoriously painful way to die. A Sioux friend of mine likes to quote, "Count no man lucky until he has had a good death." If there be such a thing as a place of rest, I hope that Robert James Fischer has found it.

I've sat for a while trying to figure out how to close. A faint glimmer of a bit of poetry had been swimming elusively in my head, just out of reach. And then it emerged.

It's from E. E. Cummings's famous poem about another lionized and legendary figure who, after triumph and glamour, also did not have "a good death": Buffalo Bill.

With Cummings's quirky punctuation, it's a short poem, with no title but referred to by its first three words: "Buffalo Bill's / defunct."

Its closing lines somehow seem appropriate here. They are:

> *Jesus*
> *he was a handsome man*
> *and what I want to know is*
> *how do you like your blue-eyed boy*
> *Mister Death*

FEBRUARY 8, 2008

A videoclip is available at http://opinionator.blogs.nytimes.com/2008/02/08/was-it-only-a-game/.

Bobby and You

Thank you very much.

That's probably the number one cliché in the world, but *merci beaucoup* is a touch affected and the great George Orwell's rules for writing include not prettying up your stuff with foreign phrases.

Disclosure Dept.: if this seems hurried—if not just plain slapdash—that's because it is. For maybe the fourth time in my life I set my digital alarm clock for evening instead of morning, and it is deadline day (another dumb practice) and time's wingèd chariot is mercilessly snapping at my fanny. My editor is a stern taskmaster and fortuitously (in the preferred sense of accidentally) here at my elbow sits the *Times*'s own article about its laying off employees. If this should now include me, as the little song says, "it's been good to know ya."

Much of your reaction to the Bobby Fischer piece even produced a tear on my part—am I becoming a sob sister?—as I read your comments. So many "moveds" and "stunned speechlesses" and the various ways of saying, as one lady did, "Thank you, Mr. Cavett, for bringing the human Bobby Fischer back into my life." There was even one "I wept." (From a famous person who would prefer not to be identified, I'm sure.)

I take a measure of delight at the reaction expressed in various ways as "Thank you for altering my nasty thoughts about Fischer formed by all the awful stuff about his later years. I had no idea there was a likable human being behind it all."

Some readers wondered: did he ever come back to America?

No, and not for a reason that is generally known, I find. He was—as the dramatic phrase hath it—a fugitive from American justice. By returning to his partially forgotten rematch with Spassky, he had defied the United States sanction against activity with Yugoslavia.

It was in the rematch that he made a blunder that, it was said, a seven-year-old—one other than Fischer, maybe—wouldn't make. A blunder one reader says he can never forget because of "Fischer's body language . . . at the moment." As one chess expert described it, "Fischer, stunned, slowly arose and offered Spassky his hand. The chess world was agog."

And, perhaps with *his* ego broken for a change, what must have been the impact on the psyche of a man whose entire life's work must have appeared to him to have crumbled? A man about whom it had once been said (by grand master Lubomir Kavalek), "He was an avid reader, devouring any chess book or magazine that came into his hands. He studied other chess giants, picking up the best ideas and improving on them. His opening play was deadly." The former world champion Tigran Petrosian remarked, after losing to him in 1971, "As soon as Fischer gains even a slightest advantage, he begins playing like a machine. You cannot even hope for some mistake."

More than one colleague of Fischer's has said that Bobby had one mortal fear in life: losing. And that this accounted for his notorious delaying antics.

Here is how Larry Evans, an American grand master, described the kid from Brooklyn who single-handedly collapsed the Soviet Chess Empire: "The most individualistic, intransigent, uncommunicative, uncooperative, solitary, self-contained and independent chess master of all time, the loneliest chess champion in the world. He is also the strongest player in the world. In fact, the strongest player who ever lived."

As we know, he went on to bury Spassky in that second match.

A bit more detail on his troubles:

Arrested at Narita airport in Tokyo for an expired passport, he was jailed for nine months, after which Iceland—the country he had put on the map—offered him citizenship. He never saw his homeland again. Somewhere late in life he is reported to have fathered a girl.

After that second Spassky match, like Edwin Arlington Robinson's Richard Cory, Bobby "was rich, yes, richer than a king." But it didn't do him much good. He lived modestly, buying no mansions or Lamborghinis. He claimed to have been variously swindled out of his fortune. While apparently destitute between the two matches and living in Pasadena, he was sometimes without a place to sleep, except for short periods on the couches of friends. He was spotted riding aimlessly back and forth on Los Angeles city buses. Usually with a chess book. Sometimes with a comic book. The lustrous world champion and world celebrity had fallen into deep obscurity.

I'm grateful to the readers who tried to make me feel better about my failure to "help" Bobby in his illness. Especially those who described their own experiences trying to get through to and help unfortunates in their own lives who suffered mental illness like Fischer's—and how futile it was.

One somewhat irritating letter does, I confess, raise a considerable point: "Has the author [Cavett] seen medical records showing that BF was diagnosed as 'mentally ill'?" You go on to say that portraying him thus may be an effort to soften the harsh effect of "BF's opinions" as those of "a lunatic or deranged man."

I don't mind being reminded that I am neither a doctor nor a licensed expert in abnormal psychology. There is too much misdiagnosis around, even by the supposed professionals—as we learn from some excellent recent articles about the readiness to diagnose depression when the patient is only legitimately but deeply sad, perhaps with grief—and the consequences of unnecessary and destructive medication.

In light of that letter, here is a depressing little item that I left out before that might easily lead to fairly confident diagnosis by us amateurs. Bobby had the fillings of his teeth removed because "if somebody took a filling out and put in an electronic device, he could influence your thinking." By my lights, unlicensed as they are, that's derangement. And as pitiful as anything I've ever heard of.

"We shall never look upon his like again" retains its popularity no matter how often it has been proved wrong. The overwhelming body of evidence suggests that—in Bobby's case—it won't be. Anybody care to bet?

FEBRUARY 22, 2008

A Most Uncommon Man

It was my freshman year at Yale. I was fresher than most—and from Nebraska—so just about everything I saw, heard, and did that year astonished me.

Mr. Cecil Lang, my English teacher, ended a class one day with the words "You might want to drop by the Law School tonight. A man I consider one of the most dangerous men in America is lecturing there." I went.

Onstage was a tall, interesting-looking man unlike anything in my experience. A speaker so vocally various, so facially vigorous, so versatile of eyebrow, so eccentric of movement and gesture—even rising virtually "on point" at times for emphasis. This was not just a speaker. This was a performer.

Only a handful of the best comic actors could display such an arsenal of physical and vocal variety. Afterward, I walked to my room, my head ringing with un-clichéd, half-understood phrases. Like ". . . and the mental spastics who read the *Nation*."

This was some kind of strange genius, alien to anything I'd ever seen and heard.

I would have had no trouble believing, as I learned years later, that at the age of eight—when some kids still write to Santa—this guy had written to the king of England, demanding certain war debt reparations.

The politics in his speech had meant nothing to me. I discovered my first editorial page that year and had to be reminded what Right and Left meant. When I thanked my teacher for having recommended such an entertaining evening, he said something I wasn't sure I understood: "Buckley's amazing, isn't he? If he had a little more of the common touch, he'd be a truly dangerous man."

I certainly never expected to meet him.

Years pass, and I suddenly find myself in the daunting world of hosting a talk show. I had seen a lot of William F. Buckley Jr. on his own show—a formidable presence on the screen—and there he was on my next week's guest list.

Because it was Buckley, I was nervous in a way I don't think I ever was before or since. If you'd asked me what exactly I was nervous about, I doubt that I could have defined it.

Then I found out.

Conversation seemed to be moving along nicely when, in reference to something he had just brought up, I said, "I'm not really familiar with that." Back came, "You don't seem to be familiar with anything."

Wham!

I think I nearly lost consciousness. It was a rotten thing to say to a beginner.

If he meant it to be funny, it wasn't. There was a kind of sympathetic "ouch" sound from the audience as I heard myself utter a feeble, "Oh, I'm . . . familiar with everything." The rest is blank, except for the thought that this new job wasn't always going to be fun. It was a moment that at a later time both of us would have been funny about. Not then. Somehow I got through the rest of the show on automatic pilot.

We now make a cinematic fast-forward jump cut to the future that will seem at first like a non sequitur bit from a confusingly edited film.

A tranquil, sparkling blue bay in the Caribbean. Several people are being pulled horizontally in a human chain through the water. Power is supplied by one of those expensive Hammacher Schlemmer toys. A sturdy little German-made putt-putt gas engine sold so rich folks, frolicking, can enjoy . . . um, being pulled through water.

Two men in the short line of swimsuited, giggling aquatic revelers are recognizable. A tourist bystander asks her friend, "Hey, can that be Dick Cavett?" "Where?" "There. In the water. The guy clinging to the naked lower calves of William F. Buckley Jr." As the latter might have

answered her with that famous and much imitated reso-
nance, "Mirabile dictu, madam, you are correct."

Obviously our relationship had taken a turn for the better.

Over the intervening years, the Cavetts and the Buckleys had become friends. Bill and his tall and striking wife, Pat—whose elegance, smarts, and wit made her the perfectly suited WFB mate—were there on their beautiful sailboat/yacht. (Pat was Patricia, of course, but I never heard anyone call her that.)

They had sailed from New York, the yacht captained by Bill, the undaunted sailor. By this time he had been an eagerly welcomed guest on my show numerous times. What he might have termed "our initial contretemps" was forgotten.

But one day I remembered it.

I felt I just had to ask him about it. I re-created it exactly. He clearly didn't recall it and seemed a bit embarrassed. I had gotten to know and to like him so much by then that I was sorry I'd brought it up. It clearly disturbed him. I quickly offered him an out.

"Is there any chance you had me confused with David Frost?" I asked.

"Precisely," he said, taking my offer and flashing that trademark wink and grin. We laughed.

It was cocktail time below deck. My wife and Bill were fond of each other and enjoyed making each other laugh. ("I do enjoy Bill," she said once. "I just wish it didn't make me feel unfaithful to Gore.") In her omnivorous reading she had downed a heavy tome on Catholicism, and she asked him to clarify some abstruse point about Saint Paul and the founding of the church that seemed to her somehow self-contradictory.

"Well, the theological question becomes . . ." he began, but he seemed to get stuck. He backed up and started a whole new sentence and came up short again. Before he could start a third, his amused spouse said, "Bill, you always like to try new things. Why not admit you don't know the answer?" After a moment, he joined in the laughter.

Later that year, in view of his striking out on the religious question, he gave my wife the *Harvard Concordance to Shakespeare*, containing every single word in the plays and every line containing that word, a monument of scholarship.

It weighed a ton, and he cautioned her about reading it in the bathtub. It was inscribed, "From one who was at a temporary loss for words, to one who—now—never need be. Affectionately, Bill."

She responded by sending him a cherished old volume given to her by the writer Jean Stafford. I hated to see it go but had to admit it was the absolutely ideal gift for William F. Buckley. Its incredible but accurate title: *The Pilgrim's Progress—in Words of One Syllable*.

She put: "For Bill, should he ever need some. Love, Carrie Nye."

MARCH 7, 2008

Uncommoner than Thou: Buckley, Part 2

William F. Buckley was a man who had a great capacity for fun and for amusing himself by amazing others.

Example: Dick Clurman of *Time* magazine, an affable gent, was a guest on the Buckley yacht in the Caribbean. After dinner, Bill B., leafing through a TV log, announced that *The Wizard of Oz* would be starting in half an hour—in English, broadcast from Puerto Rico. Clurman was delighted and confessed to never having seen it.

At the appointed time the set was switched on, but to everyone's chagrin it seemed the movie had already been on for a good half hour. Bill had read the starting time wrong. Clurman's disappointment was visible.

"Let's see if my name cuts any ice down here," his host said. The incredulous Clurman later described how his friend grabbed the phone, rang up the station in Puerto Rico, managed to get through to the engineer, explained his guest's disappointment, and asked if it would be too much trouble to start the movie over!

In disbelief, Clurman saw the screen go blank, followed by a frantic display of jumbling and flashing. And then—the opening credits and the comforting strains of "Over the Rainbow." The movie began anew. Clurman declared that never until then had he known the full meaning of "chutzpah."

I think Bill decided to let a year go by, giving Clurman time to regale all his friends and acquaintances with the tale of the Oz miracle. It was then, still reluctantly, that the magician revealed his secret. The movie had not been broadcast at all that night—except on Bill's tape deck, which he had secretly manipulated with his unseen left arm while "talking on the phone" using the other.

He was full of surprises. Once on my show we were talking about

Muhammad Ali, and Bill revealed that he himself was taking boxing lessons. The audience gasped.

"Expecting trouble?" I asked.

"No," he intoned. "But I'm ready."

Buckley enjoyed tossing literary references into the conversation, a habit not always guaranteed to make friends. Once, in answer to something I said, he injected, "As Oscar Wilde said, 'Hypocrisy is the compliment that vice pays to virtue.'"

A fine and witty remark to be sure, but one you wouldn't be wise to depend on as your opening gag in your nightclub act. And one I would guess he knew it might take the rest of us a moment to fully "get." If then.

But that's not what bothered me about it. A little voice in me whispered, "*Is* that Oscar Wilde?" In one of those bizarre coincidences life tickles us with, a French friend had given me, two days before, a volume of famous "Citations" (*see tahss ee own*) by French wits. Try real hard to believe that among the half dozen she had checkmarked as favorites was that one. Yes. The alleged Wilde.

What fun to catch my learned guest on this. But because he was who he was, I figured he must be right, and the moment passed. And because he was who he was, it was mildly heartbreaking.

Weeks pass. And he is back. All fear of him is gone. Try not to form your entire opinion of me by what I did:

Bill, I said, *I notice that on your show you hold yourself to a high level of accuracy. And that you don't shrink from holding your guests to it. I like to do the same here.* (He is too smart not to sense something. And what I did next is inexcusable.)

Last time you were here, Bill, you said, "L'hypocrisie est un hommage que le vice rend a la vertu." I forget how it goes in English. (Can you see why I was sometimes beaten up on the playground?)

Well, you get the idea. I told him that it was, in fact, "not Oscar Wilde, who was of course Irish, but François de la Rochefoucauld, who, as far as we know, was French. And I just couldn't let you go around embarrassing yourself like that again. As a friend." (*Audience chortles, then claps.*)

Bill's expression was beyond description. There was fire. Ice. And a trace of amusement.

DC: What are you thinking, Bill?

WFB (*after a well-timed pause*): Of a variety of ways to express my profound gratitude.

(*Everyone has a laugh.*)

A writer friend reminds me that, over the years, many a journalist's day was made by receiving one of the short personal notes Buckley used to send when they'd written something he liked. These cherished tidbits were only a line or two long but imbued with the full Buckley flavor.

Language was his medium and he loved to make it roll around and do tricks. I just now unearthed a copy of one of his books he had inscribed to me. He was a fan of all wordplay and had admired an unforgivable pun I had made about French painters. He wrote:

> *To Richard, in deepest gratitude for "More in Seurat than in Ingres." May I use it?*
> *With affection,*
> *Bill*

The adjective "fabulous," through overuse, has become cheap currency. But it applies to him. In the sense of "fabled." He was a character in the true sense of that word. And not of our time. He was like a creation out of nineteenth—or even eighteenth—century literature, rather than the predictable and dreary sort of folk you get these days. Not one of whom would have the class to reply to an irate letter writer demanding that he cancel her subscription to his magazine: "Cancel your own damn subscription."

If I were composing a Top Ten list of things that will never be said, I submit as number one: "Hey, I just met someone exactly like William F. Buckley."

POSTSCRIPT: *Bill would have loved this. A recent news story reported how badly our ignorant American high school students had done on a general knowledge test—failing to identify Hitler correctly, or to know when the Civil War was. Well, irony of ironies, the test itself contained an error.*

One of its multiple-choice "correct" answers was wrong.

What would our friend have done with this? He would convince us that we are all too soft from being handed things too easily, and that what would be best for all concerned would be to let the reader diligently discover the error himself, rather than to get the answer by spoon, so to speak.

So, in memory of Bill, until next time. . . .

MARCH 14, 2008

Candidate, Improve Your Appearance!

Hillary Clinton is just beginning a live speech as I type. And I just failed in my purpose.

I tried to reach the Clinton campaign to suggest that she could get a big, heartwarming laugh if she came onstage wearing a flak jacket.

I'm not sure the sight gag would have guaranteed her the nomination, but a laugh never hurts and is worth a thousand straight lines. And it's certainly funnier than the leaden, anti-Obama "Xerox" line someone saddled her with a while back. If that gag came from a staff member, he or she should have been busted to the rank of gofer. Or gofeuse, I suppose.

If I were running a campaign, I'd urge taking the mountain of money reportedly squandered on pizza, coffee, and bagels and spending it more wisely—on a talented young comedy writer. Remember Twain's "Against the assault of laughter nothing can stand"? All candidates should post this on their shaving mirrors. Or makeup mirrors. (This clumsy gender thing has to stop.)

We keep getting articles and reports of how John McCain is adored, cuddled, and all but fondled in the back of his bus by his devotees in the press, who are arranged, it sounds like, at his feet before his big, relaxing chair. His ability to create and maintain this camaraderie is surely a vastly valuable thing. One trait those "ink-stained wretches" of the press especially like about him is his candor and what's been termed his risk-taking frankness and sense of irony. This affection for him may account for why they fail to do him the favor of pointing out how badly he delivers a speech.

By speech, I don't mean his off-the-cuff appearances holding a hand mike and working the crowd, or his cool, entertaining guest shots with (the help of) Jon Stewart. Those are fine, and at those times you see the thing in him that makes people say he seems genuine and honest—a mensch saying what he believes, a real and intelligent person, as distinct from the vinyl Mitt Romney, or Boob of the Year contest winner—by a landslide—Congressman Steve King from Iowa, with his "terrorists dancing in the streets if Obama is elected" line. In short, all the things conveyed by the now so very popular buzzword: authenticity. The newest must for candidates. (How did I get this far without resorting to *sine qua non*?)

I mean those speeches from behind the lectern, center stage, requiring the three teleprompters right, left, and center. They are invisible to the audience and are supposed to create the illusion that you are not reading. And they do, when skillfully used. Ronald Reagan went to England with them when they were new. Armed with them and his acting ability he astonished the Brits with what they took to be his spontaneous speaking at length, sans text.

It's a pleasure to watch Obama's mastery of the technique. And Clinton—and I didn't say "even Clinton"—uses it much better than McCain does. And just about everybody does it better than the capering loon who does a soft shoe for the cameras while young Americans are dismembered and splattered in Iraq. What do you think would happen if, at a presidential press conference, someone like the excellent Martha Raddatz were to ask, "Mr. President, I hope this isn't too personal, but do you ever think about—maybe late at night—how many thousands of human beings would be alive today if it weren't for you?"

Sometimes when Bush speaks I can forget who he is momentarily and find myself actually pulling for him; probably from misplaced performer empathy. His speechifying has a strong odor of remedial reading about it, combined with an apparent fear that there might be some hard words ahead.

But back to McCain. Does something in him rebel at the deception aspect of doing what, when done well, tricks people into saying, "Look at that. Not even using notes"? Our John seems to actually change personalities at the lectern. Something in him tightens. His voice even goes up several notes, and he seems bogus in a way that he never does in other settings. Like an actor stuck with a part he's not comfortable in.

Politicians, if smart, would hire not just a comedy writer but an acting coach. Years ago, the gifted and classy film actor (and lieutenant commander in the navy) Robert Montgomery pulled off a miracle in this regard. Hired as a public appearance consultant for the marginally articulate Dwight D. Eisenhower—a former president, should you be among the students who scored so abysmally on that general knowledge test a while back—Montgomery transformed the man.

First he hauled the president out from behind the massive presidential desk from which it was hard not to appear ponderous and had him stand in front of it. Shirtsleeves; no jacket. To cure the rigid, military upright look of a general, he had his illustrious client lean back slightly against the desk (without sitting on it) and cross his arms casually. The actor in Montgomery knew how important stance is to the way you talk.

The success of these seemingly minor adjustments was instant. Suddenly, turgid old General Eisenhower became "Ike." A genial, avuncular fellow you might like to have over.

Although not quite considered as good an actor as Robert Montgomery was, I could still give McCain a few tips. (Few will ever be as good at it as Obama is. He has mastered the art of public speaking both off the cuff and while seeming not to use the prompter.)

If I were ever called in to coach candidates on how to give those awful stand-up speeches, here's what I would say.

Tip #1. Change all "I wills" and "I shalls" from the speech to "I'll"; also, "I haves" and "I ams" to "I've" and "I'm," etc. You'd be surprised how much this cuts down on the oratory tone.

Tip #2. Pretend you are speaking to one person. One single person. Because that's what everybody is. No one watching or sitting in the audience is an "all of you" or an "everyone" or a "those of you" or a "Hi, everybody," and no one is a "ladies and gentlemen." You, out there, are a "you." So, speaker, think of yourself as being viewed by only two eyes. (Presumably on the same person.) The most magical word you can use, short of a person's name, is "you."

The great Arthur Godfrey practiced this invariably. "How are you?" he said, is all-important. "'Ladies and gentlemen of the radio audience' is bull and reaches no one." With emphasis on "one." On radio he had millions of listeners, largely adoring women in the day-time, each convinced he was speaking to her personally. Including my grandmother. (You knew it worked because in a ruthless Nebraska summer, when all the windows were open, I could hear Arthur unin-terruptedly as I passed one house after the other.)

Tip #3. I feel almost silly when I do this one, but it works. Grab a bunch of words off the prompter and, instead of staring straight ahead, glance down and to one side as you do—in real life—when thinking just what to say next. Then look back and deliver those snatched-up words to the camera. It works like a charm. (As a beloved childhood magic catalogue of mine used to say—with unintended ambiguity—"We cannot recommend this trick too highly.")

If I were McCain's adviser I would shock everyone by having him come out carrying his script, and saying—not "Ladies and gentle-men," as we just learned, but launch right into, "You know, I don't use these teleprompters very well. I guess I'm just not one of those people who can fool you into thinking I'm making it up as I go along . . . which these things are supposed to do. I don't even fool myself. I cringe when I watch myself trying to bring off that 'electronic decep-tion,' you might call it . . . Anyway, here's my speech (*shows it*) and I'm going to read the damn thing to you. Surely I can't make even that look phony. (*Slight pause.*) Can I?" (*Laughter.*)

"Dick, what are you trying to do, get John McCain elected?" I hear you cry. I keep re-liking McCain, because he seems honest. A prince among thieves.

If I were all out for him, though, I'd need to convince myself that his continued pursuit of those twin mirages of his in Iraq—"success" and "victory"—are merely necessary devices to woo the least desir-able elements of his party. But I can't be sure.

That's why, at the moment, I like somebody else better. I guess I just can't resist giving helpful tips to a fellow performer.

(Wait till McCain gets the bill for this.)

MARCH 28, 2008

Memo to Petraeus and Crocker:
More Laughs, Please

Once again it is time to bid aloha to that sober team of mirthless entertainers, Petraeus & Crocker.

It's hard to imagine where you could find another pair of such sleep-inducing performers.

I can't look at General David H. Petraeus—his uniform ornamented like a Christmas tree with honors, medals, and ribbons—without thinking of the great Mort Sahl at the peak of his brilliance. He talked about meeting General William Westmoreland in the Vietnam days. Mort, in a virtuoso display of his uncanny detailed knowledge—and memory—of such things, recited the lengthy list ("Distinguished Service Medal, Croix de Guerre with chevron, Bronze Star, Pacific Campaign," and on and on), naming each of the half acre of decorations, medals, ornaments, campaign ribbons, and other fripperies festooning the general's sternum in gaudy display. Finishing the detailed list, Mort observed, "Very impressive!" Adding, "If you're twelve."

As speakers, both Petraeus and Crocker are guilty of unbearable sesquipedalianism, a word wickedly inflicted on me by my English-teaching mother. It's one of those words that is what it says. From the Latin, literally "using foot-and-a-half-long words." We all learned the word for words that sound like what they say—like "click" or "pop" or "boom" or "hiss"—but I'm sure the mercifully defunct Famous Writers School forbade using the *sesqui* word and *onomatopoeia* in the same paragraph. (You can have fun with both of them at your next cocktail party.)

But back to our story. Never in this breathing world have I seen a person clog up and erode his speaking—as distinct from his reading—with more "uhs," "ers," and "ums" than poor Ryan Crocker, the U.S. ambassador to Iraq. Surely he has never seen himself talking:

"Uh, that is uh, a, uh, matter that we, er, um, uh are carefully, uh, considering." (Not a parody, an actual Crocker sentence. And not even the worst.)

These harsh-on-the-ear insertions, delivered in his less than melodious, hoarse-sounding tenor, are maddening. And their effect is to say that the speaker is painfully unsure of what he wants, er, um, to say.

If Crocker's collection of these broken shards of verbal crockery were eliminated from his testimony, everyone there would get home at least an hour earlier.

Petraeus commits a different assault on the listener. And on the language. In addition to his own pedantic delivery, there is his turgid vocabulary. It reminds you of Copspeak, a language spoken nowhere on earth except by cops and firemen when talking to *Eyewitness News*. Its rule: never use a short word where a longer one will do. It must be meant to convey some misguided sense of learnedness and scholasticism—possibly even that dread thing, intellectualism—to their talk. Sorry, I mean their "articulation."

No crook ever gets out of the car. A "perpetrator exits the vehicle." (Does any cop say to his wife at dinner, "Honey, I stubbed my toe today as I exited our vehicle"?) No "man" or "woman" is present in Copspeak. They are replaced by that five-syllable, leaden ingot, the "individual." The other day, there issued from a fire chief's mouth, "It contributed to the obfuscation of what eventually eventuated." This from a guy who looked like he talked, in real life, like Rocky Balboa. And there's nothing wrong with that.

Who imposes this phony, academic-sounding verbal junk on brave and hardworking men and women who don't need the added burden of trying to talk like effete characters from Victorian novels?

And, General, there is no excuse anywhere on earth for a stillborn monster like "ethnosectarian conflict," as Jon Stewart so hilariously pointed out.

What would the general be forced to say if it weren't for the icky, precious-sounding "challenge" that he leans so heavily on? That politically correct term, which was created so that folks who are legally blind, deaf, clumsy, crippled, impotent, tremor-ridden, stupid, addicted, or villainously ugly are really none of those unhappy things at all. They are merely challenged. (Are these euphemisms supposed to make them feel better?) And no one need be unlucky enough to be dead or hideously wounded anymore. Those unfortunates are merely "casualties"—a sort of restful-sounding word.

(I have a friend who would like the opportunity to say to our distinguished warrior, "General Petraeus, my son was killed in one of your challenges.")

Petraeus uses "challenge" for a rich variety of things. It covers ominous developments, threats, defeats on the battlefield, and unfound solutions to ghastly happenings. And of course there's that biggest of challenges, that slapstick band of silent-movie comics called, flatteringly, the Iraqi "fighting forces." (A perilous one letter away from "fighting farces.") The ones who are supposed to allow us to bring troops home but never do.

Petraeus's verbal road is full of all kinds of bumps and lurches and awkward oddities. How about "ongoing processes of substantial increases in personnel"?

Try talking English, General. You mean *more soldiers.*

It's like listening to someone speaking a language you only partly know. And who's being paid by the syllable. You miss a lot. I guess a guy bearing up under such a chestload of hardware—and pretty ribbons in a variety of decorator colors—can't be expected to speak like ordinary mortals, for example you and me. He should try once saying—instead of "ongoing process of high-level engagements"—maybe something in colloquial English? Like "fights" or "meetings" (or whatever the hell it's supposed to mean).

I find it painful to watch this team of two straight men, straining on the potty of language. Only to deliver such . . . what? Such knobbed and lumpy artifacts of superfluous verbiage? (Sorry, now I'm doing it . . .)

But I must hand it to His Generalship. He did say *something* quite clearly and admirably and I am grateful for his frankness. He told us that our gains are largely imaginary: that our alleged "progress" is "fragile and reversible." (Quite an accomplishment in our sixth year of war.) This provides, of course, a bit of preemptive covering of the general's hindquarters next time that, true to Murphy's Law, things turn sour again.

Back to poor Crocker. His brows are knitted. And he has a perpetually alarmed expression, as if, perhaps, he feels something crawling up his leg.

Could it be he is being overtaken by the thought that an honorable career has been besmirched by his obediently doing the dirty work of the tinpot Genghis Khan of Crawford, Texas? The one whose foolish military misadventure seems to increasingly resemble that of General George Armstrong Custer at the Little Bighorn?

Not an apt comparison, I admit.

Custer sent only 258 soldiers to their deaths.

APRIL 11, 2008

Petraeus, Custer, and You

Clarifying statement: you may be one of the readers who asked if this column was being subjected to, as one put it, "a new kind of censorship" after last week's Petraeus/Crocker piece. The correct answer is "No." It was a case of your comments coming in so fast and in such quantity that the method of processing them and "putting them up" was temporarily overtaxed at around 200 and again at about 480. Nobody got censored, and no comments were misplaced, but some might have been briefly lost in the glut, so to speak. (What a lovely title for a song. "Lost in the Glut" . . .)

I thank you for that mass of comment and opinion, which ranged from "Hurrah, Mr. Cavett" to barely printable versions of phrases like "drop dead" and "full of."

It always quickens my pulse slightly when a comment begins *I agree with most of what you said, but* . . . This time the "but" had to do with my bad-mouthing General David H. Petraeus for showing off so many decorations, and Mort Sahl's joke about such displays. If I were a politician I would point out that it was Mort Sahl who did the joke, and that doesn't mean I agree with him.

(I do.)

I guess what bothers me about it is the ostentation. General Petraeus is greatly accomplished. So is a brilliant actor, but the actor doesn't walk around with an Oscar, an Emmy, a Tony, and a cluster of rave reviews affixed to his tunic.

Wouldn't quite a number of us be able to guess from the polished stars on General Petraeus's shoulder that he was a general and not a corporal? And that his accomplishments are surely of a higher order than meritorious K.P. or Extraordinary and Industrious Performance of Latrine Duty?

If intimidation is intended by the glittery and colorful exhibit, it certainly worked with the majority of that sorry panel of lawmakers in whom the general inspired shock and awe. And who—mealymouthed and fulsome in their praise—were virtually worshipful.

One fawning Republican senator spent his whole time composing and reciting so many verbal nosegays and sweet nothings and spoken love utterances to the general it began to resemble the balcony scene in an Elizabethan production of *Romeo and Juliet*. It was this bird who sent me straight to Turner Classic Movies. I'm not sure the television set didn't wave a white flag and switch channels by itself. Neither it nor I could stomach one more, "First, let me say this to you . . ." dollop of gooeyness.

I only dwell on this because so many readers "took me to task" about it. (What on earth does that phrase mean? To what task?) Wouldn't you wish to ask the actor clad in his trophies and reviews, "Whatever became of modesty?" I ask it of the general. (One or two commenters impertinently noted that if the general ends the war, he's out of an extremely lucrative job.) Since then, he has been assigned a new job. So far, I'm happy to say, I haven't seen anyone dare use the phrase "kicked upstairs."

I know I couldn't do what General Petraeus has done (but for one thing, once), and I admire and commend his evident accomplishments that got him all that fruit salad. And I would probably want to display it, too. But I like to think I might feel just a little reluctant to cover one pectoral with all those emblems, like roses on a parade float. Modesty, whither hast thou fled?

As for that "one thing, once," I may be, or may have been, as good at it as General P. is said to be. The one-arm push-up. In my gymnastics team days, I would have challenged him. I learned it to impress girls. Particularly Patsy Giesick. She said, "What's supposed to be so hot about that?" Patsy was a bit of a jock and I took her quickly home, fearing she might just throw a few one-armers herself.

Several commenters felt I had insulted still another general, pointing out that George Armstrong Custer didn't deserve to be in the same paragraph as George W. Bush because unlucky Yellow Hair "at least died with his men." One added that "dying with your men would never be a thing that would happen in the life of George Bush"—unless, of course, a fraternity house blew up.

There is also some scholarship on the subject of "Darling Autie" (what Custer's wife, Elizabeth, called him—perhaps partially explaining why he loved to be out on the plains with the boys) and his mental health. Some of his men had written in diaries to the effect that before and during the fatal expedition—the so-called Last Stand—he seemed "tireless" and "over-animated," singing as he rode and suddenly dashing away from the column and clean out of sight to chase an antelope. And "needing little or no sleep." All textbook symptoms of the manic state. You feel invincible and indestructible at the high end of the disease, your brain racing like a Lamborghini engine. You also feel that nothing bad can happen to you. (Or your men, I suppose, by extension.)

I guess you know that much is said of the fatally impetuous general that is the opposite of praise. He wasn't brilliant at West Point (see Bush/Yale). A special final exam had to be designed just for Autie alone in order to graduate him. Do you suppose it exists in the archives? How would it go?

CUSTER FINAL EXAMINATION
(Confidential. DO NOT REVEAL.)

———

Problem: One of your men, a thirty-year veteran of the Indian Wars, informs you that the largest encampment of Indians he has ever seen, comprising countless Sioux, Cheyenne, and a few Arapaho lodges, stretches for several miles along the riverbank and would contain an estimated 1,200 armed warriors. You have fewer than three hundred men. You should:

A. Laugh in his face.

B. Get into the center of a large city.

C. Charge into the middle of the camp and speak to those savages in no uncertain terms.

D. Wish that cell phones had been invented.

E. Give them presents. They are like children and love anything shiny. Should you have a copy of *The Golden Treasury of Poetry,* Sitting Bull is fond of Emily Dickinson.

F. Attack them boldly, kissing your men, your arse, and your scalp good-bye.

APRIL 25, 2008

Liar, Liar, Pants Aflame

Don't we all need a rest from this exhausting campaign?

You may, then, excuse me if this time I—as a refreshing change of pace—don't write about the most profound current subjects facing our world today.

I mean, of course, Rev. Wright, Miley Cyrus, and the Austrian lady kept in the bunker by the man whose offspring—or, as Bill Buckley would say, whose *progenita*—are simultaneously his grandchildren and his children.

(Shylock speaks of those who, at the irritating sound of the bagpipe, "cannot contain their urine." Just those four syllables—*Rev-er-end Wright*—affect me similarly. So . . .)

Way back on my PBS show I talked with the great English comedian (*Beyond the Fringe*), medical doctor, author, Cambridge scholar, and international opera director, the blindingly articulate Jonathan Miller. I asked if he had any great fears in life. "One," he said. "Having to take a general knowledge test. In public." (I remember Jonathan once confessing to another haunting fear: being tortured to reveal information that he did not possess.)

I had recognized my own great fear many years earlier, upon hearing for the first time of a then recent invention called a "lie detector." My fear became: "What if they asked you . . . ?"

I resolved to steer clear of them.

But once, on my ABC late-night show, I asked an eminent and famous criminal attorney, "If lie detectors work, how come they're not allowed in court cases?" Being a lawyer (and some of my best friends are lawyers—well, two), he skillfully avoided answering my question. "They do work," said Mr. Bailey. "I use them all the time." (Not in the courtroom, of course.)

"F. Lee," I challenged. "Prove that they work."

Not a man to shirk a dare, he said, "Have me back sometime and I'll bring one on the show. You can be the guinea pig, Dick."

With a compliment like that, who could refuse? Then I forgot all about it.

But he didn't. A few weeks later, Bailey brought a genuine, state-of-the-art polygraph to the show, along with a qualified and licensed operator of the machine. He was a German. I liked him right away because his accent sounded to me just like the great German character actor of a hundred movies Sig Rumann (*Ninotchka*, *Stalag 17*, *A Night at the Opera*, *A Day at the Races*).

Or maybe you know and revere as I do the classic Jack Benny/Carole Lombard/Ernst Lubitsch comedy *To Be or Not to Be*. (If you've never seen it, first things first: forget reading this and rent it.) I chose it as one of my all-time favorite films when it was my night to do so on Turner Classic Movies, getting to sit alongside the all-knowing and distinguished Robert Osborne. (If you know the film, its famous line "So they call me 'Concentration Camp Ehrhardt,' eh?" should bring Rumann instantly to mind.)

Back to our story. I was strapped into the threatening polygraph machine at my side, in full view of and facing the studio audience, wondering if I was about to make an ass of myself. (Or even part of one.) The lawyer and the German stood upstage, behind me and the machine, so as not to distract me during the test.

They listed some of the things that the machine could not cope with and that would cause it to fail: things like if the testee is drunk, exhausted, insane, or otherwise mentally deficient. "Or speaks a different language?" I wanted to ask, but didn't. I tried to be serious.

They said they would make it simple. I was to answer "Yes" to every question put to me. "Yes" would be appropriate to most but by no means all. Thus, the lies to be detected.

I supposed there would be stuff like "Is your name Dick Cavett?" (Yes.) "Are you, at this moment, in the United States?" (Yes.) "Does your mouth have teeth in it?" (Yes.) And so on. And that interspersed would be questions to which I must also answer "Yes," knowing that I was lying.

I tried to anticipate what those questions might be. Stuff like, I supposed (if I were writing them), "Is the moon made of green cheese?" (Yes.) "Are you wearing women's undies?" (Yes.) "Do 2 and 2 equal 5?" (Yes.) "Are you concealing a live toad in your clothing?" (Yes.) You get the drift.

The questions they asked were more mundane than my imaginings.

We ran through twenty or so of them as the stylus-bearing arm did its work, drawing lazy lines back and forth on the graph paper, presumably detecting. I tried my best, of course, to fool the thing. I had my heart set on it.

Guess what. At the end of the questioning, the German man removed the paper and quickly scanned it. He began to sweat. Noticeably.

Germans have an expression for how he looked, as in, *"Frau Mueller machte ein Gesicht wie drei Tage Regenswetter."* (Mrs. Muller had a look on her face like three days of rainy weather.) So did he. Perhaps forgetting for the moment that you shouldn't try to speak privately near microphones, he whispered in a sort of hushed croak to Bailey, "It didn't vork."

Wow!

The legal eagle was in a tight spot. He had stated confidently that he relied on the polygraph extensively in vetting witnesses, and so had a vested professional interest in the outcome.

He grabbed the paper from the moist German man and hastily ad-libbed, "They aren't so visible to the untrained eye, but when you know what to look for you can see the variations . . ." He pointed—but didn't show to the camera—the alleged variations.

"See right here . . . and over here . . . and . . ."

He had his wits about him, but his words were—how to say?—the opposite of true. Had he been attached to the supposedly talented machine, the arm would have been swinging wildly.

Like Saddam's WMDs, variations were there none.

I'm sorry to have to tell you the upshot of all this: sad to say, I played along. Why? What good television it would have made if I had said, "Come on, sir. Be a man. Fess up. I beat your dumb contraption fair and square. If you can see variations, you must have eyes like a high-resolution electron microscope."

So why didn't I? Maybe because I liked the lawyer in question and didn't want to embarrass him. But my failure to do so cheated the viewer out of some possible fireworks, and was also—you might even say—a miscarriage of justice. I had allowed the two of them to escape the consequences of their fiasco.

Anyway, it was all over.

(Backstage, I'm almost sure I saw both men grab a quick slug of schnapps from a hip flask.)

MAY 2, 2008

Polygraphically Perverse

Tell me your answer to this question, and I could probably come close to guessing your age: what public figure of an earlier time did you see, live on television, call lie detectors "twentieth-century witchcraft"? Want to give your memory a chance to click in? (Answer to be found later.)

I hope my causing you a week of suspense is forgivable. I mean about how I "beat" the polygraph. I can't stand the thought of your sleepless nights waiting for the answer, which, I fear, might prove to be a little drab, if not boring.

As a former magician, I am loath to reveal any secret, but here goes.

The answer to how I foiled the much reviled and much defended device is an odd one. It had to do with my mood that day.

I felt a little depressed. Not the big version—Depression capitalized—by any means, but just one of those days when you're a little "off." Not very alert, humorless, and kind of dull-headed in that way when it takes a bit of an effort to think and talk with any zest. You have to force yourself "up" a little to feel fully present and to converse, returning then into that faint haze. Again, it is not a deep thing and you can pass for normal.

As soon as the questioning started, I eased myself into my haze. I listened only enough to register what was being said, but remained mostly "away" when answering.

There was another curious element that I used to augment staying distant from the immediate present. I had to fly to Detroit after taping that night, and I let the only thing resembling a thought in my mind be a long-playing, "God, I don't want to go to Detroit."

This helped keep me even farther from the business at hand. I pretended the questioning was taking place in another room, with someone other than myself. That I was *over*hearing it.

(Just this week a chap on the street told me of his somewhat similar technique for foiling a job application polygraph: "I put myself mentally in my bedroom I had as a kid, looking around at the various objects and focusing on them in turn—curtains, gym shoes on the floor, waste basket, my picture of Roy Rogers, and so on, listening with only one-eighth of an ear to the questioner." This might work for you if the time ever comes and you don't have Detroit to help you.)

This has reminded me of something about a man far nobler than I. Somewhere years ago I read that when being tortured by his communist captors, Hungary's Cardinal Mindszenty developed a technique of what he called "putting the pain on the other side of the room."

I've developed this a bit. His Eminence's trick made it possible for me to astound my dentist by making it through a crown procedure without anesthetic. This impulse derives also from my having read eons ago that Katharine Hepburn never took Novocain at the dentist. "Dammit," I said to myself, "I'm as good a man as she is"—and I never did again, either. (Except for root canal!)

Lots of intelligent e-mail (yours) came in about the lie-detector column.

Some readers said I passed because nothing was riding on my answers that was vital to me in any way. That's largely true, except that I was keen to beat the thing. Even through the haze, I felt that strongly.

A reader suggests answering all "no" questions "yes," and vice versa, thereby messing up everything. Another—defending the device—said a lie might be missed by, say, the things measuring your pulse and your heart but not the thing measuring your breathing. Could be.

One writer added another category to the list of those whose conditions the machine can't handle (drunk, mentally retarded, thoroughly exhausted, pig stupid, etc.): sociopath. His tone suggested that he puts me in that category, but, like Hillary, I can take it. I'm glad for the information.

(On that subject, you know how at least once a week you wake up thinking, "Gee, I'm in the mood for a good book on psychopathy and sociopaths?" One of the most enthralling books I've ever read is Hervey Cleckley's *The Mask of Sanity*. The woman's case in *The Three Faces of Eve* came from him.)

A few readers wanted to know, *What is it Dick feared the machine might reveal when he wrote, "What if they asked . . . ?" in Part 1?* I'm not sure I had anything specific in mind, but I may have. It wasn't anything Raskolnikovian, since I at least can't recall murdering anyone. I know what it *could* have been, and I can't really do full disclosure on this, but can only say: I was about eight years of age and it took place in Vera Lundy's basement.

Not sure how to close out on the subject of lie detectors. A fair verdict might be that they are both valuable and fallible. That would not, of course, satisfy the "twentieth-century witchcraft" crowd.

So, who said it? It was the wonderful Sam Ervin, chairman of the Senate Watergate Committee hearings that undid Richard Nixon. R.I.P., Senator.

MAY 9, 2008

À la Recherche de Youthful Folly

Again, I offer refuge for those who, like me, feel they are being force-fed this endless presidential campaign. You might say we are being Strasbourg-goosed by it—this endless diet of the Hillster, the Obamster, and the Oldster.

I spent a recent weekend with a visitor named James McConnell of Tyler, Texas. He is the former Jimmy McConnell of Lincoln, Nebraska. And we spent the weekend bathing together.

If that gives anyone a naughty little thrill, I am not outing myself here. No, our mutual bath was one of nostalgia, reminiscence, and out-of-control laughter as we recalled and relived old times. As kids.

We lived two doors from each other. Together we played "guns" in a place we called the Jungle (a long row of spirea bushes); window-peeked at the pretty playground teacher bathing; defied the deadly summer polio scares by using the municipal pool (unbeknownst to our parents); broke school windows; blew up a neighbor's mailbox with a "three-incher"; bought single movie tickets (fourteen cents) and let the other guy in through the alley exit (if I had invested those saved fourteen cents . . .); and endless other stunts and japes, evading (with one exception) the cops. (For another time.)

Oh, and we smoked marijuana. Or thought we did. It grew in the alley, and I had a souvenir opium pipe from Chicago's Chinatown. The thrill was minor because we thought you smoked the roots.

Like all childhood recollection, much of what we remembered and guffawed about would be considered out of place for the *New York Times*. (A few of our more bizarre stunts and questionable activities would lower the tone of *Hustler* magazine.)

In the midst of our recollecting, one of us suddenly used a phrase we had almost forgotten. It was "playing out." Maybe it's regional. It has nothing to do with playing out a fish line or a kite string. To "play out" referred to that magical time in the evening, usually in summer, when, with darkness coming on, dinner was gulped as fast as parents would permit and followed by the slam of the screen door—dislodging a few junebugs—and escape to join the guys again in the cool and deepening dark for that night's adventures.

An important ingredient of the night in the Lincoln of the 1940s was the almost spooky rustling of the leaves of the great elms that lined both sides of the streets. Or they did until a citywide elm blight picked them off methodically, one after the other. To this day, darkness and rustling leaves, anywhere, take me right back to our block on South Twenty-third Street, scene of so much fun, foolishness, and occasional danger on summer nights.

The neighborhood could not have been more Midwest typical.

Nice middle-class houses whose residents never locked their doors—especially when on vacation, so neighbors could easily get in to water the plants—and who would probably have long forgotten where the key was anyway. There were no drugs or muggings. The only "crack" was the one in the sidewalk, which, if you stepped on it, would "break your mother's back."

To play out. It sounds harmless enough, but at times it was not. Kick the Can and Hide and Seek and ringing doorbells and running away were fun, but we craved more.

Neither of us is sure who introduced the thread-and-paper stunt into our repertoire. You stretched the dark thread across the street and hung the double sheet of newspaper on it just where it would meet a passing car's windshield. When a car came along in the black of night, a ghostly white thing appeared suddenly in the headlights and the driver slammed on the brakes. Mission accomplished. Except this one was a success. It didn't fail. Ever. Of course, a single instance of two cars, one just behind the other, could have spelled calamity.

Sometimes the driver got out to see what it was, snatching and crumpling and uttering curse words and phrases like "Rotten little S.O.B.'s!" Once I, the wit, responded to that one from the dark with, "How do you know we're boys?" One guy offered up the wimpy

"Dumb little butts!" How we scoffed at that one, giggling scornfully in the lilac bushes.

Jim and I began to swap memories of some of the more exciting, adrenaline-pumping times when we got spotted. And chased. Only after all these years did Jim let me in on the close-kept secret of how he managed to run around behind old Mrs. Fleming's house with an enraged driver right on his heels—and vanish into thinnest air. Sometimes the chaser was so close he saw Jim duck into a clump of four or five shaggy pine trees and figured he had him trapped. The branches inside the grove were like rungs. But even if the guy had a flashlight and shone it up the "ladders," there was no one there. The fabled Indian Rope Trick come to life.

I hope Jim won't mind my revealing his long-held secret for vanishing. Outside the grove, the branches of the big furry trees bent downward, the lowest ones appearing to lie flat on the surrounding ground. With the same move you use to slide under the covers at night, Jim slid himself under the branches. To the eye there was nothing to suggest that there was any room under them at all, let alone for a person.

(I like to fantasize that somebody reading this now was one of Jim's baffled pursuers who, with the mystery cleared up at last, can sleep peacefully again. Are you there? Drop a line.)

My own singular triumph in thwarting pursuit happened only a few yards from that clump of pine trees. We can't recall our crime but, again, we were the quarry and hotly pursued. A big fat guy was chasing me, puffing vigorously but gaining, muttering threats of what he was going to do to me.

I suddenly remembered a horizontal radio aerial of some sort of heavy wire stretched tight between two houses and only four inches off the ground. I led the guy there and, taking a few "air steps" in the dark, so as not to hit it myself and without exposing its presence, sailed over it. He did not. His overfed carcass slammed to the ground with an impact that must have registered on the Harvard seismograph.

Two guys who saw it all gave it the ultimate compliment in our vocabulary back then: "Jeez, that looked *neat*." Not until winning a gymnastics championship some years later did I accomplish anything I was quite so proud of.

Now here comes something distasteful but it's funny, which to me is always the important thing.

A nice guy named Milton Cochell served in that familiar, thankless role in boyhood of the guy the other guys pick on, humiliate, and abuse. We seemed to be endlessly initiating Milt into our gang by making him climb difficult trees, hang out of upper-story windows by one arm, eat bark, and, yes, remove all of his clothing in the dark and run across the street in the headlights of a passing car. It is with considerable lack of pride that I confess to being the author of this idea.

Milton was suffering badly not only from us but from a miserable case of ragweed-induced hay fever. It was a hot summer and a few of us were just standing around in the alley, spoiling for mischief, when poor Milt took out his handkerchief and began to blow his nose quite productively.

In midblow, Jim deftly jerked the handkerchief away.

The resulting sight was simultaneously as appalling and hilarious as you can possibly be imagining. As Milt snatched back his handkerchief and tried to tidy himself up, I laughed harder than at anything in my life. Ever. We all did, except Milton.

As Jim and I, in the present, laughed ourselves silly at the indelible memory all over again, he assured me that Milt, having survived the incident and the rest of our punching-bag treatment, has gone on to a life of success and contentment as lord of considerable agricultural acreage. God knows he deserves it.

Hey, Milt.

One more. Suddenly it was V-J Day and the town, like all towns, exploded in booming, honking, screaming celebration of our soldiers and sailors and marines and their victory over our wily enemy.

Our little gang saw fit to celebrate by hurling small water-filled balloons at passing cars. Nobody minded. With one exception.

We ran out of balloons and Jim somehow fetched up a coarse paper flour bag that held at least a half gallon of water. Winging this monster missile at our next victim, Jim missed the car. But not the driver.

The unlucky chap had his window down and the weighty projectile caught him square in the side of the head, where it exploded in a spectacular display right out of the Aquacade. He minded. We escaped.

Whoever said that you don't make any new old friends got it right.

Both of us have had some rough patches since those golden days, he far more than I. His (medical stuff) would have killed me. And yet there is Jim now, his wonderful, sunny personality still intact. Jim was my Huck Finn.

What Jim and I mean to each other, having met by sheer chance when my folks bought that house on that block and not the one miles away, can't be calculated. Considering the staggering odds against being born, let alone meeting any one person in your life, can make your head spin.

Were we happier then? That's the tough one.

MAY 29, 2008

Good to See You. *Is It You?*

Regarding full disclosure, dear reader, I feel I know you well enough by now to confide that, yes, it was at Yale that I myself learned what it means to be gay.

It was sophomore year and my friend—we'll call him David—and I were sitting side by side in front of a mirror, putting on makeup. (Shame on you. We were in a play.)

"I saw Will Geer this afternoon," he said. You may know him best from *The Waltons*. Geer—a great character actor, heavily employed in movies and on stage until heavily ruined by the blacklist in the fifties—was in a Broadway-bound musical at the Shubert Theater, right near Yale. "He was just strolling around the campus."

Jealous in my celebrity worship, I asked, "Did you actually talk to him?"

DA [*A* is for Adnopoz]: Yeah.
DC: What did you say?
DA: I said, "What brings you to the campus, Mr. Geer?"
DC: Go on. What did he say?
DA: He said, "Just lookin' at the boys."
DC (still fairly fresh from Nebraska): What does that mean?
DA: He's gay.
DC: That's nice.
DA: (*Laughs*)

I hadn't meant it to be funny and wasn't man enough to admit I didn't get it. I realized I was missing something here, perhaps having to do with the word "gay." Surprisingly, Cary Grant says it in *Bringing*

Up Baby, from 1938, but I didn't get it then either. But as in the case of any new word, suddenly it seemed to be everywhere.

David and I got to chortle over this and my other memories last week at our college reunion.

Yale '58. If you must know. I prefer to think of it as our second twenty-fifth.

I have still another friend, this one named Chris Porterfield. Roommates at Yale. He and I wrote *Cavett* together, he produced my show for a time, and then he rose through the ranks of *Time* magazine. His two best traits are (a) he is smarter than I am and (b) despite this, he generally treats me as an equal.

Reunions can be deadly, we agreed. We had seen them. While still undergrads, we had looked disapprovingly on gray and graying old fellows from, say, the class of '23, red-faced and slopping their beverages and waxing both sentimental and drunk. Not for us, we vowed. And, if we went, we would avoid as many sing-alongs and ukulele hoedowns with up-tempo renderings of "Boola Boola" as we possibly could.

But we went, and I'm glad. It can be fun to see old acquaintances.

But not always. There are the ones you recognize and then there are the ones you don't, reminding us that time does not treat people equally. Back a ways, at a high school reunion (maybe my fifteenth?), there was the shock of seeing what had become of some of the women. Some who—back in school—would be among the last choices for the prom had blossomed into breath-stopping loveliness. Balanced, alas, by former beauties who had faded. At both reunions there seemed to be a wide range of ages, even though we were all, by definition, the same age. (Except for some vets who "went in" before college.)

There were no females at Yale when I was there, except visitors like Jane Fonda, who dated a Yalie and caused the rest of us to dream and drool. Ah, Jane and the damnable sound of her high heels clicking on the bathroom tiles above our room at hours beyond "lights out" caused us no end of pain in the lower regions.

Who could have dreamed back then, staring at her in the dining hall, that one day she would engender bags of hate mail for my show in the Vietnam days? Gorgeous Jane, whom the critic Kenneth Tynan called, in reviewing her Broadway debut in *Tall Story*, "this febrile, coltish beauty." In an appearance I made at the reunion one evening I sinfully titillated the crowd by adding, after recalling Jane at Yale, "If you like trivia, Jane uses cherry-flavored ChapStick. There won't be time for the rest of this story."

There were many classy-looking wives at the reunion, some of them second, third . . . and at least one fourth. (*If at first*, eh?)

Entering the class tent opening day, I used hat and glasses to stay unrecognized as long as possible so I could observe unnoticed. (Otherwise, being "famed" causes the "Heisenberg effect" to set in. You alter the game by becoming part of it. People start saying stuff like "This wouldn't happen to *you*, of course, but . . ."—and you have tainted the conversational waters.)

Something was wrong. I couldn't figure out why this large tentful of people was different. Then it hit. From where I stood, I could take in at least seventy people and, *mon dieu!*, no one was fat! ("No one" proved to be about 98 percent correct, but a far cry from the latest 40-ish figures the national averages have reached.) Better education leads to better eating? I welcome your opinion.

After a day or so, it hits you that the star of any reunion is Time. It suffuses everything from grayed hair to the sobering number of dead classmates, their faces beaming out from the pages of the classbook in their graduation pictures, with eager looks and hopeful smiles.

Looking at them brought no profundity of thought, but stuff like "We look equally alive in our pictures, he and I, but he's not alive. Could it as easily have been me?" Then you notice that some have been dead for decades. But . . . uh-oh . . . most of those who are gone have died in the last few years. Even this year. All this brought to mind Philip Larkin's masterpiece "Aubade." Do you know it?

The poem begins:

> *I work all day, and get half-drunk at night.*
> *Waking at four to soundless dark, I stare.*

In time the curtain-edges will grow light.
Till then I see what's really always there:
Unresting death, a whole day nearer now . . .

Shameful as it is to admit, the thing I enjoyed most at the reunion was me. Perhaps I can explain. I was the "star" of the final night and experienced that treat you get too rarely in performing comedy where everything you do works. You are in the zone for sure . . . and you know it for a fact before you go onstage. You can *guarantee* you'll be good. You can feel it, and nothing can stop you.

As I walked onstage to the cliché expert's "tumultuous applause," the gods gave me my opening line. It was three days after the concession speech and I asked if anyone had had a TV on in the last half hour, knowing that they had all been at dinner. "A bulletin just now," I said. "Hillary Clinton is back in the race." (Pandemonium.)

It has to be said that in a beautiful theater setting, with a good mike and an audience that has "accepted" you from that other medium, it's pretty hard to bomb totally. But this reaction was extraordinary. I've talked to performers who've had this happen—big and small ones. No one claims it's frequent. I asked Groucho once how many times he had been euphoric in performance: where you laugh heartily at yourself along with everybody else, you're surprised and delighted at what comes out of your mouth, you feel you're in comedy heaven and wish you could stay forever, and you're repeatedly refreshed by glancing at the faces of people seemingly helpless with laughter. With surprising seriousness, Groucho answered, "It's a curious thing, isn't it? It happens about a half-dozen times in a career."

Once in a dress rehearsal of A. Miller's *The Crucible,* I came onstage and *became* Reverend Hale, scaring the hell out of the other actors. Something almost erotic and not of my making had welled up inside me and exploded. It recalled Yeats's "then awake / Ignorant what *Dramatis personae* spake."

"What happened to you out there? How did you do that?" people said. The devil of it is that unless you are born Marlon Brando or a lesser great actor, you get it only now and then—and, unlike Mr. B., you can't turn it on whenever you feel like it.

I'll stop here for now, partly because I may be getting a bit weird for your tastes.

JUNE 13, 2008

Smiling Through

Who decided that it's variety that's the spice of life?

I submit that, rather, it is *contrast* that is life's piquant condiment.

Last week, I attended two events in my home state of Nebraska that supplied both variety and contrast on successive days. A bit like the Mafioso some years ago who got married one day and began a ten-year jail sentence the next (a cynic might consider them both "sentences").

On the one hand, I addressed a group of noble citizens whose job is aiding and counseling poor devils suffering from depression. CAVETT RETURNS HOME TO DISCUSS 'THE WORST AGONY DEVISED FOR MAN' read the next day's headline in the Lincoln paper. Despite the subject matter, I got quite a lot of laughs. My credentials? Having been there myself.

The year before I had talked to a similar group of caregivers in Omaha in front of an audience that included what you'd think would be an entertainer's nightmare: a hundred or more people in the throes of the disease. I expected no laughs.

I had just gotten started telling the grim faces that I knew what they were going through when a large man—in pajamas, as I recall—stood up and slowly made his way toward me.

"Paranoid schizophrenic," someone stage-whispered to me. There was general tension in the room as the man continued to approach. When he stopped two feet in front of me and stared at me, I heard myself say, "Come here often?" Loud general laughter broke the tension. He returned peacefully to his seat—probably without having heard me or the laughter.

Miraculously, I kept them laughing for perhaps an hour. Clearly the fact that I knew about their plight from my own experience had a lot—or maybe everything—to do with it.

I was able to say to them, *I know that everyone here knows that feeling when people say to you, "Hey, shape up! Stop thinking only about your troubles. What's to be depressed about? Go swimming or play tennis and you'll feel a lot better. Pull up your socks!" And how you, hearing this, would like nothing more than to remove one of those socks and choke them to death with it.* (Laughter mixed with some minor cheering.)

The reward from this was unique in my experience. Afterward, those in charge seemed amazed and delighted. One said, "See Clara over there? She hasn't moved a muscle in her face for six months and you had her laughing out loud."

(Such inane advice of the "socks up" variety, by the way, can only be excused by the fact that if you've never had it you can never begin to imagine the depth of the ailment's black despair. Another tip: Do not ask the victim what he has "to be depressed about." The malady doesn't care if you're broke and alone or successful and surrounded by a loving family. It does its democratic dirty work to your brain chemistry regardless of your "position.")

My time with them in Omaha a year ago was not recorded, but I would rather have a tape of that day with that audience than just about anything I've done. Of the things I said to them I can recall only this story:

Personal item. Once I said to a doctor during a "session" that I wished he could get inside my head for just a minute because there's no way of imagining what this feels like. "Oh, I know," he said, "I got pretty sad when my father died."

Defying standard protocol on the couch, I arose on one elbow, turned to him—he was seated behind me—and said, "Do you think grief is even close to this?" To his credit he replied, "I'm sorry. I shouldn't have said that."

(The anger you feel at such a moment pumps a shot of adrenaline that can make you feel symptom-free . . . all too briefly.)

The fact that these afflicted people in Omaha knew me to be a "celebrity" had a good deal to do with the unexpected success of the whole thing. Some had even seen me talk about the nasty illness on television in the early eighties, or in *People* magazine. While not wishing to become the poster boy for depression, I still found the rewards undeniably pleasant, gratifying, and touching.

As in: *Dear Mr. Cavett, You don't know it but you saved my dad's/ wife's/daughter's life.* Followed by various forms of *My dad's seeing that Dick Cavett could have it made him feel he wasn't a freak, and he finally went for treatment. We are so grateful.*

Apparently one thing I said on *Larry King Live* back then hit home hard. It was that when you're downed by this affliction, if there were a curative magic wand on the table eight feet away, it would be too much trouble to go over and pick it up.

There's also the conviction that it may have worked for others but it wouldn't work for you. Your brain is busted and nothing's going to help.

The most extreme problem that depression presents is suicide. It's the reason you don't dare delay treatment. Don't mess with it. Run for help—whether it's talk therapy, drug therapy, or the miraculous results of ECT (electroconvulsive therapy, erroneously labeled "shock therapy"). The shock involved is closer to insulin shock than electric shock. It's a toss-up whether more people have been scared off it by *One Flew Over the Cuckoo's Nest* than have been scared off medication by Tom Cruise's idiotic braying on the subject on the *Today* show. (Matt Lauer should have hit him with a wet turbot.)

I guarantee that one result of recent Supreme Court decisions on guns will be the deaths of people who have a gun at home for the first time while in depression. In the depths of the malady, getting a stamp on a letter is a day's work. Going out to somehow arrange for a gun would be way beyond your capability while stricken. But having one near at hand is another matter. There were times when I longed for my ancient .22 single-shot squirrel-hunting rifle. Luckily it had been given away years earlier.

Suicide rarely happens when you are all the way down in the uttermost depths. Again, it's too much trouble. Perhaps the saddest irony of depression is that suicide happens when the patient gets a little better and can again function sufficiently. "She seemed to be improving" is the sad cry of the mourners.

Two prime victims of the disease are your libido and your ability to read. Five times through a paragraph and unable to say what it's about. But, oddly, you can read a book or article about depression with full comprehension. The two best books I know of are William Styron's monumental account of his own case, *Darkness Visible,* and Kay Redfield Jamison's *An Unquiet Mind.*

Damned if I had meant to rattle on so long on this subject, depriving you of my contrasting event, the Johnny Carson Comedy Festival in his hometown of Norfolk, Nebraska. (I'll get to that.)

And pardon me for teasing you last time about a promised tale of espionage and murder. The case is more complex than I imagined and will take some time.

And is anyone still wondering about the error by the test makers on that exam that American students performed so dismally on?

JUNE 27, 2008

Smiling Through, Part 2

The outpouring of replies to the depression column takes me by surprise. But why should it? I know that the number of sufferers is vast, but may be even more so than I thought. As the number of replies ran into the hundreds I began to think that, as with cancer, nearly everyone has been touched by it, if not personally then among relatives and friends.

Like the gay "love that dared not speak its name," depression is now shouting.

As the comments neared five hundred, the word "epidemic" leapt to mind. If it's inappropriate, it can't be by much. What a lot of hellish suffering those replies represent. And those are only the ones who wrote—always a minority.

The amount of misery reported is stunning. Humbly I thank, in turn, all those so grateful for what I wrote. That gratitude is heartwarming and makes me want to ask what more I can do for you. Or should I say us?

I think of Tennessee Williams—a major sufferer—and the vast body of genius work he was so heroically able to turn out despite the company of his own "black dog." (He credited swimming every single day as "one of my few reliable crutches.")

"I wasn't aware of it," he said on the air when I pointed out to him that in every one of his major plays a character confesses to being up against the dark wall of despair and pleads for advice and is told, in varying words, the same thing. I'll spare you my list, but in *Streetcar*, when Stella asks how she can be expected to continue her life—now with the knowledge that Stanley had raped Blanche—she is told, "Honey, you just have to go on."

The number of readers who have managed—and are managing—just to go on is touching.

Cold comfort, when you're in it. But it's some comfort to bear in mind the fact that depression is "self-limiting"—doctor talk for "eventually ends." Of course, it would be nice if they could tell you if you've drawn one of the long straws or a short one.

Having dropped Tennessee's illustrious name here, why not Marlon Brando's? As a man who had entertained a kennel of black dogs in his life, he was keenly interested in the subject. I told him about a show I had done earlier that year (this was in the mid-seventies) with—brace for another whopping name—Laurence Olivier.

Arriving for taping at his and his wife Joan Plowright's suite in New York's Wyndham Hotel, I thought, "*Olivier* for God's sake! I should be jubilant—and all I want to do is roll up in the rug."

I knew full well that I was botching it. I'd glance at short notes I'd made with no idea what they meant. My head was saying, *The Oliviers aren't stupid. They're acting like I'm okay but they can see I'm bats. I must be taking ten-second pauses, staring into space.* I just knew my producer was about to whisper, "Dick, we're going to wrap this for now. We'll get them back someday. Go on home."

But I made it to the end, murmured some sort of good-bye to Lord O. and his lady wife, and—fogged—found my way home to bed.

Dialogue in Marlon B.'s bedroom ("Talk is the thing I do best here," he said):

MB: Did you look at that show?
DC: God, no. Nothing could make me look at it.
MB: Do me a favor. Look at it.
DC: Do you know what you're asking?
MB (*with that penetrating, gnomic stare out of* Apocalypse Now): Yes. But you don't.

Back in New York, with gritted teeth, I got the show out and—fortified with the aid of a Campari and orange juice (that's what

Marlon drank, so now I did)—I hauled the tape out and looked at it, prepared to wince pitifully.

A shocker. I was fine. It was as if the show had been reshot. The sleepy pauses weren't there. My eyes were bright and, at times, sparkly. I was interested. Or appeared so. I was—and still am—amazed.

(*Back to the top of Mulholland Drive, chez Brando.*)

DC: How did you know what I'd see? What was happening to me there?

MB: I call it "automatic pilot." It takes over and does for you what you can't do yourself. Performers have to have it. Almost everybody has it to some degree. It's a relative of acting.

What good does this story do you?

Since most people can't test this themselves by taping a TV show, feeling lousy during it, and then watching it, I can assure you that whether it's enduring an unwelcome houseguest, your coworkers, or your tax man, one of the wretched ailment's mysteries is that you are in fact coming off ten times better than you feel. Or think you look.

Unless you are at hospitalization level, you can, as a number of people wrote, "fool people at work." Thanks to "automatic pilot," you can do it. And they're not lying when they say, "You seemed okay to me."

Keeping that mask on, admittedly, is exhausting. And you'll reap versions of "You don't seem bad off."

(Proofreading this just now, I recalled Woody Allen's asking me once, quite seriously, "How am I supposed to know that you have depression?")

Long-windedly, I've already gotten to where "word count" tells me to start winding down. So forgetting about style and literary flow, I'll just tick off some random shots on this subject, some from the mail.

I've decided that the single worst thing about this illness is its terrible *authority*. I mean the way it thunders at you, "*This* is the reality. *This* is how it is and how it's going to be. Any memories of fun or wellness are flukes, delusions. And will never come again. Now you have 20/20 vision and see life for the dreadful mess it really is."

Whatever wicked gods invented this torture should come down with it.

It's heartbreaking when one reader says "I need help. Can someone please tell me what to do." Ask your doctor to find you a good psycho-pharmacologist. In people talk, a pill doctor of the mind. And I don't mean an herbalist or a swami or a "psychic" or a Scientologist or a phrenologist, but someone with a degree in mind medicine. Your doctor can find one. If he can't, get a new doctor.

Although on my PBS show I once accused the Maharishi Mahesh Yogi—an endearing old coot (who developed Transcendental Meditation)—of selling water (before they actually did), I don't belittle meditation. It's good, a quickly learned discipline, and its effect is cumulative.

(As close as anything on this subject can come to humor: A psychiatrist I knew tried meditation for his depression but was poorly taught—"All I could meditate on was my suicide.")

The lady's right who pointed out that you at least do feel better when exercising. One prominent head doc urged it on me strongly, saying, "I'm a great believer in endorphins." Of course it may take an hour to find your shoes. And to tie them. And find the door. And . . .

I got a huge laugh "lecturing" to an entire audience of shrinks at Johns Hopkins—contrasting smartly with my audience of sufferers in

Omaha—when one asked, as some readers have, "Do you recommend psychoanalysis while in depression?" My answer: "Mostly you don't know what's being said to you, you can't follow the line of talk, you barely know what you yourself are saying, and you can't remember anything afterward." "A waste of time?" he asked. "Not totally," I said, "because you do get a tiny little rise in self-esteem from keeping the appointment." (I was only half kidding and a bit startled by the robust laughter.)

If you've got a solid case of it, I don't think you should drive. Not only do you forget to look left and right, but I remember thinking how easy it would be to pull in front of an oncoming car on the highway. Someone's alive because I didn't. When people are shocked at this, it's because they can't picture being unable to assign any value to themselves, let alone some faceless stranger . . . who probably also knows how awful life is anyway.

I looked forward to the dentist because by refusing the anesthetic needle, I'd be able to feel *something.*

Thanks to the lady who boldly brought up sex; or, rather, the death of it. As the old Dark Enemy approaches, the poor old libido throws up the white flag and—as they used to say—"surrenders at the first whiff of grape." (I assume the reference is to grapeshot.)

Someone noted that arousal is possible. It is, but with the devilish little proviso that you are invariably denied the, um, ultimate payoff. Sex in the manic phases can spring to life quite abruptly—sometimes dangerously—manifesting itself, as ads like to say, "in a variety of decorator colors."

Dear "Carey, US Army": Do you really think that keeping guns out of the hands of the suicidal is a serious threat to your dear Second Amendment? I may have misread you. Even Scalia, and—one assumes—his papoose, Clarence Thomas, wanted that.

Funny how people will say, "Do celebrities get depression? I mean, they're rich and famous." Most are famous and some still rich, but yes, they succumb like flies. As poor Hamlet said, "O, I could tell you . . . but let it be."

I'll tell you one. The great actor Rod Steiger, to whom Brando in *On the Waterfront* said, "Charlie, I coulda been a contenda." It was scary to hear him tell it.

In a monumental bout, which he *barely* survived, he said he lived in bed for months. ("If I brushed my teeth, it was a big day.")

After it was over, he was able to (almost) joke that at least his suicide plan was "thoughtful" and showed consideration for others. He said, "I planned to row way out off Laguna Beach, hang over the side of the boat with one arm . . . and blow my brains out. No one would have to find me. No one would have to clean up." Luckily for us, he survived to make many more movies.

Artistic types seem to be especially vulnerable and to suffer just as badly as the unlucky mail carrier who gets it. You can imagine how often the envied celebrity gets the criminal question: "What reason have you got to be depressed?" (Would these people, in an influenza epidemic, ask the shivering, chattering victim, "What reason have you got to be sickly?")

It was good to see how, as the list of comments from readers lengthened, a sort of community seemed to form. People thanked other writers for their words and offered comfort and welcome sympathy. See, for instance, Candy Asman, RN, to the plaintive and suffering Ms. Melone. If I were Joseph Pulitzer, Candy, I would give you a prize. And a Nobel, for good measure.

* * *

Deeply felt complaints about bum treatment got aired and exchanged. Dear Lisa: Your therapist should be pushing a cart in the garment district.

A woman friend named Aden Pryor, possessing both brains and wit— that combination so disconcerting to so many men—put the case quite brilliantly with "When you're in it, the brain can only process negative information."

A few admitted to resorting to booze. I almost can't type the next few words, but . . . it will make you feel better. Briefly. Then worse. And if you forget that, stitch a sampler (or get someone to make one for you) and mount it above the liquor cabinet. It should read: "Remember: Alcohol Depresses the Central Nervous System!" (Do we really want, just for that mere moment, to make things worse?)

Sorry for the length of this. It's just an inexhaustible subject.

Closing in a lighter vein, once, at Oxford, a languid Brit part-time professor (and full-time fop) was cooing to me at an academic cocktail party about what he called "this depression business."

"Depression," he announced, "is for sniveling little neurotics."

"How, then," I asked, "have you escaped it?"

I have no memory of what happened next.

JULY 11, 2008

What's So Funny About Nebraska

Among my growing list of topics promised but not delivered was a report on a comedy festival I attended recently in Norfolk, Nebraska. At the risk of sounding curmudgeonly, attending anything that threatened a forced viewing of a lot of new and largely unknown stand-up comics would be low on my list of musts, down there between dedicating a statue of Spiro Agnew and a street sale of macramé.

But this one, the Great American Comedy Festival, had good promise. Among the reasons for saying yes was that Robert Klein would be there and that these particular aspirants to the jesting trade had been expertly selected. Eddie Brill—himself a comic pro and talent hunter for Dave Letterman's show—had combed the comic woods, scanning top comedy clubs around the United States for the best available and most promising talent. And he delivered it. Brill confesses that there is something a little silly in treating comedy as a contest, but it can be fun and nobody gets hurt.

(Parenthetically to the point of irrelevance, one of Bill Clinton's lesser legacies to us all has been to make it just about impossible for anyone in public life and in the media to say *anything* without prefacing it with the now reflexive phrase "Let me say this . . ." *Who's stopping you?!* I scream at the screen.)

Anyway, let me say this: John William Carson, born October 23, 1925, in Corning, Iowa, continued his growing up in Norfolk, Nebraska, a town now famous for Johnny Carson. He died on another twenty-third—in January 2005.

For years I wrote for Johnny, and as I moved on he remained a valued friend. I've never known why I have to convince skeptics of this fact.

When Carson was eight, the family moved to the diminutive

metropolis of Norfolk. Smooth and gregarious on camera, Johnny was uneasy with most people. He wasn't with me, and our enduring friendship had a lot to do with that.

He was suspicious of journalists and columnists, and their failure to get him to "open up" resulted in some bad press and the frequent label "cold." That military brace, ramrod-straight posture of his was lampooned by those who go by the silly, pretentious term "impressionists." (You know: Rich Little, Will Jordan, David Frye, Monet, Renoir . . .)

While still writing for John C. in days of yore, I survived saying about him on one of those well-produced Smith & Hemion *Kraft Music Hall* shows a joke that began, "It's often said about Johnny that he has a ramrod up his . . . spine." During the laugh, I glanced to the side to see if the eminent victim of the roast—and my former boss— was at least smiling. He was.

It's hard to "roast" someone you really like, but our friendship survived the evening. People, including some on his staff, continued to treat me as a hallucinator with "You've actually been to Johnny's *house*? For *dinner*?" It never stopped.

"Don't for God's sake ever repeat this to anyone or tell him I told you," said the gnomish little bald man in the Cinerama-wide plate-glass specs, "at least while he and I are both alive." The speaker, who was driving, was the legendary agent Irving "Swifty" Lazar. We were heading up whatever "drive" in Bel Air led to Swifty's house, a place that was really a mini-Louvre of priceless paintings, with Picasso one of the smaller names. In Swifty's case, there was major money in book-agenting such huge-selling volumes as Richard M. Nixon's memoirs— humorously categorized under "nonfiction."

Swifty, driving in disconcerting Mr. Magoo style, delivered a thunderbolt.

"Johnny is very fond of you, you know," he began. And after another "top secret" cautioning, he went on, "I think you ought to know this. Johnny said to me once, 'Cavett's the only one who could beat me. If Dick hadn't been on a network with a short station lineup, he might have.'"

As comics say about such moments, "When they brought me to . . . and then brought me two more . . ."

That Johnny had said this was so unexpected and so startling to me—and you don't need a degree in psychiatry to understand this—that I promptly forgot it. (Yes, it came back in due course, and it still has voltage for me.)

By the way, none of this should be construed as an attempt to obscure Johnny's later, genuine enthusiasm for Dave Letterman's talents.

"We wish you were on once a week," a member of the Carson staff said to me once. "Johnny's a different man when you come on. He's even happy in the afternoon when he comes to work. And when you're out there with him, he *actually leans back in his chair*." This touched me, and does now, remembering it.

I was among the judges of the eight finalists in the comedy competition that night in Norfolk. It's the home, quite naturally, of a splendid Johnny Carson Museum, featuring an intriguing collection of photographs, some showing the pre- and postpubescent lad with his beloved magic apparatus and that then still anonymous face that was to become, often painfully for its owner, instantly recognizable everywhere.

Each day of the festival—it was the first held—the local papers were splashed with publicity and articles about the hugely successful event. One newspaper had a big color picture of Johnny on the air, at his desk, looking amused by his guest (me) in the swivel chair beside him. I'd never seen the picture before. We both look young and happy and are clearly enjoying each other's company.

The place, a handsome and good-sized theater, was packed for the gala final night's show. There was a good, smart, sellout audience of sharp local people and, onstage, excellent work by the young aspirants. At the end of the show, to my ear, both Bob Klein and I killed 'em. (The audience, not the aspirants.)

Klein and I reminisced over a western breakfast about what it was like "being on" with Johnny and how much pleasing him and making him laugh meant to a growing comic and his career. And, of course, to quite a few would-be pursuers of the comedy dream, a single smashing appearance with Johnny *made* a career.

Klein and I recalled how each time you found yourself standing anxiously behind that famous curtain with the vertical colored stripes, nerves would jangle almost audibly. At least a portion of your life flashed before your eyes.

Next, your pulse quickened a bit as you—alone and hidden—heard the familiar voice say your name and, pushing that curtain aside and taking one step into the bright lights, you were in front of America. And Johnny.

I felt sort of sorry for those sharp young comics in Norfolk that they would never have the thrill (do we still say "the rush"?) of meeting Johnny—*the* career maker of the day—and making him laugh on the air.

Of all the appearances I did with him—doubtless they are among that ton of Carson shows NBC so thoughtfully erased—I most remember one in California. He would always have me on the show whenever the latest incarnation of *The Dick Cavett Show* . . . um . . . completed its current tenure. Often on the following Monday and always with a version of the same joke in the monologue: "Our good friend Dick Cavett is here tonight. Dick's had another show shot out from under him. (*Laugh.*) I'm always afraid that if the next one doesn't take, it's going to be Armed Forces Radio for Dick." (*Laugh with capital* L.)

On such a night I made Johnny laugh, but hard. I had been the first guest out—a huge honor—and so by the end, when it was time for good-nights, and having "moved down" with each new guest, I was the farthest down the couch, cheek to cheek with Ed McMahon.

With about a minute remaining, Johnny began asking each guest what was coming up for him. And each had a big movie, big Broadway show, big something to plug. I didn't. I hoped the clock would run out before my fellow Nebraskan got to me.

Every comic can report a few "gift from the gods" moments. Here came one. "What are you doing, Richard?" he asked with a kindly smile, and I sensed he knew I probably had nothing to brag about.

Then, a miracle bred of panic: I heard myself say, "I'm working on an idea for a sitcom, Johnny. It's a humorous version of *Gilligan's Island*." The reaction would have broken a laugh meter.

Several columnists quoted the line, but—since an ear for nuance is not mandatory for such employment—invariably misquoted it as "a *comedy* version," thus karate-chopping away the line's finesse, if I may so say.

But the important thing was Johnny's reaction. He did that thing where he exploded with laughter that sent him sideways stage left off his chair. I felt like a stock market must feel going through the roof, or the space shuttle blasting off.

For a (comparative) youngster, still making his way in our cut-throat business, a lottery win would have paled in comparison. Oh, how I'd love to have a tape of that moment to wear out in repeated viewings.

Well, our hour is about up. Maybe next time we might explore why, despite all this, anybody in his right mind would want to be a comedian.

JULY 25, 2008

Mamas, Don't Let Your Babies
Grow Up to Be . . .

still want to be one.

But there is good common sense in the question I promised to deal with in my Johnny Carson column: Why would anyone want to be a comedian?

Obviously those who burn to be professional jesters mean that they want to be *successful* comedians. And those are always an elite, microscopic portion of the population. But oh, how they try. And in droves. It is a profession where, as the saying goes, many are called, but . . .

There can't be many professions where the aspirant risks so much. Or where you can get such instant, smack-in-the face humiliation. And get it time after time for a long time.

Coming up through the ranks of any calling can be rough, but that battered soul who survives the early years of courting the comic muse comes close to knowing what only the soldier knows: what combat is like.

What puts that vulnerable soul up there in the most brightly lit part of a room, clutching a microphone, to be judged by skeptical and often hostile strangers?

Desire to be loved is surely part of it, cliché though it be.

What better substitute for real love than a sea of eager faces, beaming, laughing, applauding, and celebrating your existence?

The contrast between the moments with them in front of you and the feeling, alone back in your room, whether it's at the Waldorf or a roach motel outside Minden, Nebraska, is stark.

For the extremely neurotic performer, that contrast between "on" and "off" gets worse with time. Judy Garland did my old ABC morning show shortly before she died. (That tape is gone. It was reused to tape *Let's Make a Deal*. Trust me.) I think it was her last television appearance—1968.

And what a comedian! She was garrulous, witty, and wickedly, wickedly funny. What they say was true. She made you feel you were an old friend, while keeping you in stitches.

But afterward we couldn't get her out of the dressing room. I left the theater and later walked back well after tape time, and she was still there.

She couldn't make a false move on stage and so did all she could to delay leaving it; and, equally, leaving the cozy womb of the dressing room. She was home in those two places.

Leave them, and you are back in so-called real life—where it seemed poor Judy made only false moves.

I did stand-up while still working for Johnny Carson in the mid-sixties, thus gaining the advantage of at least getting laughs from him about how I hadn't the night before.

When you're a club comic on the road, nightly fighting your way toward the golden sunrise of the Big Time, the hotel can be particularly lonely and depressing. Even if you didn't happen to bomb that night. Going from the laughing throng to your often dismal lodgings is at best a jolt to the psyche.

In a blizzardy, knee-deep-with-snow week playing the Act Four in Detroit, I learned that you can owe your survival to an animal. The fact that I had a small dog along to greet me in the hotel room after the show may well have been the one thing that kept me from twisting the shower curtain into a rope.

The gifted-without-limits Darrell Hammond of *Saturday Night Live*—the man who fiendishly "does" everybody while seemingly changing the very structure of both his head and his face—said quite straight-facedly when we met, "Your book *Cavett* saved my life." He actually credited reading my accounts of the horrors of the road with saving him—while on that road himself—from despair and its unpleasant consequences.

Few comedians kill themselves. (Maybe because audiences so

readily do it for them.) Young Freddie Prinze comes to mind. At least two in recent years have indulged themselves to death (in different ways)—John Candy and Chris Farley—but I think the legendary funny folk outlive the general population as a rule. And I guess you could say Lenny Bruce—whose alleged genius largely escaped me—did himself in. And of course John Belushi, for whom I had great affection. But by and large (will anyone ever explain that phrase?), comics are long-lived. (See Hope, Burns et al.) Quite a few hundreders.

Comic genius rises to the level of art—as with Groucho—all the way down to Aunt Martha who says, "Tell the one about that was no lady, that was my wife." (Just in passing, can the human mind conceive of anyone funnier than Jonathan Winters?)

When I was coming up in clubs, wise old heads would bore you to idiocy on talk shows with two favorite old standbys: "Where are the new comedians going to come from?" And "There's no place to be bad anymore."

The first can be answered in two ways: "When they get here we'll ask them" and "Aren't there at least one or two more urgent questions facing the human race?"

No place to be bad? Try Comedy Central, or your favorite comedy club. (Yes, of course: both have lots of crackerjack talents.)

Another convenient place to be bad was *The Ed Sullivan Show*. (Ed loved comics, and he stood about six feet to your right, looking at you, not the audience. Being hard of hearing and an optimist, he assumed the audience was laughing, and so he invited the good ones and the clunkers back equally. Does that clear up that mystery?)

One defensible reason to be a comedian. In the words of my legendary (now retired) manager, the incomparable Jack Rollins: "Succeed at comedy and money will pour down on you like a golden waterfall."

And when it works and when, as the great Lynn Fontanne—of that unsurpassed pair of stage comedians Lunt and Fontanne—phrased it on a show of mine, "on those nights when you're going high," the thrill is one you don't get in the pants business.

That doesn't mean I agree totally with a comic who said some-where recently, "There is no thrill that compares with getting a big laugh."

Really? I can think of at least one.

AUGUST 15, 2008

Cavett Dodges the Chair

Our locations today are two, both in Nebraska: THE LINCOLN PVBLIC (*sic*) LIBRARY and the Prescott Elementary School playground. If Nebraska, a library, and a playground sound pretty dull, you've been duly warned.

I have no idea why Herbert Langhus and I got in a fight. I suppose we might have seen ourselves as rivals over a dainty hand, but it seems unlikely. We were in fifth grade and probably still felt that girls were pretty boring, if not that other awful thing: "stuck up."

What passed as a fight in those days, even among the big guys, bore no resemblance to a fight now. There were no knives, chains, brass knuckles, blackjacks, saps, clubs . . . none of the current props employed in performing what was once termed, among gentlemen, "fisticuffs."

And there were no guns. Guns were things you knew from the movies, unless Dad was a hunter. I didn't know anyone who'd ever seen a handgun except on police. In that innocent time, could you even imagine a day when you could get shot dead in a dispute over a parking place?

There weren't even *fists*. Fighting was as described in the taunt "I'll bet I can *get you down*." Nobody ever delivered a knuckle sandwich to his opponent's features. You struggled and grappled and pushed until you got the enemy down and held him there, demanding, "Do you give?" If you were the unlucky party underneath, hurting and wondering how you'd explain the destruction of your new shirt, you "gave." Vowing, of course, revenge.

Hoping to impress a friend in a heated argument in an amusement park over God knows what—and influenced by neat-looking movie brawls—I defied the taboo and eagerly hit a guy as hard as I could—in the face! His identity unknown to me then as now.

He didn't budge, looked surprised, and I broke a small bone in my hand. It was baffling to me why the bare-knuckle brawlers on the screen, like John Wayne, never hurt *their* hands delivering a dozen punches to sturdy jaws.

Anyway, for whatever lost-in-the-the-mists reason, H. Langhus and D. Cavett were wrestling and scrabbling in the playground dirt and gravel, surrounded by cheering fifth-grade onlookers. Suddenly, the awful thing happened.

But first we must backtrack a bit.

A darkened movie theater. My friend Jim McConnell and I—both still grade schoolers, this was about a year earlier—were watching *Blood on the Sun* for about the fifth time. The setting is prewar Tokyo: James Cagney is involved in the search for a secret Japanese document that would reveal Japan's war plans—"The Tanaka Document." (After all these years, I still get a little chill in typing those three little words.)

What we loved about the movie was the judo. We first see Cagney working out in a Tokyo dojo, expertly dispatching onrushing opponents. The movie ends with a life-or-death judo free-for-all. If all prints of *Blood on the Sun* were destroyed somehow—and I was having trouble remembering what I did yesterday (technical term: Alberto Gonzalesitis)—I could still describe that last scene frame by frame, from long shot to medium to close-up.

As a bookish boy, I had special permission to use the adult part of that old, old LINCOLN PVBLIC LIBRARY. (When a substitute lady librarian asked, "Aren't you looking for the little folks' room?" I snarled in anger, "I hate little folks' rooms. And little folks.")

I scoured the place for martial arts books and found the one capable of altering my life forever.

Modern Judo had, despite its title, been published in 1918. It became my bible. I learned the Japanese names for the various throws we perfected. (*Uki goshi*—hip throw—we perfected; I can still do it, but so far haven't found the opportunity.)

One hold in particular became a favorite. It was a neck hold described under "Strangling Techniques." But unlike any of the familiar ones that involved pressing the neck between the two forearms, one front, one behind, this one was unique. It was a diabolical neck hold and we learned to practice it with extreme care.

Let us return to the playground, fight in progress.

While pretending not to be bothered by getting scratched and abraded by the gravel as Herb and I scuffled, on and off our feet, I suddenly remembered the hold. Wrenching him about so I was standing behind him, I applied it. Forgetting its effectiveness—and with all that adrenaline pumping—I really clamped it on him.

He went limp and dropped to the ground, lying there in a kind of fetal position. His color turned an awful wet cement gray. The guys around us stepped back. There was a gasp.

I froze.

I had never seen anyone dead before.

A single tear appeared at the inside corner of one eye and rolled down his inert cheek. Nobody breathed, least of all Herb.

And then he trembled a little and resumed breathing. Groggy and unable to walk, he had to be helped, between two guys, to the nurse's office. I don't remember anything beyond that, except that for a good stretch of time thereafter I was treated with unaccustomed awe. Strangely, I don't remember ever seeing or speaking with Herb again. I guess we both preferred to forget what was almost so unforgettable.

Decades passed before I learned, from a Japanese aikido master, that that specific hold had been—even by the time I wielded it— banned from judo for, as he put it, "excessive fatalities."

It may not be too self-dramatizing to say that by neither naming it nor describing it here, I might just save a life or two. Part of its lethal nature is that it requires hardly an ounce of strength. It breaks the voice box first, while stopping the victim's breathing.

What can be learned from this for the benefit of, say, a concerned parent?

This: *Keep young kids on the streets and out of the library.*

AUGUST 29, 2008

Experience 101

Dear Reader: It may be time to give up on writing about current events in this space. When you think how news travel time has been telescoped, it's dizzying. It took *days* for even the rumors of Custer's annihilation at the Little Bighorn to reach the east. Now any news over two hours old isn't news—it's "olds." Anything from the day before is virtually archaeology.

In reading what follows, be aware that nothing here is exactly meant to be a "this just in" bulletin. And so, the inevitable phrase: "By the time you read this . . ."

Or, for short:

B.T.T.Y.R.T.: Sarah Palin will doubtless have been outed even further from the witness protection program in which her handlers have kept her secreted since her smasheroo solo performance on That Memorable Night.

There's no denying that she rocked the place and, as her enthusing boosters said, "She really delivered the goods."

So she did, even if some were shoddy.

Back here in the past, when I'm writing this, we have just seen part one of her quizzing by Charles Gibson, with mixed reviews for both. So far I have not seen her confronted with some of the things about which she has been, to put it in that awful Diplomatically Correct phrase, "somewhat less than fully truthful." (Typesetter: If space is scarce, use "lying.") As in claiming "no thanks" to the bridge money while failing to disclose that she kept it.

"Performance" is the *mot juste* for what she did at the convention. And I admit that even my own jaded and cynical showbiz heart leapt up as she wowed the adoring crowd with a show-stopper display of charm and personality. I even laughed at two or three of the two or three too many insults directed at Obama. Don Rickles could not have snapped them out better.

Watching a woman slight of build and full of pizzazz so thoroughly bedazzle a vast audience is entertaining. Something chimed in my memory when she brought that crowd to its feet with frantic and worshipful cheering.

Ah, yes. I had seen it all before.

It was Judy Garland at the Palace.

And yet no one offered *her* the vice presidency. (Fact checker: Am I right on this?)

I wince and feel for her over the reports of how she is being tutored, guided, and taught in marathon cram sessions of what might be called a crash course in Instant Experience 101. There's something almost funny in the idea that she is being speedily stuffed, Strasbourg-goose-style, with knowledge she should have had before she was selected.

You can't help wondering about her current tutors and coaches and experts. Will they collect their checks and depart? Or will they still be around should she have to make a quick decision about things like troop movements, new surges, or whether or not to reduce Iran to a cinder? Or any number of other matters requiring résumé items more complex than those faced by a mayor of Wasilla.

I'd love to have the chance to ask her how being able to see Russia from parts of her state apparently qualifies her to deal with that vastly complex country more effectively than those scholars and diplomats who find themselves less proximate to its shores.

Every time I nostalgically try to regain my liking of John McCain, he reaches into his sleaze bag and pulls out something malodorous.

If there were a prize cake available, McCain's lowbrow ad attempting to paint Obama as a virtual pornographer and peddler of sex to kindergarteners would take that pastry. Plate and all.

And it might be, if not instructive, at least fun to give McCain's trash-peddling Karl Rove acolytes some truth serum and ask them if—in their heart of hearts—they really think Obama meant to call our Sarah a pig.

To believe that, wouldn't you have to be at least as dumb as Georgia

Republican Lynn Westmoreland? The man who used the word "uppity" about Obama?

Westmoreland, a living embodiment of that stock cartoonist's character the Good Old Boy southern congressman—complete with slouch, beer gut, and eyes over his bags—courageously claimed ignorance of any racism in that favorite term of those who murdered Emmett Till and Medgar Evers. Anything involving Westmoreland and ignorance is unlikely to be disputed.

McCain is in on a pass with a large chunk of the press. It's said he owes that to his friendly *kaffeeklatsch* manner in the back of the plane, sleeves rolled up, chummy, not averse to a dirty joke or two— one of them a stomach-turning jest about a recent president's daughter uttered at a public gathering.

His remedial-reading clumsiness with the teleprompter sometimes affords amusement. On Sarah: "She's worked with her hands and knows"—pause, making it sound exactly like "hands and nose"— then, realizing, ". . . and knows what it's like to worry about mortgage payments, and health care, and the cost of gasoline and groceries." (Did YouTube and Stephen Colbert miss that one?)

But enough of this carping. There is one good thing you can say about Sarah. She seems to have hit upon something that might bring relief to the hordes of suffering souls with the wolf at the door and their homes in jeopardy: collect per diem for nights spent in your own house.

SEPTEMBER 12, 2008

'Tis But a Man Gone . . .
but What a Man

hate having to say good-bye to Paul Newman.

He was one of the last of the giants. It's as if a sequoia has fallen.

And, corny as it sounds, he was on that shortest of short lists: real good guys.

His good deeds, charities, and availability for worthy causes should get him into anybody's heaven.

If his artistic talents were short of Brando's—and whose weren't?—he was a hell of a lot better steward of his acting gifts than the man Jack Nicholson always called "the Man on the Hill." And he, Brando, never once returned to the stage, where those lucky enough to have seen him there make you envious, saying, "If you think Marlon was powerful in the *movies* . . ." Mr. Newman delighted theatergoers by repeatedly returning to Broadway.

He and I first met on my old daytime show, which he had discovered early and lent support to when people of his caliber didn't yet. He kept coming on through the years and was the ideal guest. He would be funny, even silly. And, as easily, dead serious and even profound.

It was fun to watch the faces in the audience when he stepped onto the stage. It was as if they were seeing a deity. Once I saw (and heard) an astonished woman down front say, "Oh, my *God*! There he *is*!" (I almost asked her, "Did you think I was kidding?")

(I lied a moment ago. I just remembered that, in fact, we had briefly met before in New Haven. I was a "freshie" at Yale and had just seen him onstage at the venerable Shubert Theater in the Broadway-bound *The Desperate Hours*. Three times at $1.20 each—mid-fifties prices. Front row, second balcony.)

Those startling good looks could take most of your breath away. I found that out when I all but smacked into him on the street. About a decade later I asked him, on the air, if he remembered a flustered freshman type who blurted, "Great performance, Mr. Noonan!"

"Was that you?" he jested.

I wince a bit, remembering how much I kidded him once on the show about sweating. He had just come from the gym and perspired like a lemonade pitcher in August, apologetically daubing his face with his handkerchief. I remember playfully calling attention to it, saying, "I only allow my guests to sweat *back*stage."

I sweat now, recalling this. But such impertinence seemed okay because his complex, congenial charm made you feel like an old friend, even a buddy, right from the start.

Once he came into my dressing room before the show and put some kind of drops in his eyes. I asked if they were the ones Peter O'Toole used that supposedly enhanced the blue in his eyes. He denied this and then, stepping back and looking at his reflection— and feigning sudden discovery—said, "My God! No wonder everybody wants me."

He wasn't kidding. When he first came to New York, bipeds of every known sex hungered for him, as they had for that other male beauty, Marlon Brando. "You must get that, too," Paul said once, with a smirk. I admitted it was true, but probably to a lesser degree. "Because you're half a foot taller than I am," I suggested—as if that were the only difference.

"Gays, too?" he asked.

"Especially," I said.

Wickedly, he had a bright idea: "Hey, why don't you and I date each other a few times in public and maybe they'll all leave us alone."

We got to laughing ourselves silly over the idea.

PAUL: Will you be embarrassed if I call before we go out and ask what *you're* going to wear?

DC: Not at all. I'll probably say, "I'm wearing something mauve and clingy . . . and a simple veil."

By that time we had all but convulsed ourselves over our saucy alleged humor. I said that we must have looked "like two Deke frat boys, howling with laughter over belching, upchucking, and the passage of gas."

"You just described a former me," he said. "Just a different frat."

Paul's fondness for elaborate pranks and practical jokes lasted, some felt, a bit too long. A famous friend who might prefer not to be ID'd said that while Paul was a responsible and mature adult, "his sense of humor froze at about seventh-grade level."

He and Robert Redford had become friends with *Butch Cassidy*. And Redford had a beloved sports car. In a move that few real seventh graders could afford, Newman managed to have it towed away—under cover of darkness—and *compacted*. The massive block that resulted was returned to Redford's front lawn.

Nobody needed to guess who had done it, least of all Bob "Rarely Anyone's Fool" Redford. The following morning the ugly monolith of glass and steel was gone from the Redford lawn. Dawn revealed it: it had suddenly and mysteriously found its way to the Newman residence, where it could be plainly seen . . . on the roof.

Paul's ire was kindled by lots of things, ranging from autograph hounds to Richard Nixon. Despite having been draped with awards, he convincingly maintained that his appearance on the Great Unindicted Co-conspirator's "Enemies List" was his favorite honor. As one similarly honored, I believe that.

He refused to ratify the oft-assumed showbiz rule that celebrities are honor-bound to gratify every pest who feels entitled to a chunk of any celebrity's time, whether the bothered and famous one is strolling, eating, or, um, attending to nature's demands. Paul was hilarious in describing how once in an NBC men's room an astonished fan realized whom he was standing next to, turned ninety degrees while still in midstream, and said, "Wow, Paul Newman."

Newman: "I was ashamed of what they were going to think at the cleaners."

* * *

For way too long, our paths failed to cross again. The last time I saw him was at a party here in the city for some noble cause. It was at the Johnson apartment (as in Johnson & Johnson) on Park Avenue. As usual on such occasions, Paul stood apart, his back to a wall, observing.

We chatted. Years earlier he had confessed to the practice of dunking that famous face in ice water each day, "for preservation purposes."

It must have worked, because there was no doubt who—at just short of eighty—he was but, standing with him, I felt something was wrong with the picture.

Then I realized what it was. And how many years had gone by. And how time is nobody's friend.

Paul Newman and I were, for the first time, the same height.

OCTOBER 3, 2008

A videoclip is available at
http://opinionator.blogs.nytimes.com/2008/10/03/tis-but-a-man-gone-but-what-a-man/.

Anger Mismanagement

I just watched the two candidates at the Al Smith dinner on YouTube. What a strange and disorienting experience it is to see the bitter rivals laughin' and scratchin' and gigglin'. Both had good gags, good writers, and, for non-comics, good delivery. Both brought down the house; or, in this case, the hotel.

It's fun to watch the two men joking. Maybe the whole campaign should be done in jesters' caps and bells, eliminating those possibly life-threatening rises in our blood pressure from yelling in rage at the TV screen. For a brief interval you can say to yourself that maybe this isn't so serious after all.

If only that were true. The laughter will be quickly forgotten, the sniping resumed.

Nothing could have convinced me a few days ago that I could find myself laughing at (and with) and liking John McCain. For moments on end. The distance between the Al Smith/Letterman McCain and the debates McCain is, to me, both vast and puzzling. And two people.

In the same way that a badly adjusted set of binoculars gives you two overlapping images, the two McCains don't come together for me. It must be frustrating for his handlers to be unable—due to some internal blockage in the candidate—to get the amiable self onstage instead of the less palatable one who shows up for debates and now hollered speeches.

Because the one is affable and funny and handles himself skillfully before an audience.

The once seemingly genial John has appeared less frequently of late. John Number Two is a remnant—the snappish, scowling, sour husk of the man I could once see myself voting for. (But as Hamlet put it, "And now, how abhorred in my imagination it is.")

Now someone has actually tallied Senator John's eye blinks in that last debate, coming up with a total that runs into four figures beyond normal. Sometimes they come in rapid flurries, leading to the thought that between his blinks and her winks he may never have seen Sarah Palin.

Laughs aside, unfortunately, I realized during the last debate that watching the two of them together on the screen I would think anyone, even a non-lip-reading, non-English-speaking viewer with the sound off, could see at a glance which man is presidential.

Partly because the word "angry" is so often applied to McCain these days, I decided to read up a bit on anger. And it made me mad.

At myself, I mean. Because I have a goodly portion of it in me, and reading about it has shown me how dangerous it can be. Over the years I've seen articles with titles like "Getting Angry Can Kill You," and sick-making cute titles like "Your Ticker Wants You to Be Glad, Not Mad." I have now read one too many.

It comes as a sort of relief that, according to the experts on anger, we can often blame this, too, on our parents.

One authority, a Ph.D. professor with the fun-to-say title of—hold on to your hats—"behavioral epidemiologist" (would the old *What's My Line?* panel have ever gotten that one?), says that "children who are angry often come from families where there is a lot of punitive blaming, a lot of high emotion and anger expressed." This, he says, happens when adults take things personally rather than simply recognizing that the kid is just being a pain in the posterior nether regions. (Not the prof's exact words.)

The scarier stuff on anger is the evidence of what it can do to your vitals. I know full well that I am laying down deadly plaque in my arteries when enraged: as when you're late and the cabdriver lets other cars in ahead of you—causing you the acute pain of sitting through a green light while the cars he let in glide into the distance—all the while murmuring and nattering into his cell phone in no known language.

Similarly, although I like most women, I can momentarily loathe them all. Irrationally, of course. As when I, late for something, am hurrying along the sidewalk and one gets in front of me with a hairdo too wide for peripheral vision.

As I try to pass, she diabolically wanders left and right, blocking me on both sides, over and over. Defeated by her coif, I even get mad fantasies involving a pair of hedge shears. (Harpo would produce them from his coat and make short work of those hirsute blinders.)

Unpleasant reading on the subject of anger tells us that there's not really anything wrong with it. In limited amounts. It can even be a good thing. A pressure valve. Then, just as we angerable folks sigh with relief on reading this, there comes a vivid technical description of how our major snits can lead to heart disease, diabetes, and "other major health problems."

Like, perhaps, the irritating one of getting smashed in the face with a Coke bottle by the object of your anger?

A cause of anger you, reader, might identify with could be people who promise something in their column that they fail to deliver.

Remember that test a good ways back that was said to show how ill-informed and poorly educated America's young folk are? (Perhaps, like me, you have small reason to dispute this. A youthful graduate of the esteemed Bowdoin College recently asked a friend of mine who wondered how he'd liked *The Iliad,* "Is that the one about ancient Rome?") A natural philosopher of my acquaintance, Charles Roos—a computer expert by trade—supplied me with the following. The funny thing: this smugly erudite test makes a mistake. It claims Ralph Ellison wrote *The Invisible Man.* Ahem. Ralph Ellison did indeed write *Invisible Man,* but *The Invisible Man* was H. G. Wells.

I have a long list of things that make me mad. Maybe if you send me some of yours, we can have some fun, laugh, and save our hearts, if not minds. And I promise to never once use that mimsey little junior high newspaper interviewer's inevitable phrase: "pet peeve." I flustered one once by telling her my pet peeve was nuclear war.

I have room for a few more of mine.

Paper cuts.

Weathermen who can't pronounce "meteorologist" and say *meterologist.* These same ones have never noticed that the word "Arctic" has two *c*'s and so should their *Ant-ART-ic.*

Oldsters who still say "President ROOZA-velt." (Why? No more excuse than for saying "Lyndon JENSON.")

The waiter who, when you are late and want the check, vanishes to another country.

This one deserves caps: AOL HAS UNEXPECTEDLY QUIT. (Remove the "Un" and you have the galling truth.)

Men's shirts without a pocket.

President Bush.

OCTOBER 17, 2008

Fright Night

A smarter person would make this column about dogs, or Tina Fey's good looks, or stamp collecting, or the Hanseatic League.

But I fear it has to be about Tuesday night and all that that entails. Since this column has to be turned in to its editor on Friday, you have the advantage of me. So bear in mind that I don't know what's happened since noon on Friday.

Soon it will all be over but the celebrating and the sobbing.

And high time. It's all been sort of fun until recently. I, for one, am now heartily sick of the whole mess.

And I am sensitive to the accusations—"screams" might be more accurate—of media bias by the right-wing "base." So I will say right now that I don't care who wins.

Just as long as it isn't He and She.

Just about anybody else will do.

It's not been easy being the offspring of English teachers, and few would agree with me, I fear, that assaults on the English language are a major crime. But would you agree that it's at least a little unpatriotic to treat our glorious language sloppily? The language of Lincoln, Jefferson, and, of course, that unpolitical man who, despite the lack of a college education, somehow turned out *Hamlet* and *Henry V*?

I salute Rachel Maddow for being alert to crimes against the mother tongue. For noting, for example, that among the dwindlings of John McCain has been his joining the ranks of those who think "pundits" is pronounced *pundints*. That one mystifies me. Do those who favor this aberration refer to "road agents" as "bandints"? In their "wallents," do they carry their "credint cards"?

And does it work in reverse? Do they fear for the future of their "descendits"?

Never mind. Let it pass.

Better to worry about Sarah Palin's taking over the role of Another Oval Office Occupant Who Can't Pronounce "Nuclear" Correctly.

Herewith, a favor to you, gentle reader, if you dig this sort of stuff. Should you have missed it—in school or out—look up George Orwell's "Politics and the English Language." It's one of those essays so brilliant and entertaining that you'll return to it as the years go by. (Like me, you may even crib from it.)

Back to our story. There's one thing virtually nobody questions about John McCain and that is his heroism.

Some well-meaning readers have forwarded stuff to me that questions that heroism during the war. Much of it reeks of Swiftboatism and rankest hearsay. Some would say, of course, *But where there's smoke, there's fire*. This, in itself, is demonstrably untrue. Who hasn't seen smoke without fire?

In alluding to this nasty McCain stuff I feel a bit like one of the numberless right-wing radio "personalities" (a misnomer, in most cases) who, when rapped for unfairly bringing up something out of someone's past that has been thoroughly disproved, protests, "I'm not bringing it up, I'm just mentioning it."

Among the individuals who, like those on the "little list" from Gilbert and Sullivan's *Mikado*, will not be missed: that new comet on the horizon, Joe the Plumber. This unfunny Ralph Kramden—not officially a plumber, or even a Joe—seems to have effortlessly captured the imagination of those without much of it to spare.

What will history make of this until recently anonymous figure who has been elevated by the McCain forces to the level of a cultural icon, whose every utterance is treated as if from on high? (Many of his fans, waving their placards in Sarah Palin's whooping throngs, favor an alternate spelling—"plummer"—of his revered profession.) Did you hear that he has recently acquired a "manager"—presumably for lecture tours and seminars and think tanks—and a recording contract? (Will he have backup singers? "Joe and the Plumber's Friends"?) Risking the appearance of rudeness, I expect America's ambitious plumber will soon be down the drain.

Is it ungentlemanly of me to confess that I will not miss the pause-free stream of unparsable flapdoodle that issues from the woman chosen by McCain as capable of holding the office held by Jefferson, Lincoln, and the others on Mount Rushmore? Might those carved worthies be scowling in their granite majesty at the thought of someday having to move over a little to make room for Wasilla's wonder woman?

A recently discovered addition to the list of semi-desirables whose departure from the scene won't be hard to take is someone called Michael Goldfarb, identified at the bottom of the screen as the latest "McCain spokesman." Talking to CNN's Rick Sanchez, the just-a-touch-goonish Mr. Goldfarb asserted that Obama hangs out with many undesirables, including those who are, in his rendering of the word, "anti-Se-MET-ic."

Repeatedly challenged by Sanchez to name just one such, he proved unable. He kept repeating, "We all know who that is." I didn't. (I assume, on reflection, that it's Reverend Wright. I and others have been giving the McCain squads credit for at least not throwing him in among their desperate closing thrusts. I hope it isn't just that John can't think of his name.)

One question I have failed to see John McCain asked when adrift in his pipe-dream world of "victory" and "success" in Iraq is this: What went through his head when his idol General Petraeus said that "victory" and "success" are not words to be applied to the Iraq situation? Maybe there is still time for that question.

Do you recall with relish, as I do, the moment when dear Tim Russert, attributing some controversial words to Senator John, was told by McCain, "I don't know where you got that quote"? Russert's reply: "I got it from John McCain." Then he read it out, from one of McCain's speeches. The senator blinked. A YouTubeist has conveniently collated this and similar stuff in a priceless item. You might want to use it instead of Christmas cards.

But the scariest thing McCain has said—worthy of Scotland Yard's "Black Museum" of horrors—is one I've barely seen commented on.

I heard him say that when the White House phone rings at the dread three o'clock in the morning, you don't want someone picking it up who has to take time to "think and analyze the situation, but someone who will *act*." This, coming from a man with the thinking and analyzing traits of a snapping turtle, cannot help but bring the Cuban missile crisis to mind—and what the world might be today had the Arizona senator been in charge. If it (the world) would even *be* at all.

On his program at this very moment (that is, in your recent past) I can hear the humor-free Rush Limbaugh saying that he is "being told by my gut"—which is in evidence—that "things are moving McCain's way." Interesting, to say the most.

But enough of this bridled hilarity. Soon it will be time to start cutting sandwiches and perhaps selecting a tranquilizer for Tuesday night. And note that I, for one, am not making any confident predictions.

I am just old enough to remember that awful night when Dewey defeated Truman.

OCTOBER 31, 2008

The Wild Wordsmith of Wasilla

Electronic devices dislike me. There is never a day when something isn't ailing. Three out of these five implements—answering machine, fax machine, printer, phone, and electric can opener—all dropped dead on me in the past few days.

Now something has gone wrong with all three television sets. They will get only Sarah Palin.

I can play a kind of Alaskan roulette. Any random channel clicked on by the remote brings up that eager face, with its continuing assaults on the English language.

There she is with Larry and Matt and just about everyone else but Dr. Phil (so far). If she is not yet on *Judge Judy*, I suspect it can't be for lack of trying.

What have we done to deserve this, this media blitz that the astute Andrea Mitchell has labeled the "Victory Tour"?

I suppose it will be recorded as among political history's ironies that Palin was brought in to help John McCain. I can't blame feminists who might draw amusement from the fact that a woman managed to cripple the male she was supposed to help while gleaning an almost Elvis-sized following for herself. Mac loses, Sarah wins bigtime was the gist of headlines.

I feel a little sorry for John. He aimed low and missed.

What will ambitious politicos learn from this? That frayed syntax, bungled grammar, and run-on sentences that ramble on long after thought has given out completely are a candidate's valuable traits?

And how much more of all that sort of thing lies in our future if God points her to those open-a-crack doors she refers to? The ones she resolves to splinter and bulldoze her way through upon glimpsing the opportunities revealed from on high?

What on earth are our underpaid teachers, laboring in the vineyards of education, supposed to tell students about the following sentence, committed by the serial syntax killer from Wasilla High and gleaned by my colleague Maureen Dowd for preservation for those who ask, "How was it she talked?"

"My concern has been the atrocities there in Darfur and the relevance to me with that issue as we spoke about Africa and some of the countries there that were kind of the people succumbing to the dictators and the corruption of some collapsed governments on the continent, the relevance was Alaska's investment in Darfur with some of our permanent fund dollars."

And, she concluded, "Never, ever did I talk about, well, gee, is it a country or a continent, I just don't know about this issue."

It's admittedly a rare gift to produce a paragraph in which whole clumps of words could be removed without noticeably affecting the sense, if any.

(A cynic might wonder if Wasilla High School's English and geography departments are draped in black.)

How many contradictory and lying answers about the Empress's New Clothes have you collected? I've got, so far, only four. Your additional ones welcome.

Matt Lauer asked her about her daughter's pregnancy and what went into the decision about how to handle it. Her "answer" did not contain the words "daughter," "pregnancy," "what to do about it," or, in fact, any two consecutive words related to Lauer's query.

I saw this as a brief clip, so I don't know whether Lauer recovered sufficiently to follow up or could only sit there, covered in disbelief. If it happens again, Matt, I bequeath you what I heard myself say once to an elusive guest who stiffed me that way: "Were you able to hear any part of my question?"

At the risk of offending, well, you, for example, I worry about just what it is her hollering fans see in her that makes her the ideal choice to deal with the world's problems: collapsed economies, global warming, hostile enemies, and our current and far-flung twin battlefronts, either of which may prove to be the world's second Thirty Years' War.

Has there been a poll to see if the Sarahites are numbered among that baffling 26 percent of our population who, despite everything, still maintain that President George has done a heckuva job?

A woman in one of Palin's crowds praised her for being "a mom like me . . . who thinks the way I do" and added, for ill measure, "That's what I want in the White House." Fine, but in what capacity?

Do this lady's like-minded folk wonder how, say, Jefferson, Lincoln, the Roosevelts et al. (add your own favorites) managed so well without being soccer moms? Without being whizzes in the kitchen, whipping up moose soufflés? Without executing and wounding wolves from the air? And without promoting that sad, threadbare hoax—sexual abstinence—as the answer to the sizzling loins of the young?

(In passing, has anyone observed that hunting animals with high-powered guns could only be defined as sport if both sides were equally armed?)

I'd love to hear what you think has caused such an alarming number of our fellow Americans to fall into the Sarah Swoon.

Could the willingness to crown one who seems to have no first language have anything to do with the oft-lamented fact that we seem to be alone among nations in having made the word "intellectual" an insult? (And yet . . . and yet . . . we did elect Obama. Surely not despite his brains.)

Sorry about all of the foregoing, as if you didn't get enough of the lady every day in every medium but smoke signals.

I do not wish her ill. But I also don't wish us ill. I hope she continues to find happiness in Alaska.

May I confess that upon first seeing her I liked her looks? With the sound off, she presents a not uncomely frontal appearance.

But now, as the Brits say, "I'll be glad to see the back of her."

P.S.: Lagniappe for English mavens: A friend of mine has made you laugh greatly over the years. David Lloyd is a comic genius (I can hear you wince, David) who wrote for *The Mary Tyler Moore Show, Cheers, Taxi, Frasier,* Jack Paar, Johnny Carson, and me, not necessarily in that order. As a language fan, he has preserved many gems for posterity in his prodigious memory bank. Here comes my favorite:

A navy lecturer was talking about some directives on the black-board that he said to do something about, "except for these here ones with the asteroids in back of."

Even David couldn't make that up.

NOVEMBER 14, 2008

How's That Again, Guy?

Y'all's mass reaction to the Sarah Palin column was a bit overwhelming. I may not have gotten to your own comment even yet, but I shall.

I had resolved to follow it with a switch-hit, hoping to tap out something utterly frivolous as a change-up. (Forgive the mixed baseball metaphor. My jockness was in gymnastics.)

An allegedly "all fun" column draws urges to "get serious, Dick." Predominantly serious ones produce pleas to "frivol" it up again. For sheer fun, I had planned to write, this time, about the joys of Spell-Check. (Mine, for example, instead of "nytimes" urges "nighties.")

But the Illinois governor is too hard to ignore.

The question overhanging this sordid mess, you might agree, is, "How did such a specimen ever get elected?"

It's as if a soldier, tested for his fitness as potential combat leader, passed his physical despite scurvy, pyorrhea, jake leg, leprosy, the quinsy, contagious influenza, and at least two trick knees.

(We all know from childhood that it's not nice to make fun of people's appearance. So I will confine myself to merely observing that whatever covers the governor's head looks to me like a bowling ball cozy.)

Is humor out of place on this subject? Probably. In Rod Blagojevich, we are dealing with a sick man. Or, in medical terminology, extreme pathology.

I felt the need to get some expert opinion on just what the ethically challenged governor is a case of. I sought the counsel of the eminent Dr. Willard Gaylin, longtime practitioner and author on such matters—once entrusted with the care and feeding of my own tender psyche. He filled me in.

He described what would now be called a "sociopath," a modern-day term for the older "psychopath." It's a complex, hard-to-treat ailment, and "antisocial" is the key term here.

Among the prominent traits of one so afflicted is the absence of any sense of guilt or shame. Empathy is unknown. The truth may be told, but only when it serves the often bizarre purposes of the teller. Never for its own sake.

The governor's astonishing dare—"Go ahead and tap my phones"— brings to mind the much more normal Gary Hart's "Follow me." (They did.) It is explained by the sociopath's absolute conviction that he is somehow immune from being caught.

This appears to be connected to the sociopath's trait of confusing his lies with reality. Unable to distinguish between the two, he proceeds on his brazen way, willing, like Richard Widmark in *Kiss of Death*, to push a wheelchaired old lady down a flight of stairs to gain his purposes.

Gaylin reminds us that sociopaths are not always obvious misfits, as evidenced by their being found, for example, running major institutions. Often they have the acting skills of award-winning thespians, can exhibit great charm (though not in this case), and can fool even experts.

To give but one example of the bizarre and extreme forms of the disease, I cite a case from Cleckley's famous work on the subject, *The Mask of Sanity*.

A man, having been lengthily and apparently successfully treated for sociopathy, was at long last released. His relatives delighted in his apparent recovery, the resumption of good grooming, the return of his cheerful personality, and his entertaining and humorous discourse, polite manners, and social affability.

Some weeks into his recovered freedom—at his sister's wedding—he politely made his way along a row of seated wedding guests to the aisle. There, he defecated.

Does this mean there can be more surprises in store from the governor?

My revered former boss Jack Paar said once, "Kid, if you get a bad review that you haven't seen, don't worry. It will always be brought to your attention by a friend."

Thus has come to my attention my excoriation at the skilled literary hands of the excellent Camille Paglia. She's sore as hell about my Sarah Palin piece.

After praising my TV work—and even plugging the DVDs of it—she lays into me.

Responding to such things is a thing I just love to do. Maybe next time? I am always advised against it by wiser heads. I'll never know what damage I did myself years ago by my criticism of the *Times*'s television critic in a letter the newspaper printed. I was told that he was especially stung by my criticism of his writing. I'd said that "his prose has all the sparkle of a second mortgage."

Some of what Ms. P. says is so dumb that I assumed, at first, it was meant to be funny. But I think I'm wrong. It would be strange of her—considering the number of arrows already in her daunting intellectual quiver—to suddenly attempt humor.

I've always loved Camille.

Maybe I should have told her.

DECEMBER 12, 2008

A Better Sort of Insult

I haven't ever found any great writing on that wonderful and often unappreciated art form, the insult.

There are two kinds of insult. "I was bored by your book" is one kind. "Your book? Once I put it down, I couldn't pick it up" is the other.

Although both are insults, only one is witty. Or, at least, funny. I suppose we should reserve the accolade "wit" for the very highest practitioners of the art—Parker, Wilde, Shaw, Twain, Kaufman, Levant, Marx et al. Some would include Rickles. (As when Sinatra entered a club while Don was onstage. Rickles: "Make yourself comfortable, Frank, hit somebody.")

While on the subject, I believe it was writer/critic Clive James who is said to have remarked, when a man punched Sinatra in the face one night outside the stage door, "That's the first time the fan hit the . . ."

If there is a Top Ten list of insults, Churchill's most famous one would be at least number three. It is, of course, the well-known exchange between Sir Winston and an irate lady MP.

Often botched in the retelling, the correct version, according to an MP who claimed to have witnessed the notorious exchange, was:

> *Mr. Churchill, you are drunk.*
> *Madam, you are ugly.*
> *Mr. Churchill, you are* extremely *drunk!*
> *And you, Madam, are extremely ugly. But tomorrow, I shall*
> *be sober.*

Somewhere the witless got hold of it and added "and you'll still be ugly," shamelessly spelling it out for the slow to catch on. The stress on "I" needs no further help. The boobish add-on sinks it.

* * *

Great humorists are great insulters.

Someone should do a book, or thick booklet at least, of the collected cracks by Mark Twain sprung from his lifelong lack of admiration—to put it mildly—for the French.

I cannot find this sentence again but shall do my damnedest to get it as right as possible for you. The sentence includes a reference to something that "shone with that rare combination of lust and envy that burns in a Frenchman's eye when it falls upon another man's *centime*."

A lesser writer might have had it "another man's coin" or "another man's money": but the rhythm would be off. And the finesse would be gone.

Comedians are sometimes resentful of their writers. Probably because it's hard for giant egos to admit you need anyone but yourself to be what you are. Some of the funniest insults I've heard were whispered from one comedy writer to another while in a meeting with an unpleasant star comic shortsighted enough to be nasty to his writers.

Here come three gems from my small but cherished collection of well-deserved toxic bombs dropped on giant comic egos by fed-up writers.

The comic who received the following poisoned arrow was known on both TV and radio, nationwide. Let's leave his largely forgotten name aside, should he have surviving relatives who may not have heard this. (Note: It was not Arthur Godfrey. I liked him.)

Let's call this fellow "Don."

I met him but twice. He was unpleasant. He was known as a good ad-libber, cordial and amiable on air. Additionally, he was known as a horror. Think of one you know. Don was worse—snide, insulting, and contemptuous of those vital employees whose talents nourished and enhanced his reputation as a funny man.

At a meeting with his staff of four writers, his contempt for them and their art became too much for one guy. Don was a marked man, about to inspire an insult of the deadliest variety.

First, a required fact. The comic had an unfortunate disfigurement of the face and was self-conscious about it. Makeup made him look okay on the air, but in person the small craters in the facial flesh were the worst I've ever seen. They were virtually holes.

On the fateful day, he said something so infuriating that one of the writers resigned on the spot. Uttering a decidedly unwitty expletive, he jumped to his feet with a loud "That's it!" and stomped out, slamming the door.

Then the door reopened. He reappeared, momentarily.

"Hey, Don, I've always wanted to ask you something. What's par for your right cheek?" (*Exit.*)

You'd think that insecure comics—and this category includes some huge stars—would know better than to open themselves up as targets to the very people who can both make them appear witty and, at the same time, most memorably wound them.

I was a huge Jackie Gleason fan, despite friends who wondered how I could admire both Groucho Marx and Gleason, whom they considered crude. Watch him in *The Honeymooners* or, if you prefer, in *The Hustler* and see the definition of the phrase "never makes a false move."

Contributing to his collection of neuroses was the fact that, when he was quite young, his father went away one day and never came back. It's said that Jackie went to great lengths to find his lost father, even trying psychics and trance mediums.

One of Jackie's writers had been summoned to the penthouse offices of the Gleason show in the Park Sheraton in Manhattan. (In my youth I used to hang around there in hopes of glimpsing the Great One.) From experience, the guy knew he could expect a chewing out.

The writer was on time but the star was not. An hour passed. And then another.

The writer, presumably with an already ample list of grievances over this sort of treatment, apparently decided that employment in a salt mine would be no less pleasant than the current gig. He'd had it. It was time to quit.

He announced this to Gleason's secretary and headed for the door.

"What shall I tell Mr. Gleason when he finds no one here?"

The writer vented his accumulated bile with but a few words:

"Tell him his dad dropped by."

The comedy writer, and my friend, David Lloyd and I worked on the staff of a popular TV show. There were four writers, one a particularly loathsome specimen. The modesty of his talent may have nourished his other traits: jealousy, gossip, rumormongering, and an inclination to knife his colleagues whenever he was alone with the star.

I've forgotten exactly how he went over the line with David, but I came around a corner just in time to hear, "Al, your parents owe the world a retraction."

David asked me if I remembered what I had said about this same loathed writer. I didn't. David: "We saw him come out of the men's room once, and I asked what you thought he does in there. You said, 'That's where he puts his best stuff on paper.'"

As a sort of sweetener from the brutality of the above blowgun darts aimed at fellow human beings, let us close this subject—but only for now—with something a bit milder. It's from the man who once complained to me, "I can't insult anyone anymore."

Mistakenly, I thought Groucho was being contrite. But no. It was that things he said when seriously angry, and meaning to wound and leave a scar, failed to injure. Instead, he got the reaction, "Oh, thank you, Groucho! Wait till I tell my friends what Groucho Marx said to me."

"It's almost ruined my life," Mr. Marx only partially jested.

Upon leaving a stuffy Beverly Hills party thrown by a socialite, Groucho said to her, "I've had a perfectly wonderful evening. But this wasn't it."

Does it get any better?

JANUARY 9, 2009

I'm Not Weeping; It's an Allergy

These foolish drops do something drown my manly spirit.
—SHAKESPEARE, *The Merchant of Venice*

I had neither planned nor expected to cry.

If it's true, as some maintain, that men who cry are pantywaists, then I stand condemned.

Not being one of those whose tear production is either quick or voluminous, I was amazed at how many times, watching the all-day spectacle, I lost it.

And it wasn't just at the easy times like, say, during a sudden close-up of a tear-streaked elderly black face in the crowd, but also at moments that were just plain "for the country."

"Historic" and "historic moment" and "historic day" were repeated mercilessly, but remained true. Only a zombie could fail to feel the truth of it.

It seems, doesn't it, that there are two kinds of tears.

There's the kind produced by the death of your dog (which just happened to me once again, and about which I always offend someone by asserting that the reason the death of a pet is worse than the death of a human is that you have mixed feelings about *all* people), or by the loss of a loved one. And there's the almost opposite kind—but still tears—produced by watching Astaire and Rogers, the young DiMaggio and the young Ali, a sudden Picasso, Ol' Blue Eyes's voice, the Twenty-third Psalm, or any performance by Meryl Streep. Or Obama's grin for his daughters.

Music bypasses the brain and goes straight to the heart. I wish my life had more of it. Once, years ago, I was taken along to Tanglewood for a concert by the great Zino Francescatti, a name scandalously unknown to me the day before.

Somehow we were in the front row. I was not on TV yet or I would have been even more embarrassed when, repeatedly and to my total amazement, the virtuoso violinist caused me to, as suddenly as a hiccup, give forth an audible, gurgling sob. Beauty tears, I guess you could call them. Tears of joy.

Aretha can make me cry. So could Ella, and Etta, and Ruth and Billie, and Carmen and Lena, and, and . . . the list goes on and on of female black singers who have unlimited access to my emotional innards.

And yet somehow I was never moved—a limb confronts me and I am about to venture out upon it with a dangerous confession—by the sanctified Marian Anderson.

Her affectations and regal bearing I found embarrassing. It takes a heart of stone not to be moved by just about anybody's rendering of "He's Got the Whole World in His Hands," but her choosing to make "hand" sound too much like "hahnd," and her queenly personal use of the royal "we" and "our" in both speech and writing sort of put me off. (Sorry to those for whom this admission will place me beyond redemption.)

The refreshingly robust delivery of "Amazing Grace" by Wintley Phipps last Tuesday got to me big-time. And I always worry for that great song, fearing it might grow stale through overuse. It gets trotted out to give instant depth of feeling to mediocre dramas that can't otherwise spur emotion. One year, it was the theme music of *three* feature films.

I find most "sacred music" pretty dismal. I don't have a strict policy of "nothing sacred." Once past the overly familiar "Mine eyes have seen the glory" stanza of "The Battle Hymn of the Republic," at least a dozen lines in the sublime later verses—even just reading them—can make me gurgle and (since I don't own one) ask for a hankie.

At least a dozen lines and passages in it simply cannot be read impassively, from "I have read a fiery gospel writ in burnished rows of steel" to whole stanzas like:

He has sounded forth the trumpet that shall never call retreat;
He is sifting out the hearts of men before His judgment-seat:
Oh, be swift, my soul, to answer Him! be jubilant, my feet!
Our God is marching on.

One moment in that stirring hymn never fails me. Though not much of a believer, I have only to think and hum the first line of one of the less familiar stanzas to induce instant throat stricture.

In the beauty of the lilies Christ was born across the sea,
With a glory in His bosom that transfigures you and me:
As He died to make men holy, let us die to make men free
While God is marching on.

Why was Julia Ward Howe not forced to turn out at least twenty more hit singles?

I felt bad when George W. Bush was booed.

But only briefly. My sympathy for that man has a half-life of about four seconds.

There was a surprising number of outpourings of sympathy for his having to sit there and, as it was too often described, "take it on the chin." Was there ever a chin more deserving of taking it?

"You have to feel sorry for him," someone cooed. "No. You do not!" I shouted at the screen. I know he "tried" and he "did what he thought was right." But so does the incompetent surgeon.

What does that excuse?

His brief discomfort "sitting there" can't have been less endurable than the discomfort of the young soldier describing on the news how he watched helplessly as his gut-shot buddy bled to death on the sands the smirking Texan sent him to.

And a hearty sayonara to that other fellow.

Do freshman philosophy classes nowadays debate updated versions of the age-old questions? Like, how could a merciful God allow AIDS, childhood cancers, tsunamis, and Dick Cheney?

As with all good entertainments, there was unintended comic relief.

Not since Robert Goulet forgot the words to the national anthem has there been a moment to rival the Chief Justice's blowing his lines, turning the Oath of Office into an Abbott & Costello "Who's on First?" routine.

The giggling schoolboy side of me thought it laughable as hell. What would the funny man do next? Drop the Lincoln Bible on his foot?

Yet the increasingly curmudgeonly side of me frowned and found it inexcusable. It isn't as if some tipsy, third-rate actor did it. It was *the Chief Justice of the United States!*

And he was playing to perhaps the largest audience in world history.

Nerves? Stage fright?

How nervous could a man in his position possibly be? As one of the dozen remaining people in the country with job security—and for life—oughtn't he to be at least relatively calm?

(My favorite game regarding the Supreme Court is waiting for the day when the brilliantly dangerous Antonin Scalia and his papoose, Clarence Thomas, disagree on *something*.)

All in all it was, to put it feebly, a day to remember.

And, remarkably, I heard, the mobs of millions produced not a single arrest. All kinds of history was made that day.

What this—as Tennessee W.'s Blanche DuBois says—"young, young, young man" can do for the country and the world is yet to be revealed.

But for starters isn't it nice having someone in the Oval Office with smarts? And class?

And syntax?

Writers Bloc: When Updike and Cheever Came to Visit

You can count yourself lucky in life, I guess, if certain things happen to you that happen to only a few. Good things, that is.

Winning the lottery, of course, or taking Olympic gold, or the Oscar, or the Nobel Prize. Part of the fun, if that's the word, is that few other people in the world get the chance that you did. If you're a nice person, you may even take a moment to feel sorry for them.

In my life, a rare thrill of a different order recurred a few times: the chance to sit, on television, between two great writers.

A recent obituary brought memories of one of the best of those times. Though a bit more genteel than my notorious Norman Mailer / Gore Vidal show, this one was no less thrilling.

"What if we could get John Cheever *and* John Updike?" someone said. "Together. On the same show!"

The fantasy came true.

Much of the pleasure of sitting, as I did in 1981, flanked by two articulate and entertaining literary giants, is in knowing that a vast number of lucky—and grateful—people at home are getting to see it and revel in it, too.

I've had noted and famous pairs of guests on together, each of whom, I knew, had a low opinion of the other's viscera. But side by side on national television, they could be counted on to spout flowery compliments at each other. ("This woman sitting here defines the phrase 'movie star,'" etc.)

These two great writers sitting there demonstrated the real thing. They praised each other, but in a way that transcended the usual embarrassing chat-show, face-to-face, fulsome public flattery. (Both would strike out about a half pound of my intensifying adjectives from that sentence.) They elevated praise to an art form.

Updike and Cheever. Two literary giants who deeply admired, and even envied, each other's gifts and talent. Seeing them say so was a treat. (Here, too weak a word.)

Each literary genius spoke—from the heart—of the other. First, Updike said how much he admired Cheever's writing. Moments later, Cheever said that he refused to review books, a thing Updike did voluminously. I put Cheever on the spot, mildly, by asking what he might say if he *did* review Updike's newest novel, *Rabbit Is Rich*. During his answer, Updike glowed.

I had Cheever on the show, by himself, another time. I'm pretty sure I didn't bring up sexual ambiguity, but I may have. I did ask him about a remark Updike had made about running into him, plastered, at some ceremony and finding him all but unrecognizable. "I was fairly certain that the John Cheever I knew was in there somewhere," Updike had said.

Unfazed (seemingly), Cheever quickly answered, "I don't remember where John made that remark," and went on to talk toughly about his alcoholism, hitting bottom and saying to himself, "This is not me, nor the life for me, and I enrolled myself in Smithers"—where he kicked the booze after some hard months. I regret not having asked him more about his admiration for certain writers and his detestation of J. D. Salinger.

The price exacted by booze, drugs, and the wear and tear of leading a double (triple?) life of bisexual adultery while maintaining a family and brilliant writing career was writ large on the raffish Cheever face. Looking at the two writers sitting side by side in the green room backstage, waiting to go on, I saw that Cheever's somewhat rumpled appearance contrasted noticeably with that of the prim and preppy Updike.

A note on John U. and bad habits: Either before or during one show, someone lit a cigarette, and Updike said, "I could have sworn in court that I am not smoking these days. Then yesterday I edited some pages and, amazed, looked down and there were eleven butts in the ashtray."

John Updike died of what doctors abbreviate "ca. of the lung." Maybe docs, especially, like to avoid the dread word.

There is dispute about who gets credit for "Envy no man until he has had a good death." (Euripides? Shakespeare? Soupy Sales?)

Neither man did. Cheever's "ca." was of the bladder (possibly also thanks to the tobacco industry) and it had metastasized. At Cheever's last public appearance, upon receiving a major literary award at Carnegie Hall, Updike reported, "We acolytes out front were horrified by his gaunt appearance." He goes on to say, "On that night John announced, 'Literature is invincible.'" My notes, alas, don't have Updike's exact next words, to the effect that "we were all astonished at this optimism."

Speaking of loss, there was a "Dick Cavett Night" once at that great, historic forty-room mansion on Gramercy Park that is now the National Arts Club. My honoring speakers were (gulp) John Cheever and the great Agnes de Mille. I keep meaning to find out if there is any record of that night.

My memories include my wife's being charmed and enchanted, getting to sit next to and chat with Cheever—whose works she knew—on the dais.

I remember a huge laugh I got, perhaps somewhat cruelly. In thanking a list of people out front, I came to the name of a gent who had spoken earlier. I recall his last name: Montmorency. His first may have been Rupert. If not, it should have been.

Coming to him on the list, I heard myself say, "And next, Mr. Rupert Montmorency. If, indeed, that is his name." The laugh was robust to the point of regrettable. Cheever produced tears.

The one sad note of the evening: Out front afterward, on the dark sidewalk as people were leaving, I thanked and said good-bye to Cheever for the last time. He started away and then came back, reached inside his jacket, and handed me his typed copy of the wonderful and witty remarks he had just made about me. As I recall, I tucked them inside my blazer pocket, making a mental note to take good care of that sheet of paper. A cleaner may have been the last to see it.

Damn my sloppiness to deepest hell!

I do have some other cherished items, though. Cheever was the master of the terse, witty note of but three or four lines. A favorite had to do with some unflattering remarks made about me by the writer

Francine du Plessix Gray that had appeared somewhere. Cheever had answered them, defending me. In the mail came:

> Dick,
>
> I'm a little worried about my remarks, about Francine du Plexxis [*sic.*] Gray. She is a member of the French aristocracy and a crack wing shot. There is no cover on my land.
>
> John

FEBRUARY 13 & MARCH 2, 2009

Videoclips are available at
http://opinionator.blogs.nytimes.com/2009/02/13/writers-bloc-when-updike-and-cheever-came-to-visit/
and at
http://opinionator.blogs.nytimes.com/2009/03/02/a-last-look-at-updike-and-cheever/.

Conjuring Slydini

made more money in high school than I ever have since.

Or so it seems.

Entranced by a pitchman at the Nebraska State Fair when I was eleven, I bought a trick deck of cards, known to magicians as a "Svengali deck." It set me back a dollar and a quarter and before I wore it out it paid for itself a hundredfold—and more.

Magic became my life.

Let me assert right here that magic may be the greatest hobby for a kid. It's all-consuming. Get your problem child interested in it. The first time your kid masters a trick and performs it—and an adult, genuinely amazed, says, "How in heck did you do that?"—your potential juvenile delinquent will be hooked and too absorbed in the new hobby to steal hubcaps.

I'm not saying a Svengali deck given as a bar mitzvah present would have spared us Bernie Madoff. Nor am I claiming that a magic deck popped into Dick Cheney's or Donald Rumsfeld's Christmas stocking would have spared the world their predations. But it's possible.

As I got more stuff from those newly discovered wonders—magic catalogs—I developed an act. Shows in church basements, Elks Clubs, and birthday parties in Lincoln, Nebraska, and environs jumped quickly from free gigs to netting a princely ten dollars! Soon, my fee jumped to twenty-five dollars. Eventually I hit thirty-five dollars. And they were 1950s dollars. I was rolling in it.

When my schoolteacher parents' decrepit '38 DeSoto finally threw a rod, Cavett, the Magician (as my business cards read), their early-teens son, was able to lend them $750 toward a new Studebaker. (No youthful reader, or youthful parent, will believe the following statement, but here goes. This amount, a few years later, equaled three-quarters of my freshman tuition at Yale. Where did that world go?)

By great luck a wonderful man named Gene Gloye, studying at the university, financed his graduate school expenses working as a local conjurer and took me under his wing. I owe him a lot. He opened my world to the wonders of magicians' magazines, national magic organizations, magic books, magic catalogs, and, best of all, magicians' conventions.

At one of these, in St. Louis in 1952, I won, at fifteen, the Best New Performer trophy in the rope category, beating out the new president of the International Brotherhood of Magicians. The *Lincoln Journal* headline screamed, YOUNG LINCOLN SHARPIE BESTS MAGICIANS' GROUP HEAD. (Taking out the fading remains of that clipping—complete with three photos of a beaming, bow-tied youth—can still send me into a dream state.)

I'm just old enough to have seen and met some of the last of the legendary mystifiers from an earlier time. Blackstone (the elder) came to Omaha with his full evening show. I cut a day of school to see it twice. (The great old-style full-evening touring magic show—with its pretty girls and its handsome assistants, its floating ladies and other grand illusions—is a thing of the past, killed largely by the musicians' union's demands for a full pit orchestra.)

Other greats I got to see (I feel I should say "witnessed") were the legendary Cardini (in his last performance ever), Dai Vernon, Okito, the Great Virgil, Bert Allerton, Al Flosso, and Jack Gwynne. Not household names to you but gods to me.

I was too young for Houdini, of course, and Thurston, and Chung Ling Soo (William Robinson on his passport)—a man who affected offstage and on his Chinese guise, including (onstage) a wide-stance walk in Chinese robes and makeup. Without revealing anything, I can tell you that the stance made it possible for Chung to produce a huge, tub-sized, gleaming crystal bowl of swimming goldfish from, seemingly, thin air.

All magicians have had a trick go wrong, but Chung paid the highest price. He was accidentally shot to death on a London stage by an audience volunteer while performing the "Bullet Catching."

I couldn't have imagined that a life without magic would ever happen, but my new magical worlds—Yale and New York City and the theater and television—pushed magic out of my heart and mind.

Years later, when I had a show on PBS, I went to see Doug Henning's evening of magic on Broadway. Backstage in his dressing room after the show, I barely noticed a smallish man standing to one side. Suddenly he said what sounded like "You D. Cava?" I horripilated. Before me stood the god I haven't mentioned yet. There, in the flesh, stood Slydini.

Instant gooseflesh. He'd been one of the giants in the pantheon of magic for decades. I would sooner have dreamed of meeting Beethoven.

Slydini. Just typing those three syllables even now gives me a frisson.

This legendary conjurer, born Quintino Marucci in Italy, found close-up magic wanting and simply reinvented it ("I wanted to take out all the phony-looking stuff"). He toured the world, working in several languages.

What had sounded like "D. Cava" was, of course, my name, and I loved that Slydini knew it. I knew that he refused to do television. A bad experience in Europe, with cameras in wrong places and lousy editing, had soured him on that, and, a perfectionist, he wouldn't risk again having his work tainted.

I was thrilled when, having heard I knew magic, he said that maybe I would "be the man to give me what I need" and asked if he should consider doing my show, "If-a you are interested." (Guess.)

Suddenly Doug Henning said, "Tony's doing a special demonstration for some magicians tomorrow night at Vesuvio restaurant. Come."

Tomorrow night finally came. For the magicians, sitting for nearly two hours at that table, sudden gasps and intakes of breath abounded.

It was like seeing a man walk up a wall. Nothing prepared you for it. Right at the start, a solid, heavy silver dollar, held before my eyes, vanished into thinnest air. And by no method I knew of. Certainly no sleeves. The two hours flew too quickly.

* * *

Not long after, Tony appeared on two half-hour PBS shows with me. He wanted a few people at the table and I invited actor friends I'd just worked with on Broadway. I think they may have tired of hearing me rave about my new friend and wondered if anyone could be that good. It became a case of "Those who came to scoff remained to pray."

I felt shamelessly proud of being able to preserve on two shows this great artist's work. The magicians' mecca, the Magic Castle in Los Angeles, gratefully made me a lifetime member. (One minute after the first show aired, an exuberant Johnny Carson called me from California.)

Tony was a bit bowled over by the reaction on the street the day after the first show aired. He was particularly delighted by a phone call from Johnny Carson that morning. At his tobacco/newspaper shop, where he said he'd been anonymous for decades, he was now lionized. "Dick, you make so I can't-a go anywhere," he mock-complained. And then he did complain: "But, Dick, I'm-a look-a so old." As a young man, he'd been a handsome dog.

A week after that show aired he went to France, Spain, Italy, and Japan. Home recording of television was not all that common back then but, he said, "Everywhere I'm-a go they go to a machine, push a button, and up comes Dick Cavett and Slydini. How they get I don't know." (Magicians cassetted that show all over the world to one another.)

Out of gratitude, Tony offered to take me on as a student, "If-a you have time." I kvelled. I felt the way a young cellist might if asked by Yo-Yo Ma if he "had time." (I once rudely asked YYM if I could call him by his first Yo.)

Slydini lived in a tiny old ground-floor apartment on West Forty-sixth Street in Manhattan: mecca for his students, some of whom commuted from distant cities for their treasured sessions. At the center of the small living room was a custom-built padded table where you sat, across from him, for tutoring.

Tony's generosity in teaching other magicians and his young

students sometimes ran up against the problem of their being unable to do his stuff, even when he showed them how. This related not only to his phenomenal digital dexterity, but to a central element in the world of magic. It's a thing based in psychology and learned human behavior. It's called "misdirection": in brief, putting the attention where you want it.

This is old ground for magicians reading this, but the easiest to fool are the intelligent; the hardest, the dumb. (And, in some fascinating recent scholarly research, the insane.) Misdirection relies on learned responses. Point to a lamp and your intelligent friend looks at the lamp. Do the same for a dog, a small child, or an imbecile, and they look at your hand. (Tony knew that his superb acting skills and strong misdirection were fully acquired by only a few of his prize students.)

I couldn't wait for evening to come the day of my first Slydini class. I knew I would leave his place able to do some dazzling miracle and tried to guess what it might be. I was in for a surprise. In fact, for a (foolish) disappointment.

I couldn't believe what he said: we would spend our first hour or two together "learning to take a coin from your hand." (I almost cried. And almost said, "I *know* that one.")

Giving me one of his famous six silver dollars that he'd used for decades so that they had a lovely patina—the ones he used in his "Coins Through the Table" masterpiece—he said, "Dick, hold-a the coin, lying in your left hand, take with your right hand and show to me." (I'll keep the dialect to a minimum, but it's hard because I hear Tony's voice.) "Hold with your four fingers and your thumb. Keep-a the coin hidden behind the four fingers when you show the hand so I don't see the coin, but it's there."

I took and showed.

"Good. Do again. Fine. Now do again, but this time, no take."

I tried. Tony, in his affectionate but critical tone, said, "That's-a no good. When you show me the right hand that's suppose-a have the coin, why you keep your left hand tight if it's supposed to be empty?" I had begun to learn.

Tony now did the move himself over and over, each time asking, "I'm-a take or no take?" I never could tell. They were identical.

There were a half dozen more "tips" and "subtleties," all enhancing the illusion of taking the coin into the other hand. Space allows one more.

"You see what your body does when you no-take?" I didn't. "It stays with your left side where you know the coin really is. Your body knows. When you no-take to the right, lean a little to the right, like you do unconscious when you really take."

One more: "Here's a help. Sounds crazy. When you pretend it's in the right hand, you have to believe it." Leaning his head ever so slightly to the right toward the (non) coin and, yes, listening. "Just for a moment, hear the coin there. It's help-a the acting."

I was getting a master acting class. Hundreds of these physical and psychological subtleties in his performing added up to his infallible deception.

An element of Tony's personality was his goodness. He taught kids who couldn't continue to pay instead of taking new students who could—although he needed the income.

He was a superb chef. His spaghetti was on a level with his magic, and he made a point of always feeding young students he felt were scrimping on food to pay for their lessons.

He saw me admiring the (apparent) marble parts of his living room. "Isn't that stuff expensive?" I asked. "Not spensy for me," he chuckled. "Look-a close." It was trompe l'oeil, painted by him.

The voice on my Hollywood hotel phone said, "Richard, let's go to the Castle. I'll pick you up." It was my former boss John Carson of *Tonight Show* fame. The absolute Dean of All Magic, the great Dai Vernon, joined us at our table. After convulsing us with personal stories of what a schmuck Harry Houdini was, suddenly he looked wistful. "I realized the other day what my one wish would be," he said. (Vernon was in his eighties.) "If I could just be fooled one more time before I die."

It was sort of sad.

"Nobody can fool Dai Vernon?" I asked.

"Nobody," he said. And then, "Well, Tony can."

There was a fluid beauty in the Slydini hands. They never moved fast. You could be taught the same moves, but your hands didn't look like his. Any more than a skilled dancer, duplicating Fred Astaire's steps and moves, looks remotely like Astaire. I asked him about this. "I have one student," he said, "he can-a do." I was jealous.

He liked the fact that I brought famous people to see him: Woody Allen, Robert Redford, Sophia Loren. (He nearly purred when she caressed his cheek.) I asked Tony to come by the studio to meet Muhammad Ali. He had Ali tie two white handkerchiefs together, with multiple square knots. He sensed the champ was being nice. "Tie tight. Tight!" he commanded. Holding one end, with Ali holding the other, he had the only three-time heavyweight champion of the world "pull really tight." They both pulled. "C'mon-a champ," he said, "you can pull harder than that. Hard!" Both pulled hard, making a loud snap.

"How long you think would-a take me to untie those knots?" Tony asked.

"Two years," Ali replied.

Tony took both handkerchiefs and immediately and gently handed them back. Separately. Ali beamed. "Hey, Dick, this guy's a magician!" he said. The champ got a teacher and took up magic.

Tony and I never spoke of his personal life. I'm sure he was lonely. There were rumors of his having been a spy in World War II, or a prisoner, of a lost wife and child. All sorts of things, none confirmed.

Inexplicably, I drifted away from him for a time and learned he was in an old-age home in New Jersey. (He died there in 1991.) I visited him there, and it was sad. He said he didn't even have his beloved coins with him, and it looked like he did little but sit on the bed, in his customary crisp white shirt and tie. "Nobody in this place ever hear of Slydini," he said.

Thank God, I had one of my few good ideas. I sent cassettes of the shows to the home, and they played them for the assembled residents.

I visited for what proved to be the last time. "Dick, you do it again," Tony said. "I was-a nobody here. Now I'm-a the star."

MARCH 27 & APRIL 10, 2009

Videoclips are available at
http://opinionator.blogs.nytimes.com/2009/03/27/conjuring-slydini/
and at
http://opinionator.blogs.nytimes.com/2009/04/10/conjuring-slydini-part-2/.

Seriously, What Are the Odds?

A friend of mine was meeting his soon-to-be in-laws for the first time. They had driven from a faraway state. Their license plate, he saw, consisted of an unusual, arcane scientific term: something like GENTFRETS. Let's call it that.

Nothing strange so far, except that the families had never met, and my friend's father's license plate, relating to his profession, also read GENTFRETS.

That baffling phenomenon—coincidence—intrigues me more and more as instances spice up my own life with their mysterious improbability. I've had some doozies.

I'm told of, but haven't yet found, a recent book on the subject that raises the question: are coincidences more than coincidence?

The idea that they are is akin, I suppose, to those who like to say, pointedly and accusingly about a significant and injurious mishap, "Freud says there are no accidents."

This tiresome note is eagerly sounded by its adherents when you spill hot soup on your disliked cousin, or when the wife's pot of geraniums slips from her hands from a third-floor window sill and brains her husband. And in less dramatic instances, slips of the tongue: as when one says "wife" for "life" in saying what one is sick of. (Perhaps not less dramatic.)

First of all, Freud never said it. Or, if he did, it has escaped the notice of at least two acquaintances of mine, well read in the works of the man V. Nabokov enjoyed calling "the Viennese quack." Both my sources for this are licensed, Harvard-educated practitioners of the shrink trade.

What Freud *did* say, they tell me, is that there is nothing in behavior that doesn't have a cause. Obscure and difficult though it may be to discover. Maybe a less than perfect understanding of that concept is where the cherished "no accidents" idea comes from.

I love my own coincidences and love to hear other people's stories. Or let's say I love *most* of mine.

What I don't love is when one happens that combines wonder and chance with face-scalding embarrassment. An instance follows.

A thick fog blanketed Long Island's east end. Alone in a shared summer house, I sought that morning's Sunday *Times* for companionship.

As I headed for the newsstand's rack of papers, so did another man. A bit ahead of me. He snatched up the remaining copy. Instant hatred. As I cursed my luck, he put it back and took *Newsday* instead.

Grabbing that last *Times* up, I paid and got back in the car and tossed the weighty bundle ineptly toward the passenger seat. A cascade of sections slid to the floor, leaving only Arts & Leisure exposed.

I glimpsed but one headline. It announced a coming Broadway musical to be adapted from a popular and fairly amusing book of that time. Let's pretend its title was, say, *How to Be Sexy Tho' Bald*. That info was taken in at a glance. I saw nothing else on the page.

Something urged me to drive to the beach and take a lonely seaside stroll in the fog. It was super thick and of the kind where a tree, for example, appears instantly and magically, two feet in front of you, invisible until that moment.

The lovely sensation of walking along the water's edge, utterly hidden and feeling like the only person in the world, was suddenly shattered. The figure of a man appeared, those two feet before me. We startled each other and nearly bumped.

He looked familiar, but not overly. I couldn't match his "Hey, Dick" by greeting him by his own name. After the obligatory exchange of "How ya doin'?" and "What's happ'nin'?" I was stuck. I needed to say something to cover the embarrassment of facing a stranger who knew who I was.

In a sort of panic, I grabbed for the only thing in my head. "Can you believe the junk that gets to Broadway these days?" I said, needing to say something.

"Like what?"

"It's in today's paper. They're actually going to make a musical out of *How to Be Sexy Tho' Bald*."

"You're kidding me, of course," he said, with a sort of sorry look.

"No, I'm not. It's in today's *Times*."

"You know I wrote it?"

Just typing that line decades later makes my face hot to the touch.

I went on to do the coward's "I've got to stop kidding people this way" sort of pitiful, cheese-eating-grin-accompanied attempt to save the day. But it was without salvation.

Exactly how we parted is lost in memory's own fog.

I went home and somebody had left a *World Almanac* on a coffee table in the rented house. I looked up how many people there are in the world.

Theoretically, at least, I could have run into any one of *them*.

Couldn't I?

MAY 8, 2009

Why Can't We Talk Like This?

How many people have you met whose conversation is instantly publishable?

There can never be more than a handful of such people living at any given time. My peculiar line of work has allowed me to meet a few. Of those I had the great good fortune to sit with on the air, first to mind come Noël Coward, Peter Ustinov, and Jonathan Miller.

Robert Benchley said that you can divide people into two groups: those who divide people into two groups and those who don't. Another such group pairing would be: those who were blessed to have seen *Beyond the Fringe* on Broadway—and everyone else.

In 1962, four British lads fresh from Oxford and Cambridge—Peter Cook, Dudley Moore, Alan Bennett, and Jonathan Miller were their names—hit Broadway with a bursting bombshell of hilarity.

A few minutes into the first act, a tall, thin, gangly, somewhat stork-like figure with barely kempt hair lurched to center stage and brought down the house with an improbable narration about a true incident in which a huge, unidentified load of men's dark serge trousers appeared mysteriously in a London railway storage room—admittedly not a subject usually seen in a comic's repertoire. In Miller's hands it left you weak.

Dr.—as he then was—Jonathan Miller decided after some soul searching to put his budding medical career on hold to appear in the comic revue that the quartet had so successfully put together. He planned to allow himself a year or so to "cavort and caper upon the public stage" before returning to serve mankind, Hippocratically.

As Jonathan's—now Sir Jonathan's—seventy-fifth birthday bears down upon him, he still suffers guilt at never having returned to medicine. He takes comfort in the fact that his wife, Rachel, remained a doctor, so at least one of the Millers continued, until retirements, to aid the stricken. (He has added to his list of accomplishments becoming an internationally sought and acclaimed director of opera.)

The thing about Jonathan is that his comic gift is accompanied by another trait that is certainly not required of a rich comic talent.

He is one of the most formidable intellectuals in captivity.

In that capacity he has fathered many books and articles in scholarly publications on science, physics, religion, politics, the arts, medicine, psychology, mesmerism, and just about everything else. With his knowledge of medicine and anatomy, he did a stunning series seen on public television called *The Body in Question,* all about every part of you and me.

I wish I had daily access to Jonathan's thoughts on significant current events. On one taping with him on my old PBS show, the news had just broken of the attempt to ban the teaching of "the theory of evolution" in schools.

I archly asked him if he would submit his own children to the "poisonous teachings of Charles Darwin." He said that he would, as readily as he would expose them to "the poisonous teachings of Isaac Newton." That to deny the truth of the thing for which there is more proof than perhaps anything else in the universe would be, as he politely put it, "to be in error." He stated his "respect for people's religious beliefs" but not for "this particular bit of nonsense." (He did a brilliant series for the BBC some years ago on the history of atheism.)

Jonathan observed that referring to the "theory" of evolution is like saying the "theory" of gravity.

Jonathan spouts original insights and observations on just about anything. Once, as we waited backstage to go on together at the Ninety-second Street Y, I pointed disapprovingly at his lit cigarette, causing him to talk entertainingly about some of the ironic rationales of the smoker who's aware he's doing wrong: "I know these will kill me. I'm just not convinced that this *particular* one will kill me."

MAY 29, 2009

A videoclip is available at
http://opinionator.blogs.nytimes.com/2009/05/29/why-cant-we-talk-like-this/.

Miller Talks Again

Lots of readers were stimulated by Jonathan Miller's talk about the surprisingly still volatile subject of the teaching of evolution. It had just re-erupted in America. He'd said that talking about the "theory" of evolution is like talking about the "theory" of gravity. He marveled that things that are facts—or laws—seem to be required to serve "a sort of apprenticeship as 'theories' before they can graduate, after a period of probation, to earning the full title of 'facts.'"

The idea of evolution, he said, is not sitting around waiting for accreditation. "No credible scientist or biologist questions it. Creation is not a hypothesis. Not something that can really be taken seriously." He went on to say, in his tolerant, nonranting tone, that it would be "extremely difficult to think of anything more plausible to explain how things are than Charles Darwin's works on the subject. How creatures, by gradual alteration and modification, became what they are today."

This jogs a memory, just now, of my Old Testament course at Yale in which Professor B. Davie Napier explained that Genesis, correctly seen, can be thought of as a poetic creation, stating that God's relationship to man is as personal as the potter's is to the clay from which he fashions his vase. Not as an attempt to insist that God slapped man and the world together in a week.

It's probably just as well that Jonathan was not on the show with a long-dead near-relative of mine who remained undisturbed by evidence like carbon dating, prehistoric arrowheads and hide scrapers, and fossils dating back to the dawn of time. "Those," he said once in my presence, "are easy to explain. They were put there by the devil." For what reason, I wondered? Should I have guessed his answer? "To confound man."

I decided to ask where the devil got hold of those bundles of mystifying artifacts. Did he design (!) them? Did he distribute them personally, or use some sort of Hades-dwelling delivery boys for their dissemination? Smart-ass questions, of course, bred of my teenageness. That time of life when you are smarter than you will ever be again.

MY CRUSTED RELATIVE: He just scattered them all over the globe.
DC (*smirking*): Was he the only one back then who knew it was a
    globe?
(I seem to recall ducking a swat.)

I was always delighted when Dr. Miller would hold forth on topics like mesmerism, his fear of the procedures of medicine when it comes to himself, and why, in America, medicine should be so ruinously and unnecessarily expensive—remarks deliciously ill received by his stateside sawbones colleagues and that dedicated enemy of public health the American Medical Association, those tireless opponents of sane national health care.

JUNE 12, 2009

A videoclip is available at
http://opinionator.blogs.nytimes.com/2009/06/12/miller-talks-again/.

Sky's the Limit

June and July always contained my two favorite days of the year.

The first of them, chronologically, was that longed-for, ached-for day when both hands of the old-fashioned roman-numeraled one-click-a-minute school clock on the wall hit III. The magical 3:15 that cued Miss Gabus, or Miss Fuchs, or Miss Swanson, etc., to utter the words "Everyone have a nice summer."

I can almost bring back that glorious feeling, exiting Prescott School in Lincoln, Nebraska, brimming with joy that months would go by without having to sit half-brain-dead in a dun-colored room, acquiring such vital knowledge as the principal export of Argentina from, alas, generally colorless teachers. Absolutely nothing in life even remotely resembles that particular thrill: a whole summer ahead.

Not all states let you out of school at the same time. I was in one of the luckiest. Our last day might even have been in May, because I recall my father's saying, more than once, "We may not make much money [my parents were teachers], but by God we get paid on a year-round basis, with three whole months off. How many people can say that?"

(I'd love to know what my parents made, teaching in the 1940s and '50s. It had to be a good bit more than my dad made during the Depression, when he beat out some twenty or so desperate competitors for the honor of teaching high school English in Comstock, Nebraska, to mostly farmers' children, for a sorely, sorely needed $900 a year. For no extra remuneration, he was granted the privilege of also coaching football, baseball, and basketball and staging the senior play.)

The only problem with the last day of school (oh, how those words still resonate!) was that June still had to be gotten through before the Fourth of July.

* * *

Fireworks!

The word still raises the hair on my arms. (The forearms, mainly.) Fireworks of all kinds were legal back then in Nebraska, and the opening of the first fireworks stand at the edge of town meant infinitely more to me than the first crocuses did to the flower worshipper, the robin to the bird lover . . . well, you get the point.

I didn't like fireworks. I *loved* them. (Pyrotechnomania?) And I don't mean the stuff that girls and sissies liked: fountains, sparklers, pinwheels, and those infantile "snakes." I mean the big stuff. The heavy ordnance. Cherry bombs, torpedoes, aerial bombs, two-, three-, and even six-inchers (jumbo firecrackers). And, once, a twelve-shot repeater aerial bomb.

Because I was rich—yes, richer than a king, from doing magic shows for up to $20 a Kiwanis Club or church basement appearance—I was able, one memorable year, to buy from the fireworks catalog the "Jumbo Assortment." The company name may have been "Spencer Fireworks," or something, somewhere in Ohio. I'd love to know what my order in, say, 1949, cost.

And one day, a mail truck pulled up in front of the house and unloaded a box. Judging from its size, I guessed my folks had bought a living room easy chair. It was *feet* in every direction.

It took an hour to unpack: rockets, Roman candles, aerial bombs, "ash cans" and cherry bombs, pinwheels, bushels of brick-sized packages of every brand of firecracker. And, topping everything, a single one-pound aerial bomb. Also, negligibly, a generous amount of the despised "safe & sane" fountains, sparklers, and snakes. For little kids and girls.

LAY ON GROUND. LIGHT FUSE. RETIRE QUICKLY.

I pity anyone for whom those printed words were not a feature of youth. (Could that familiar phrase from the life of everybody who ever bought Chinese firecrackers have contributed to a current language problem? I mean the one where, seemingly, somewhere between seven and ten people in the entire populace know the difference between "lay" and "lie"?)

Let's admit right now: firecrackers and fireworks can be hellishly, horribly dangerous.

Nevertheless, my friend Jimmy McConnell and I, our pockets loaded with super-powered cherry bombs, set out to do some damage. These cherry bombs were the kind you could throw into a lake, pond, or stream and they, having sunk—and thanks to their waterproof fuses—would explode below the surface. They were too powerful to blow a tin can ten feet into the air the way a firecracker would. They'd simply blow it inside out before it left the ground. As most kids know (even if not firsthand), they can be flushed down a toilet, as someone did when I was at Yale, thereby removing a considerable amount of venerable plumbing. And not just on one floor. (Mercifully, there were no reports of anyone's having been seated at the time.)

On this particular unlucky day, I wedged a "cherry" between the upright leg of a farmer's heavy wooden sign and the sign itself. Standing ten feet away proved insufficient. I thought I felt something hit my face. "Look at your shirt," Jim said. My white undershirt was dotted with red spots where tiny chunks of wood had entered it—and me.

Failing to learn from this—and under the illusion of immortality that goes with extreme youth—we found a potentially much worse object for demolition lying beside the road. Someone had thrown out one of those concrete Christmas tree bases—at least ten pounds of solid concrete, shaped like an immense gumdrop, white, with a hole for the sawed-off trunk.

What we expected was not what happened. We tossed a cherry bomb—or possibly it was an equally powerful ash can—into the hole and retired quickly. *Baroom!!* A jagged chunk of the thing the size of a clenched fist whizzed, screeching, past my ear with about five inches of clearance. The closest I was to come to knowing what vets described when bullets or grenade fragments zipped past their head. One step to the left and you'd be reading someone else right now.

On that July of the Jumbo Assortment, Jim and I were allowed to sleep out on his porch the night of the third, which, it felt to us, had taken eons to come. I had already sold pounds of fireworks from the mammoth assortment. (Jim pointed out my business acumen: I had marked one of the items spread out on a bed for viewing—a small pack of firecrackers—as "10c. each \ or 2 for a quarter.")

We awoke on the porch about 4:00 A.M., not having slept much. It was going to be a clear, hot Nebraska summer day. I doubt that it had occurred to either of us that God might wreck our Fourth with rain.

I should note that I don't recall our parents' ever expressing any particular worries about our detonations. My dad made the rocket trough and did remind us that his dad, in showing him and his little brother how not to hold a firecracker, dispensed with part of a finger. (We did impress girls, or so we thought, by squeezing little "lady-finger" firecrackers tightly by the butt end between thumb and finger and letting them explode without letting go.)

Jim and I had fondled and cradled and caressed the star item in the assortment: the single one-pound aerial bomb. We began the big day with it. It was just before sunrise. There was no one else up. We lovingly carried it to the nearby grade school playground, lit it, and stood back.

With the propelling explosion on the ground, the payload the size of an orange rose upward in what seemed a slow and stately ascent—and went off. Shock waves. Only a modest yet gratifying number of school windows broke. We ran.

In later years, I had two fireworks-related adventures. I got, through some connection I've forgotten, to be on the Grucci fireworks barge at a display on Long Island. It was scary. The aerial bombs made Jim's and mine look like ladyfingers. And the lighters, scrambling around on deck setting them off, were constantly showered with sparks. So were the unlit fireworks. I stepped partway over the side and lowered myself behind some protection from what seemed like the inevitable conflagration. This was a good bit after the year a Grucci barge did blow up in the Hudson and onshore spectators, unaware of the deaths, applauded the wondrous sight.

George Plimpton was, like me, also queer for fireworks. (Mayor John Lindsay had made him unofficial "Fireworks Commissioner" of New York City.) At one of Plimpton's annual displays at his place on

Long Island, I left the crowd and sneaked down to near the fire trucks and launching area, getting there just as a rocket changed course and, NASA *Challenger*–like, went sideways instead of up. It landed on an onlooker's blanket in a magnificent explosion of red stars, winning her $60,000.

Back in Nebraska. One awful year, suddenly, it was all over. The state legislature did its dirty work. Not a total ban. Just no more big stuff.

In some states, do-gooders have legislated away everything but sparklers—oblivious, apparently, to the fact that the gentle sparkler, with its 1,000-degree temperatures, causes more severe injuries and third-degree burns than all other fireworks combined.

Every year when the Fourth approaches and I long for the good old days, as I know Jim does, I find it hard to believe that the resonant date will pass and I won't light a single fuse. I know you can't legally buy firecrackers in New York City, and I know it's not wise to confess to potential crimes, but if someone were to emerge from a doorway today, hawking a verboten package of Zebras . . .

Anyway, let's all have a great Fourth! Somehow.

JULY 3, 2009

Who's Afraid of Richard Burton?

He was sitting in front of his dressing room mirror after a tiring performance of *Camelot,* removing his makeup for the who knows how many thousandth time. Paler, with the greasepaint cleansed from the famous face, he managed to look simultaneously handsome, vibrant, and worn.

"Richard has been entertaining the idea of doing your show, Mr. Cavett," a man who appeared to be both valet and companion said.

"And letting the idea entertain him," the Welshman intoned in that unmistakable voice.

In fact, Richard Burton was still pondering whether to do my show, and it was thought that my visiting him backstage informally might help.

I tried to imagine what fears or hesitations Burton might have about appearing with me. Could he be afraid that the rich voice, those rugged good looks, the manly erotic charm, the hypnotic blue eyes, the articulacy, the fine wit, and the ready storehouse of classical and modern literary quotations and allusions were not quite enough to qualify him for sitting next to Cavett? (Did anyone think, just now, that I was describing myself?)

Could he really think that maybe a boy from Nebraska—who had only been to Yale and not, as he had, Oxford—might outshine all those charms? As my Aunt Eva would say, "The very idea!"

Hoping for the effect of light humor, I said, "I hope I don't frighten you, Mr. Burton."

"No, Mr. Cavett, you do not. I do that to myself."

I liked him immensely.

Even under regression hypnosis, Richard would probably not have recalled how we had briefly met about a quarter of a century earlier when only one of us had a familiar name, but more of that anon.

Memories of that night backstage: Richard's expertly flipping a single, long Marlboro—the mendaciously advertised "light" version—from its box, contemplating it for a moment in a manner that brought to mind an actor holding Yorick's skull, and saying, as if a little embarrassed to be lighting up, "Looks like these lethal goddamn things will be with me to the end of my days."

"And hastening them," I decided not to say. Later, when we knew each other better, he wouldn't have minded and would have had a wry response.

Then came the best thing.

Leaving the theater by the stage door required crossing the wide New York State Theater stage. The *Camelot* sets had been struck for the night and the house and stage were dark; dark except for the murky bulb in a cage on a stand downstage center—the thing known in the theater world as "the ghost light," an aptly named light that somehow manages to make a vast, dark space seem darker and spookier than it would with no light at all.

What happened next was in the too-good-to-be-true category. Burton stopped near the light, his coat draped over one shoulder, gazed out at the empty house, tilted his head back, and, with the famous full chiming resonance, began, "O for a Muse of fire, that would ascend / The brightest heaven of invention"—and went right on through that ringing prologue to *Henry V* (known to actors as *Hank Cinq*).

Gooseflesh manifested.

He was standing no more than a yard from me, and I thought, "Talk about front row seats!" Unforgettable.

Maybe our meeting did the trick. A day or two later, Burton agreed to do the show. But, sadly, he requested that there be no studio audience. I felt sorry for a bunch of strangers I would never meet who would never know what they missed.

You can do a good show without an audience, but I knew from experience that audiences sometimes buoyed guests who at first feared them.

"What if I made a deal with you?" I dared. "Since they already have their tickets, why don't we start with them, and if you feel uncomfortable, we'll tell them there's a technical problem and we have to stop for that day and see them out?"

This gambit could accomplish one of two things: (a) he would feel sorry for the disappointed folks and relent, or (b) I would learn how to say "bugger off" in Welsh.

He accepted the offer.

I introduced him with a glowing quote from a prominent British critic about a past performance, never dreaming—since I didn't know that Richard had disciplined himself to shun all reviews, good or bad—that I was bringing it to him for the first time. He confessed to enjoying it.

At his entrance—which he artfully delayed for just a few anticipatory seconds—my usually sedate PBS studio audience went nuts. The mikes didn't truly report the intense burst of applause. (Happily, this was taped before the later craze of piercing, high-pitched cries and shrieks from talk show audiences that have replaced applause as we knew it. Today, when a guest—of whatever high or low consequence—steps out, the air is ripped with screaming. Why? Who started this?)

I love to watch audiences when famous figures appear. Burton's charisma radiated. At the moment of his entrance, I watched a highly respectable looking lady in the audience slap her hands to her cheeks, let her purse slip to the floor, and slide down in her seat. A staff member reported seeing a woman grab for smelling salts.

I once had a guest hate the audience, lean over to me, and whisper, "Let's dump the creeps out front." I knew Burton still might opt for that, although in somewhat classier terms, probably whispering something more like, "Richard Cavett, I'm experiencing a modicum of discomfort. Let us enforce our gentlemen's agreement and politely dispense with the assembled onlookers."

It didn't happen. When he got that all-important first laugh, every muscle in the Burton face relaxed visibly and I knew we were in for a good half hour.

The show went by fast, leaving me wanting more. The man who wasn't sure he'd do the show at all agreed to do a second one. At the end of that one, I asked if he thought he had one more in him. He did. And, definitely pushing my luck, I snagged a fourth.

Sadly, I was too chicken to ask for the one that would have made a full week. Downing his sixth diet soda, Burton talked away a fifth show backstage in the green room. I owe you one.

There's a lot more to say about this man, but I'm electing to withdraw for now.

JULY 17, 2009

A videoclip is available at
http://opinionator.blogs.nytimes.com/2009/07/17/whos-afraid-of-richard-burton/.

Richard Burton, Take 2

Richard Burton mentioned that he refused to read his "notices," stating that "the good ones are never good enough and the bad ones are upsetting." Looking at those shows again, I had almost forgotten how damn charming he was. I'd almost forgotten one of the most surprising things he said—that he scrupulously avoided seeing the movies of two men interchangeably described as "our greatest living actor," Marlon Brando and Laurence Olivier. His reason: "For fear of becoming unduly influenced. And imitative."

You can tire of the constant comment about Burton, "Those eyes!" But it was true in spades. When describing something intensely dramatic, he seemed to see it before him—with a look that suggested Macbeth seeing Banquo's ghost.

We had first met years (and years) before.

I got to Yale in 1954. One of the treats of being in dreary New Haven—and in those days it would be hard to think of another one—was the presence of the Shubert Theater. It was only a few steps from the campus, and that gloomy city was a tryout town for shows on their way to Broadway. I saw them all. Some died there. (Moss Hart once said, "New Haven is like something that never got out of New Haven.")

The Yale Dramat, the undergrad drama organization, would invite the stars from the Shubert to a cocktail party, and often, to my amazement and delight, they accepted.

Richard Burton came with his costars in *Time Remembered*—Helen Hayes and Susan Strasberg. I had lost my heart to Susan in *Anne Frank*, and yet, like everyone else, I was drawn to Burton. Even with two other stars in the room, the current seemed to carry everyone to him—including the two other stars.

I'd just seen him as Alexander the Great on the screen and been thrilled by him in the play, and there I was, standing by him, mesmerized by his easy chat, good humor, friendliness, and personal dazzle.

Someone mentioned Laurence Olivier. Richard said that he and Olivier had worked out a song-and-dance duet with hats and canes that they performed at those all-star charity events the Brits love so much, where stars would come from their plays and do a "Midnight Matinee."

"Our 'Larry and Dickie' big number used to stop the show," he said. "Larry and I used to look very much alike. If not exactly twins, brothers." And then he added something that has stayed with me, that struck me as strange: "Until he got old." (Olivier got a great deal older. This was in 1956.)

We asked him about various actors and he willingly and freely held forth.

I hate all "most" questions ("Who was your most interesting guest?" etc., as if there could be a clear winner, as in the hundred-yard dash.) So I wince when the remembered sophomoric voice in my head is my own: "Mr. Burton, who is your"—and let's hope I didn't say "most"—"favorite actor?"

The Great Triumvirate (John Gielgud, Laurence Olivier, Ralph Richardson) were all alive, so everyone expected him to pick from that immortal trio, but no. I'm reasonably confident that I worded it, "Do you have a personal favorite?"

"Yes," he said. "Paul Scofield."

He was not alone in that. Many lucky enough to have seen the superb Scofield in his great variety of stage roles agree.

Alas, I saw him tread the boards only once, in *A Man for All Seasons*. And, of course, in the film. (Maybe the least disputed Oscar in history.)

His towering King Lear was generally agreed to be the one for all time. For contrast, see him as the thoroughly American academic Mark Van Doren in Robert Redford's *Quiz Show*. Or the Nazi commander Von Waldheim in John Frankenheimer's *The Train*.

How I would love to have done a show with him. But this explosive—onstage—actor was shy of such things, shunned them, and preferred to go from the stage door straight to his country home in Sussex, where he loved to wander the moors in solitude. (Light reading for him was probably Thomas Hardy's *Jude the Obscure*.)

Burton disclosed a curious tidbit about Scofield: that he was kept out of military service because of his deformed toes. Burton: "I got a glimpse of them once and it was quite awful. They appeared to have been brutally broken by some torturer and then forcibly tucked under." He went on to describe how they affected this great actor's ability to walk, demonstrating a kind of swinging stride that was Scofield's: "I thought it was quite a powerful walk, but"—he laughed here—"poor Paul worried that it looked a bit faggoty."

Told in the Burton voice and with the Burton feeling, what follows was more powerful than it will appear in print and will be best appreciated by actors. Still talking of Scofield, he said, "Any decent actor of twenty can play eighty. But to play *forty* at twenty. Good God! Sheerest genius."

JULY 31 & AUGUST 28, 2009

A videoclip is available at
http://opinionator.blogs.nytimes.com/2009/07/31/richard-burton-take-2/.

Strange, Dear, but True, Dear

We were living in an icehouse that winter.

(That sentence is not about a power failure, but is the result of my favorite high school English teacher in Nebraska, Esther Montgomery, who advocated trying for an arresting opening sentence in writing a story. I hope you are arrested.)

I could as easily have begun with "It was an icehouse, and it had been inhabited by Franklin D. Roosevelt."

Clarification: my wife and I had been offered a place to go on winter weekends to recover from the weekly grind of taping five ninety-minute shows in four days on ABC. It was, in fact, a former icehouse on the property of a majestic old manse in, I think it was, Stockbridge, New York. Its walls were at least a solid foot thick, and it belonged to the eminent Canadian actor Donald Davis, abroad for the winter. He had fixed it up into a cozy dwelling, surrounded by woods. Memories of older neighbors confirmed FDR's having used it as a sometime retreat for himself and a lady friend. (Unfortunately, the walls could not talk.)

You are about to have your credulity strained, on a topic in line with an earlier column. One that caused readers to send their own similarly bizarre incidents.

It was a bright winter Saturday morning and I'd gone into the small town to get the paper. Not having done this before, I realized in returning that I hadn't paid attention and was not sure how to get back. I was lost. All streets looked equally likely, so I picked one of many for no reason.

I picked wrong, but that led to what followed.

In front of a schoolhouse there were a lot of parked cars and people milling around among tables, apparently shopping for whatever was on display. Seeing the words "Village Book Fair" made me want to stop, but for some forgotten reason I was in a hurry. It was clearly a popular event but, sadly, there were no vacant parking spaces for even a quick inspection, so I chose, reluctantly, to move on. But suddenly a car obligingly pulled out right in front of me, and I pulled in.

Twenty or so card tables held a sea of books. Still in a hurry, I decided to check only the nearest table that chance and the exiting car had placed before me. Without looking at any titles, I picked up a clearly used volume, mainly to see the quality and condition of the books offered. I didn't even notice the title, but let it fall open somewhere near the middle. My eyes fell upon the following words: "Harrison was disappointed. Montauk would not show its face for the fog, and he so wanted me to love the adored place as much as he did." The author went on to say that they spent the weekend, fogbound, in the old house on the mist-shrouded cliffs.

Gooseflesh.

A glance at the spine revealed the book to be an autobiography from the 1940s: *Who Tells Me True*, by Michael Strange. "Harrison" was Harrison Tweed, an eminent attorney at the historic and prestigious Wall Street firm of Milbank, Tweed, Hadley & McCloy and (chance again) a friend of Roosevelt's.

I like to think that one or two perhaps elderly and steeped-in-literary-knowledge readers among you would realize that the combination of "Michael" and "Harrison" does not indicate a gay partnership. "Michael Strange" was the *nom de plume* of Blanche Oelrichs (1890–1950)—poet, playwright, actress—a bohemian woman of letters of the 1920s and '30s who was married to John Barrymore for a time, and to Harrison Tweed for another. The daring lady had been known to startle the few neighbors in the remote area by the unheard-of practice of going topless on the Montauk cliffs.

The McKim, Mead & White historic house referred to in Ms. Strange's book had been nicknamed "Tick Hall" by Tweed and his law-colleague fishing buddies—owing to the unwelcome presence, even back then, of the pestiferous local arachnid later notorious for spreading Lyme disease. The surf-casting weekend occupants of the house referred to one another as "Tick Tweed" and "Tick Morgan" and, quite likely, "Tick Roosevelt."

Not an incredibly remarkable story so far, I admit.

Why the gooseflesh? I had purchased that house from ninety-one-year-old Harrison Tweed. Three days earlier.

Being a victim of innumeracy, I don't know how you would calculate the odds against such a happening. In such instances, is there maybe something operating other than sheer chance? Does anyone know a good book on the subject?

A skeptic might begin attacking the almost supernatural quality of the thing with the picking up of the book. Even though in hoisting it I didn't consciously look at the title, maybe in my deep unconscious I had somehow registered the title years before?

But did the same force make me open it to the only page that concerned me? Adding to this the randomly chosen street, the unexpected book fair, the unexpected parking place, the one table among the many—and I suppose you could add the double Roosevelt connection (icehouse / Tweed friendship) . . . putting all that together, you get odds comparable, I should think, to those against people foolish enough to dispose of needed dollars in the lottery. (I like the idea that only in a society "illiterate" about numbers could the lottery exist at all.)

What the hell is coincidence anyway, in its most astonishing instances? A subject worth pursuing at another time? Thinking about it fogs my mind, and makes me recall something that's haunted me for years. It's a koan-like thought from my class with the reincarnated Socrates of Yale, philosophy professor Paul Weiss: the idea that, logically, there is no such thing as a possibility that did not take place. In what sense, then, was it possible?

And what, then, do you call things like my Tweed house incident? A possibility that was not caused?

Keep your answer brief, but pithy.

P.S. No more Burton teasing. Next time, including a hilarious story.

P.P.S. Could I buy someone in Philadelphia a season ticket to boo Michael Vick for me?

SEPTEMBER 11, 2009

A Third Bit of Burton

Let us all rejoice that Richard Burton is back.

I almost felt guilty accepting a paycheck for the privilege of sitting next to and being so greatly entertained by this master of conversation as he voiced choice recollections of Bogey, John Huston, Garbo (they chatted for a while before, embarrassed, he realized who she was), and, yes, Elizabeth, whom he married. Twice. A highlight was when I chanced asking if he would talk about booze. He delivered a generous and riveting monologue on the subject, saying to "fellow victims out there" that he sympathized and fully identified with "the horror that you live with."

One thing got to me especially.

Most actors' claims of "Why does everybody say I'm so talented?" strain credulity to the snapping point. But why wouldn't a young boy from the mines of Wales be amazed by the towering gift placed in him by the gods? How could Burton not be stunned to receive a rave review in his first job from a major London critic for the way he, with bucket and brush, wordlessly scrubbed a floor, largely with his back to the audience?

I don't think he ever lost that wonderment about his great gift.

I raised the idea that even one so lavishly successful as he was might fear the disappearance of all that fairy gold and fame and talent, the old Greek idea of being struck low by the envious gods. He chilled me with his look and tone, saying, "You mean hubris? Overweening pride and all that?"

He called it a frightening thing.

His fear of it was there to see when he told of running into a man he had worked with at the Old Vic. Those eyes did their stuff as he said of this fine actor, "He hadn't had a job in fourteen years."

This points to a thing I've found to be true of many great actors. Admitting to a kind of bad dream about waking up some day and—as with the dread "block" that writers get—having that magical "it" not be there.

It's somehow tied up with another term from the Greek, *charisma*. It can't be learned and is over and above talent. It's that mysterious *x* factor that the handful of the very greatest have. It's that extra something you can't describe but can feel emanating from them, on the stage, on the screen, and certainly sitting next to them.

Brando had the most of it. It's what made an acting teacher I knew tell of seeing him enter in a play, way back before his name was known: "Suddenly a man came on the stage whom I had never seen or heard of. Before he even spoke, it was as if a leopard had entered the room."

That says it best for me. That's the intangible "it" that made the brilliant Jack Nicholson once say, "When Marlon dies, everybody moves up one."

SEPTEMBER 25, 2009

A videoclip is available at
http://opinionator.blogs.nytimes.com/2009/09/25/a-third-bit-of-burton/.

Richard Burton: A Regretful *Au Revoir*

Here is a choice story. I got it from my fine actor friend John Cunningham, who vouches for its total authenticity. I have never gotten a bad vouch from Cunningham.

A much-missed friend, the late and wonderful Jerry Orbach, best known as Detective Lennie Briscoe for so many years on *Law & Order*, is a main player in the story.

Jerry and his wife had just come to New York, hoping to "make it" in the big time and the Big Apple. It was before Jerry got his break in *The Fantasticks*, from which all followed.

The Orbachs were invited to a party in Manhattan and, virtually on their way there, learned that it was a birthday party—to their distress, since buying any sort of present would tax their meager holdings.

Passing a sort of novelty store, Jerry's wife, Marta, spotted an inexpensive but decent-looking small kaleidoscope. "We'll tie a ribbon around it," she said, "and let it be our present."

Arriving at the party, they noticed that the assembled guests included quite a few theater notables, including—to their amazement—Richard Burton, the birthday boy himself. He was starring in *Time Remembered* on Broadway, with Susan Strasberg and Helen Hayes. Susan was at the party.

The Orbachs submitted their present and passed into the kitchen in time to catch a scene out of soap fiction.

A half-dozen women had Susan surrounded and were berating her vehemently with such dialogue as "You're ruining your life" and "You're mortgaging your future happiness." The subject: her current affair, while still in her teens, with an "older, philandering, womanizing, married man."

The birthday boy.

While she was absorbing these presumably—or shall we say possibly—well-meant and (just possibly) jealousy-inspired psychological body blows, the villain himself entered the kitchen.

He began a brief but eloquent monologue, beginning, I would guess, with something like "Jerry, I fear it may exceed my verbal capacities to sufficiently thank you for your thoughtful, marvelous gift."

The room fell silent, as it usually did when the Welsh organ tones began to sound, and Richard went on to say that he had never had or held a kaleidoscope before. You'll have to imagine the spontaneous poeticism, lost to the ages, as he compared the colored-glass-filled instrument to life itself, in its constant, changing variety; its unexpected, startling delights; its ability to—like life itself—dazzle and surprise in its random, colorful spectacle, etc., etc.

No kaleidoscope ever had it so good.

The kitchen occupants stood rooted and mesmerized, the female berating team as breathless and taken as everyone else. Richard finished and exited, and Susan said, "And that's just the talk."

Burton was ailing during those shows we taped, but I didn't know it and he didn't show it. He had been praised in the *Camelot* he was then appearing in for his "economy of motion"—a phrase that recurred in the reviews. Swinging the heavy sword onstage with a slow-motion deliberateness was effective in the way Kurosawa's ingeniously conceived slow-motion sinking to earth of a mortally wounded swordsman in *The Seven Samurai*—the dust slowly rising as he fell—was so inventive and effective. (And so flatteringly stolen in countless dramas and Westerns thereafter.)

Few knew that Richard's limited physical ability at the time accounted in large part for those effective slowed motions. His "choices," as actors call them, were in part bred of pain. That "accomplishing the largest effect with the smallest effort" he referred to in our interview was not, in this case, entirely by choice. All this had been kept from public knowledge.

Shortly after the shows with him, I heard details about the illness from an actor friend of his. I think it was Richard Harris. A surgeon I knew, skirting medical ethics perhaps, filled me in: "The poor guy needs a bad operation." (Maybe not his exact words. He probably used the popular medical euphemism "procedure." Sounds a lot more fun than "surgery" or "operation.")

"Don't you touch him!" I wanted to say. I asked what specifically needed to be done to Richard. It was then and there that I learned the chilling word "laminectomy." When I admitted to being "unfamiliar" with the term (and why don't we ever just say, "I don't know that word"?), the sawbones dropped euphemism dramatically: "We go in through your neck and take out part of your back."

If I didn't pale, it felt like it.

Camelot finished its run, and Burton was in Los Angeles, preparing for his surgical ordeal. I learned he was in L.A. the same day I was about to leave there for New York, and I called his agent, hoping to pass on good wishes. Coincidence strikes again.

She answered with "Dick Cavett! I simply cannot believe it's you calling!" She went on:

"Less than twenty seconds ago, I just finished showing the last of your four shows with Richard to a group of his brothers who've come over from Wales for the operation. Maybe *ten* seconds ago. Your theme song is just fading from the screen."

(At a dinner with Jonathan Miller recently in London, we talked about coincidence. "Do coincidences mean anything, beyond just coincidence?" I asked the sage doctor. Miller, with unaccustomed brevity: "Of course not." Now we know.)

History shows, by the way, that the operation was a success and a pain-relieved Richard lived out the rest of his too-brief life span.

But before hanging up, I asked the agent if I could talk to one of the Burton brothers, wanting to see if he sounded like Richard. He didn't, of course. The lilting Welsh accent I find so pleasing to the ear was, unlike Richard's, unadulterated. He was a slyly amusing man and I laughed when he accused me of "callin' from the next room," because of the uncanny timing. And he got off on a laugh.

"Ya know somethin', Mr. Cavett? We never knew Richard was so interestin'!"

OCTOBER 9 & 30, 2009

A videoclip is available at
http://opinionator.blogs.nytimes.com/2009/10/09/richard-burton-a-regretful-au-revoir/.

Dangerous Substance:
Sample with Care

He captured the world's attention and it intoxicated him.

Him, I mean. The nit who pretended to have sent his son aloft in the helium balloon.

He said he wanted to be famous.

There's a lot to be said about fame. And wanting it. And getting it.

While on ABC, I used to like to go, on weekends, to a remote Long Island beach where you could shed your clothes and jump into the sea unobserved. Or only lightly observed. There was seldom more than one other person there, maybe a nude sunbather at the other end or maybe a lone surf caster.

Usually I had it to myself, except for Bucky, or Buck—a good-looking, well-built youth who showed up now and then. He wore a long ponytail, a former girlfriend's name on a pectoral (back before tattoos were everywhere; when checking out the girls, he put a Band-Aid over it), and a pleasant manner, a sort of stock character of the early seventies, content to bum around, do some yard work for "bread," and invest it in a nickel bag he convivially shared. His main activity, otherwise, was surfing. Probably a dropout with a middling IQ, I figured.

This friendly lad enjoyed spotting me, solo, on the beach and stealthily slipping up behind me with a "Boo!"

Although I had the feeling he lived and slept in the woods, he had usually somehow seen a recent show of mine that we'd chat about.

I liked talking with him. I quickly relieved him of the need to call me "Mr. Cavett," and he provided a nice relief from the semi-reality of my celeb-riddled life.

One day, he announced he'd had a revelation about why he envied me, and about what he proposed to do about it to add the needed, missing element to his own life.

"I'm going to save up, get all my money together, and spend it all on getting lots and lots of pictures of myself made with my name on 'em and put 'em up everywhere and make myself famous."

This was sad.

Where was the "everywhere" he would put them? On the beach? On trees and lampposts? Locally, or from New York to Los Angeles?

Was this cannabis, or acid, talking? I couldn't help wondering how long before the effects of those and his other recreations would begin to show in the decline of his still healthy-looking, athletic physique.

I had to say something.

I suggested that before he blew all his amassed mowing and pruning earnings on Fame, he might want to think about it a little more.

"Fame is a mixed blessing," I said.

I knew. As a kid in Nebraska, I craved it. And a guy named Carson had already achieved a good dose of it while still at the University of Nebraska, emceeing campus shows and performing his magic and ventriloquist act. Then he achieved a lot more of it in New York.

A middle-aged radio announcer at a local station where I sometimes worked had puzzled me once, saying, with what I later realized had to contain a trace of envy, "You, young man, are going to get up and out of here the way Johnny did."

Lincoln was large enough to attract big-time touring shows and entertainers. Having laid eyes on the visiting Bob Hope, Spike Jones, Charles Laughton, Louis Armstrong, Basil Rathbone, Henry Fonda, and even Elvis, I couldn't imagine that anything could be wrong with fame. When those people left town, I wanted to go with them.

"What are some of the bad things about being famous?" Buck asked.

Having become "famed" myself relatively recently, via the (then) small screen, I felt qualified to list a few negatives with sincerity.

"For one thing, you lose an awful lot of freedom."

This gave Buck pause and put him into a kind of reverie. We watched the waves roll in on the incoming tide to just short of where we sat as he thought awhile.

"Like how?" he asked. "What freedom do you lose?"

"For one, the freedom to not be recognized everywhere," I offered.

"That's bad?"

The initial delight of being spotted lasts about a week and four days.

It's nice when it produces a friendly compliment; less so in major ways and a hundred little ones, as when you stumble on a curb and get applause and a "Way to go, Dick." Or, thinking you're alone and are caught with a finger in a nostril (your own, at least) or scratching yourself intimately. Or when leading any sort of double life. One hears.

Then came the thunderclap.

"Wasn't it Fitzgerald who called fame the 'Bitch Goddess'?" he asked.

A breeze-wafted sparrow feather would have knocked me over. My impression of him did a 180. My assumption—that he was a simple fellow—might need revision.

Had I actually heard "Fitzgerald"? What was he a case of? What was I dealing with here? A once educated brain, probably being depleted by aimlessness and unhealthy substances? (God knows his generation had plenty of that.)

And are our snap estimates of people often that wide of the mark?

I looked forward to his appearances now, eager to find out what other unsuspected resources might be inside that ponytailed head.

A couple of weeks passed. I asked around but nobody had seen my friend. I didn't want him to vanish from my life, and I hoped he hadn't from his. Janis and Jimi had just OD'd a few weeks apart, and I hoped young Buck wasn't facedown somewhere in the woods.

I even kept an eye out to see if maybe he had posted some of his quest-for-celebrity pictures, but no. He wanted to be famous and I had never bothered to ask his last name. I never saw him again.

If he's gone, I wish I could have saved him. I never admonished him about drugs. Maybe my bloody fame would have given it impact for him.

Did he have parents? Was I somehow a surrogate for them? What, ethically and morally, might I have been obliged to do for the boy? Adopt him?

I still think of him.

Hey, man, I hope you're out there.

NOVEMBER 13, 2009

The Ghost Ship *W.W.*

Your responses to my column about the lad Buck and the subject of fame delighted, amused, and moved me. What explains the fact that there is so much good writing among the readers? (Even "You are not very funny, Mr. Cavett . . ." got to me, providing good contrast, lest the compliments turn my head.) There is stuff in those "letters" that is as good as anything turned out by us alleged pros.

Dare one say sometimes better?

Several readers raised the subject: what of the time when fame has fled? I'm grateful to them because it reminded me of an almost vanished memory of that very thing.

Readers who've achieved a number of years nearer the minimal end of the age scale might feel the need of a dose of Wikipedia upon hearing the moniker "Walter Winchell." It had been a name to strike terror into the cardiac area of even the powerful. (Burt Lancaster's character J. J. Hunsecker, the powerful newspaper columnist in *Sweet Smell of Success*, was based on Winchell.) This notorious figure, in his time as household a name as can be, outlived his fame and died forgotten. And widely unlamented.

There was quite a stretch between the time I first tuned in—with most of America—to the distinct and famous voice on Sunday night radio and my meeting him.

For some reason, I recall that my dad and I were in our Nebraska basement, shelling black walnuts we'd gathered in the woods. On this particular night, the famous voice, akin to heavy dice being rattled in a metal cup, fired off at lightning speed the show's signature opening: "Good evening, Mr. and Mrs. America and all the ships at sea, let's go to press! Washington . . ." Etcetera.

On that memorable night, "W.W." stunned the nation with the

unthinkable words ". . . and a president who does not know what the *h-e*-double-*l* is going on." (HST was the sitting White House occupant so described.)

It was a bombshell, almost as if full frontal nudity had been displayed on the cover of the *Reader's Digest*. But Winchell's accreted clout at the time was sufficient armor. He was a media figure full of unprecedented power. Among other things.

Much of Winchell's fortune was his voice. Sharp, tangy, forceful, and dramatic, it produced goose bumps over the radio, where voice was all. It was a favorite of "impressionists" (not Monet and so forth, you understand).

Walter Winchell had been a veritable king and he had a good, long reign. Then fame ended. But he did not, doomed to years and years of has-been-ism.

He was old and I wasn't when we met. The mirror had turned around: I was on TV by then, so the faded Winchell knew of the hot kid on the cover of *Time* who had shelled walnuts in Nebraska to the sound of his voice.

I got a close-up look of what it means when fame has fled. It ain't a pretty thing.

Surprised that he was still alive, I had him on my show. This must have been in the late sixties. He was elderly but not creaky, and gamely agreed to exhibit a bit from his early vaudeville dancing days. The old boy brought down the house with a skillfully executed tap routine. My wife cried watching it. His celebrity was by then a dim memory, and he was grateful to me for causing some renewed recognition on the street after a very long time.

My reward? An evening out with Winchell at the Copa. Yes, the legendary Copacabana nightclub, which, like him, had seen better days. The headliner, the popular (and cheerfully bibulous) Tony Martin, warbled a medley of his past hits for us, surrounded by the renowned and luscious Copa Girls—many now Copa Grannies, I should think.

W.W. had collected me, driving his own car. He was fadedly elegant in a tuxedo not of the latest cut, the butt of a snub-nosed .38 peeping from the cummerbund.

"Expecting trouble, Walter?" I ventured.

"Always, my boy. In my game, you have to."

Winchell had fear-induced influence most everywhere, and in his heyday had acquired from his cop friends the sort of official police car radio forbidden to ordinary citizens, allowing him to habitually cruise the night and, upon hearing of a crime in progress, speed there for a column item.

"They never give me a ticket for speeding," he boasted to me. A moment too soon. Minutes later, we got one. Somewhere on lower Park Avenue, while responding to a police call.

To his chagrin, my companion of the night's name and visage cut no ice with the young rookie.

Despite the lives he purportedly ruined when at his peak—careers made and destroyed with a few words in his column or on the air—it was still sad to see the old lion now toothless. At one precinct we'd visited earlier, where in better times a chorus of "Hey, Walter!" would have gone up, only an ancient sergeant knew who he was. Walter devoured the scrap.

To the young cops, he was a cipher. My knowledge of his past victims—said, even, to include a few suicides—at that moment didn't matter. That evening, as I accompanied him on his nightly prowl, I felt like quietly paying someone to say, "Hey, ain't you Walter Winchell?"

And then it happened. At one precinct, a young gendarme with a good ear suddenly said, "Hey, Pop. Say something else! Talk again." He did.

"Oh, my God! I know who *you* are!"

W.W. beamed.

"You're the announcer on *The Untouchables*!"

Someone had been smart enough to cast the uniquely voiced Winchell—an excellent actor with once the most instantly identified voice in America—to narrate *The Untouchables*, the then popular TV crime series about the tough cop Eliot Ness in Prohibition Chicago. Winchell's staccato delivery was perfect for the intermittent narration bits.

At the moment of recognition, Winchell grinned and seemed to visibly drop twenty years. To almost anyone not a victim of his past predations, it would be hard not to be moved by that moment, seeing the effect on the old fellow. Fame—though vastly reduced to a voice-over—had administered a craved injection.

Delighted, the former giant grabbed a pen and, eagerly and gratefully—although it had not been sought—signed an autograph.

DECEMBER 4, 2009

Almost Nothing About Tiger Woods

Wasn't it Francis Bacon who said, "He that hath wife and children hath given hostages to fortune"? (Sometimes misquoted as "hostages to fate," but it amounts to the same thing.)

So has the person who has acquired fame given hostages, and when trouble strikes, the famous may wish that fame, face—and even their suddenly burdensome name—could be dispensed with. At least temporarily, until the bad dream eventually fades.

(I'm pretty sure that it was on a show of mine that the great Mort Sahl said of a then presidential candidate, "I just read that years ago, Barry Goldwater changed his name from 'Goldvasser.' You have to admire a man who's not only Jewish but does something about it.")

Just now, the bearer of the initials T.W., appearing daily on tabloid front pages, might be as heartily sick of his name as I am. The bigger the name, the worse it is when trouble calls. O, to be John Doe when your self-inflicted calamity outs you as a bimbophile. I actually felt sorry a while back for "Senator Wide Stance" of unwanted men's room fame, and do now for relatives bearing the burden of the name "Madoff."

Some readers of an earlier column in this space on the subject of fame admitted they would be willing to risk the dangers inherent in being recognized everywhere. Think at least twice if a genie exits a bottle and offers to endow you with that near-relative of the Midas touch, vast visual recognition. (More commonly, "famous-faced.") It can be a bit of a Faustian bargain.

While still writing for Johnny Carson on *The Tonight Show* and while dropping that day's monologue jokes on his desk, I asked if he'd like to join me to go see something—in public—that I knew would interest him. Memory has swallowed whatever it was, but it doesn't matter. What I remember is his somewhat poignant answer, "I'd love to go there with you, Richard. But with this face?"

I felt for Dave Letterman when he so adroitly and directly dealt with his "trouble" in a way doubtless envied by so many other public figures who bungled similar situations with transparent denials and attempted cover-ups. (Do you enjoy it as much as I do when a moralistic figure of the religious right is caught with descended trousers?)

The un-famed, when caught in a *scandale publique*—and when the ensuing atmosphere at home is inevitably tense—can at least take a walk or go to a movie. But the owner of, say, the Letterman visage is denied seeking the heart's ease of a Central Park bench for respite and contemplation. He would risk incurring the index-finger-scraping "shame on you" childhood gesture of the censorious. Or the unwelcome "Right on" or "Way to go, man" of the passing yahoo.

When Robert Redford made the leap from being a reasonably well known television actor to an overnight megastar with *Butch Cassidy and the Sundance Kid*, he suffered mightily as international fame came down on him in its most extravagant form. Envious, of course (the bugger kept getting my movie parts), I once asked Bob if such a Niagara of fame wasn't a bit of an annoyance.

He didn't disappoint me.

"You can't imagine it," I remember Redford saying. "You work like hell to get yourself ahead in the business. You could go anywhere before, and suddenly you can't go anywhere. It's like being a cartoon character."

When Jack Benny first came on a show of mine, I suddenly blurted, "Isn't it a drag, Jack? Constant recognition?" To my surprise, he blurted back, "I like being famous!" A rare admission at any time.

He elaborated: "I go to a nightclub, I get a good table. I go to the theater, I get the best seats. At the country club, the steam room attendant gives me the best towel." Then came, delightfully, "And ya know, kid, what the best part is? People are generally glad to see me."

I declined to remind the great man of something I had witnessed years before when I was writing for Jack Paar. Mr. Benny, as I then called him, was on that night's Paar show, and when taping was over I made my habitual point of getting into the elevator with one of my heroes. So did a bunch of audience members. The son of Waukegan looked smart in his belted classic Burberry.

For what follows, younger readers will need help with the trademark Jack Benny references, so dear to the memory of those of a certain age.

First, someone asked "Do you still drive the Maxwell?" Then came "Are you really cheap?" This of course triggered "Do you really keep your money in that underground vault?" Before we reached the main floor there was time for several more, including the inevitable "Do you really not pay Rochester much?"

Realizing that he must have become numb to being asked these same questions for decades, you had to admire the gracious way he nodded and smiled. He was a very nice man.

When the doors opened, the civilians all rushed out to astonish their friends with reports of whom they had met and actually spoken with.

Jack put his arm around my shoulder and in that soft voice said, "Ya know, kid, sometimes ya jes' wanna tell 'em to go fuck themselves."

Oh, the wonder of it! And the innocence of it. It's a sweet story and only a misfit would find it dirty.

Hearing that voice, famous from childhood, that issued from our old two-minutes-to-warm-up Majestic radio, employ one of George Carlin's "Seven Words You Can Never Say on TV" (now you can, thanks to cable) was a rare experience. More so from him, because Benny, as comedians say, "worked clean." Cleaner, maybe, than any other giant comic. And he was smart enough to realize the shock value of a naughty word from the mouth of the former little Benny Kubelsky from Illinois.

How lucky I was to have been there. (I feel almost heroic being able to bring this gem to you, dear reader.)

What a treat!

DECEMBER 18, 2009

Why, I Oughta . . . and I Did

've never seen you lose your temper."

I've been told this, but it's not entirely accurate.

An inherited nasty temper has flared on the air only a few times, but much more frequently in "real life." So far I have managed to escape having my salient features rearranged. (A thing worth considering in this regard is how frequently friends and neighbors of those who commit hideous murders observe, "I never once saw him angry.")

One of those odd memory jogs that release a long-buried incident has happened.

The advent of the book *Cavett* in 1973 brought with it that mixed blessing known as the book tour. You go around the country flogging your tome on local book-chat shows, both radio and television, doing press interviews, and signing copies for fans in bookstores. Lucky authors get to do the late-night network shows. I got to do "Johnny."

Although the tour sells books, some authors are just not up to the ordeal and stay home. For those submitting to the thing, it's a chance for housebound authors to see some of their country. Downside-wise, you endure constant travel from town to town on plane after plane, endlessly answering the same questions. Like "Why did you write this book?"

And you get to learn a few things about publishers. Like the fact that all of them have mastered the trick of failing to get the books into the towns you visit and the bookstores where you were supposed to sign them.

One big store had received several hundred copies of Lawrence Welk's book instead of mine. I signed about fifty of them ("Dick Cavett, from Nebraska just like Lawrence") and left.

The experiences with local radio and TV hosts are often delightful, sometimes less so.

Even when you're doing it, it's hard to keep track of what town you're in due to jet lag, sleep deprivation, lousy and hasty food, and too much coffee, so after all this time I can't remember for sure where what's coming happened. Detroit? Minneapolis? Beaver Crossing, Nebraska? Take your pick.

Let's call my TV host, wherever it was, "Raymond." Adjusting to the varied personalities of the hosts was part of the limited fun. Usually.

Up to that point in the tour I had been treated, in the main, with adoration bordering on worship. I guess the fates decided to provide me with a little contrast.

Raymond sported an aggressively loud green plaid jacket and matching tie, not exactly in perfect tune with the hip threads of the seventies. Also thick glasses that magnified beady eyes and a wig that said "bargain basement." And possibly "Buy One, Get One Free."

Technically, Raymond's tonsorial deception was a hairpiece, delta-shaped, disconcertingly thick, and devoid of the merest hint of verisimilitude. I had to work to keep my eyes off it. It reminded me of an artifact from earlier times, when I trudged about Manhattan clutching the out-of-work actor's bible, *Casting News*. An ever-present ad went, as I recall, something like, "Balding? Get More Jobs With THE TAYLOR TOPPER."

Our studio session began fairly neutrally. Then Raymond shifted gears.

His technique seemed to be "soften 'em up awhile and then start with the slip punches." It became clear that the best compliment one could pay him would be "Hey, man, you're not afraid to play rough with the celebs!"

The softening period ended. Here is how I remember the darkening atmosphere as our time together proceeded.

"Why does it bother you so much that you're so short?"

I'm not *freakishly* short. I had, on my show, used shortness as a joke subject; it didn't really bother me. But somehow I was unable to say these things just then.

Then came—and he always began with "Why?"—"Why do you think going to Yale has made you smarter than other people?"

I didn't, but said so feebly. Accumulated fatigue had made me feel I'd been injected with some kind of weakening fluid. I felt uncharacteristically defenseless.

To make things worse, I could see a nice lady sitting nearby, looking at me with pity. And, curiously, she looked like my beloved Aunt Esther, thinking "Poor Dickie."

Don't most people, maybe especially men, hate to be seen as pitiable? I did, then, but seemed to have come without my gun belt. There was a kind of emasculation effect. I was getting the distinct feeling that I could have sung countertenor.

There are two ways to handle such situations. Either pummel back with your wits (but mine had fled) or remain nice to make him look awful. Sadly, that one—with much to recommend it—seems not to be part of my nature. And aggressive wit was unaccountably unavailable.

His next "Why?": "Why did someone on your staff say in the *Time* magazine cover story on you that you're a prima donna? Are you? Why would they say that?" I mumbled something.

"Why do you think you're as good as Carson? The ratings don't seem to think so."

Somehow, that functioned as the dromedary's back-breaking straw. I awoke.

"Raymond, is it? 'Why' seems to be your favorite word. May I do one?"

"Sure."

"Why do you wear a rug that looks like a wedge of blueberry pie sitting on top of your head?"

It's rare to hear, from inside a studio, laughter and cheering coming through the supposedly soundproof glass of the control room. Raymond heard it, too. "Aunt Esther" clapped. The mike boom man nearly fell to the floor. From how he looked at that point, Raymond's blood pressure had surely hit "perilous."

A kind of creamy, mirthless grin spread only partway across his mouth and he seemed to be struggling for air. I decided not to add, "Here's another 'why': Why don't you finish the show yourself?"

What I did say was, "I'm glad I was able to bring some pleasure to your coworkers," added "Good day," and headed for a nap.

I never learned how Raymond filled the remaining minutes. I would almost rather have a recording of this than just about anything I ever did on television. If you, out there somewhere, by some miracle, recorded it—and back then it would have been on reel-to-reel—let me know. I'll trade you something for it.

Oh, one other thing: your opinion. Should I feel guilty for what I did?

JANUARY 8, 2010

Awesome, and Then Some

(WARNING: *Good friends have refused to believe a word of what I'm about to relate. Your credulity is about to be strained.*)

The setting was the Universal lot in Hollywood, and I was preparing a prime-time special to be called *Dick Cavett's Backlot U.S.A.* We'd somehow lured Mae West out of her most recent retirement. We had Mickey Rooney and Gene Kelly. We needed another big-name guest.

Someone came in with a message and casually dropped the words, "The Duke is shooting over on the Western street."

I was fairly sure that by "Duke" he didn't mean Edward VIII. Before there was time to even think "Feets, do yo' stuff," I was all but out the door. My producer, the splendid Gary Smith, didn't need to ask where I was going. He just said, "Get him for the show."

"Sure thing," I said, laughing.

I hit the ground running. A man carrying a fake tree pointed the way. It felt like that heavy slogging one experiences in dreams. I knew I'd be too late. I got through a section of London, the New York street, the New England village . . . and there it was up ahead. The square of an old Western town. *The Shootist*, which proved to be John Wayne's final movie, was being filmed.

Somehow—although it seemed I had met all my heroes and non-heroes in the biz—I had always been certain, deep down, that I was destined not to meet John Wayne. It was just not in the scheme of things.

If the word "icon"—used daily now for just about everybody, even me—ever applied in its fullest force to anyone, it was to the man embarrassed as a kid by his real name, Marion Mitchell Morrison.

How could I ever hope to find myself standing beside the star of *Sands of Iwo Jima*, seen five times by Jimmy McConnell and me in our Nebraska youth? (Later, we'd "play" his Westerns, taking turns being the Duke, our bikes standing in for horses.)

How could I expect to meet the "Ringo Kid" from *Stagecoach*? Or the man in another one of those great Monument Valley John Ford classics (*She Wore a Yellow Ribbon*), riding toward the camera, the cavalry column behind him, the storm overhead. Surely this mythic figure could not occupy the space right next to you.

And yet there he was.

The gods had smiled and arranged for my first glimpse of him to be the ideal one. Mounted and in full cowboy drag: the chaps, the boots and spurs, the neckerchief, and the well-worn Stetson atop the handsome head. He was waiting for the scene to begin.

I moved, or rather was moved, toward him. He saw me gazing upward.

"Well," he said—in John Wayne's voice!—"It sure is good ta meet ya."

I reached up to shake the mounted man's proffered hand. It enveloped mine like a baseball glove.

He was instantly likable and, although it seems almost the wrong word for such a fellow, charming. We chatted for several minutes until shooting resumed. I watched him ride off for the next shot. I figured that was it. I was satisfied.

Meanwhile, I had forgotten about the special, and I started to leave. I couldn't wait to phone Jimmy McConnell.

Suddenly, the Duke—preceded by his shadow—came up behind me, on foot now. As with the Great Pyramid at Giza, nothing prepared you for his size. (And there was a rumor that he wore lifts in his boots. I was not about to ask.)

"I'd enjoy talking to ya but I've got a scene to shoot with Betty Bacall," he said. "D'you want to watch?"

The answer came easily. And my new friend led me inside to the set.

It was the old West, and the scene was in the kitchen of the house belonging to Lauren Bacall's character. She was about to serve him a meal.

"Ya wanna run your lines, Duke?" asked an assistant.

"No thanks, I know 'em. Most of 'em, anyway." (Crew laughs.)

I was a few feet from him, in the shadows. They were still setting up and Duke was humming to himself, and—I guess unconsciously recognizing the tune—I began to hum along. He spotted me and chuckled. And the following dialogue took place. On my solemn word. (I went straight home and wrote it all down before it faded.)

WAYNE: Wasn't he great?

ME: Who?

WAYNE: Coward.

ME (*startled, realizing now that the tune was Noël Coward's "Someday I'll Find You"*): Yes.

WAYNE: I've always loved his stuff. Remember the scene in *Private Lives* when they realize they still love each other?

ME: Yes, and did you know there's a recording of Coward and Gertrude Lawrence doing that scene?

WAYNE: Gee, I gotta get that. I guess I've read most of his plays.

ME (*still not convinced there isn't a ventriloquist in the room*): I'll send you the record.

WAYNE: Well, thank ya. I like the line (*he switched to quite passable upper-class British*) "You're looking very lovely, you know, in this damned moonlight."

ME: I did a show with Coward and, as he introduced them, "My dearest friends, Alfred Lunt and Lynn Fontanne."

WAYNE: I sure would love to have seen them in *Design for Living*. (*Mentally I reach again for the smelling salts.*) And, damn, I'd love to see that show of yours.

ME: I'll see that you do. (*Jesus! Did I? Oh, I hope so.*)

WAYNE: That'd be awful nice of ya.

ME: Did you ever think of doing one of his plays?

WAYNE: Yeah, but it never got past the thought stage. I guess they figured that maybe spurs and *Blithe Spirit* wouldn't go together. Can't you see the critics? "Wayne should go back to killing Indians, not Noël Coward."

As I looked around for someone to pinch me, the mood was shattered by a sharp, barking voice: "Okay, people. Places for forty-three."

It required the common sense of Woody Allen to put the whole thing into perspective. When I burbled the story to him, he seemed disappointingly unastonished.

"It reminds you that he's an actor," he said. "Not a cowboy."

JANUARY 22, 2010

Oh, What a Lovely Mess!

You may be among the e-mailers who have written, in effect, "Let us hear what Dick has to say about this. He's in a unique position to comment on it."

The "it," of course, being NBC's Hindenburg disaster. (Throughout the bloodbath, I kept hearing a voice crying "Oh, the humanity!")

The "unique position": my having been one of that handful fingered by the fates to experience the joys and horrors of hosting a five-times-a-week late-night talk show.

Hoping that those who have requested my views on this are not the only few people left in America who can bear to hear another word on the subject of what happened to the curious triumvirate of Jay/Conan/Dave, I'll try.

I thought it was a dumb idea from the git-go.

I can't think of another example of what happened to Jay. Of a star's being told that a time is coming when we aren't going to need you and your profitable and successful show. In five years.

In a medium where careers come and go in but a few years, this might seem generous. But the psychology of it! Not to mention the insensitivity.

Granted that network biggies rarely have an inkling of the psyche of the performer, but this broke some kind of record for dunce-cap thinking.

Allegedly, a major factor in all this is what I think of as the Myth of the Young Viewers. That precious chunk of the population that advertisers are said to salivate over.

Just for fun, take a moment and ask yourself how the ratings services can claim to know the age makeup of a mass audience. Do they send out squads of window-peekers to see if it's Grandma or Junior sitting before the set watching Dave, Conan, Jay, Ellen, Craig, Jimmy, and Jimmy? Or to see what percentage watch while using yo-yos vs. ear trumpets? Who is twittering and who is tatting? (Perhaps someone in on the secret formula will share it with me?)

And isn't there something a little dubious about the notion that the young are the ones with all the money? Someone please enlighten me.

This whole mess was like an election where everybody lost.

And how about that cynical get-lost offer they made to Conan? It didn't require his Harvard degree to perceive that what they dangled before him—a show starting at 12:05 A.M.—past midnight—couldn't with much accuracy be called *The Tonight Show*. *The Next Day Show* maybe, or *The Tomorrow Show*, or *The Really, Really Early Show*—but hardly *Tonight*.

Appearing by remote from New York on Larry King's show at the height of the confusion, shock, and turmoil, I claimed to be able to see NBC's building from the studio window: "They've hung out a banner, Larry, that says 'Mission Accomplished.'" The joke worked again on Imus. (And, I hope, here.)

Despite what everybody seems to have concluded, there is one thing this sorry episode did not prove: that talk can't work in prime time. Merv Griffin throve for years midevening with his syndicated chat show. And before Merv's show, way back in time, someone at ABC had the not entirely indefensible idea of seeing whether talk could work on a major network in prime time. They decided to launch the experiment: a talk show "across the board" (Monday through Friday) in prime time. "Let's put Cavett on for an hour, prime, and see where we come out." And they did. In the summer.

It did okay. It might have done even better if, in one of those baffling examples of net-think, they hadn't shed some of their nerve. Apparently someone decided, just in case it doesn't work, let's only be embarrassed three nights a week instead of five. So the experiment was compromised going in.

It might take you a week to imagine what else they did. They did put it on three nights a week, but guess what? On nonconsecutive nights. Like Monday, Thursday, and Friday. (Or was it Monday, Tuesday, and Thursday? They're even hard to say, let alone remember.)

Groucho came on and did a great show, remarking, "I love watching you this summer, but you need a secretary to know when the show is on."

It was touching in a way to see how common was the reaction to NBC's crass behavior, as in letters to editors asking, "Don't people keep their word anymore?"

There are but two explanations: *money* and *greed*. But it's sweet to think that there are nice people out there who would expect those two magic words to take second place in the television industry to that old-fashioned value, keeping your word. (Pardon my muffled laugh.)

It can't be much fun to be the one, or ones, to have designed a catastrophe that TV's annals may record as NBC's *Titanic*. Considering the wholesale damage done to Leno, O'Brien, and the network's image, it really should win some sort of prize. Knowing how such things traditionally go, I'd say it can't be more than a matter of days or weeks before those responsible for the thing are given hefty raises and promoted.

My favorite irony is the fact that all of this was about keeping the threat of David Letterman at bay. Dave's having been a once treasured NBC employee (and then "screwee") spices the irony. NBC's clearest unarguable accomplishment in this *Believe It or Not* specimen of ineptitude? A whopping increase in Dave's ratings, making him an even more formidable enemy. A shining lesson in strengthening the opposition.

And they've put their returning *Tonight* man in the awkward position of perhaps, with the network's assistance, failing to equal his former standing.

So much damage in one fell swoop. A kind of unwanted home run with the bases loaded.

Or with *somebody* loaded.

FEBRUARY 5, 2010

More Awesomeness, or
John Wayne, Part 2

I've been reminded that, in my earlier column on what to me were three glorious days spent in the company of John Wayne, I said that there is more to the story. Here's what I meant.

I hurried through all my duties in shooting my special to hang with my new friend as much as possible. Just at this moment of typing I've identified the feeling I was having then. It was as if a seventh grader (me) had been befriended by the popular, big, tall, jock upperclassman. And wished everyone could see us together, maybe with his hand on my shoulder.

(Did anyone just reach for an airsick bag?)

The picture *The Shootist* was his last. There is debate still about whether Wayne knew at the time that he—like the legendary gunfighter he was playing—was dying of cancer. Most agree that he did.

Here was a greatly talented, highly intelligent, college-educated, well-read man of immense personal charm and humor. I think we can agree that he knew.

There's a rough-going scene in which he asks Jimmy Stewart, playing his doctor, not to spare him the details of what will happen as the disease progresses. It's fascinating, if true as some say that he had not been able to do this in life but—by requesting that the script be sharpened in detail on this point—chose this route to the information.

If I had to pick ten highlights of my life, one would be my arrival on the set at almost the instant this scene was shot in the doctor's office. The crew knew their longtime friend was not well. There seemed to be more people than usual standing around watching. When Stewart delivered the line with the dread word in it—the one even doctors will euphemise, as in "ca. of the breast"—a burly stagehand-type near me had to quickly cover his mouth, apparently fearing that the sort of tearful, involuntary snort he emitted might have been picked up by a mike, spoiling the take. Similar moments on the part of crew members could be seen all around.

A second consequence of my time on the set with John Wayne: It's early afternoon on the Western town square set. Costumed extras relaxing, smoking, gossiping, strolling, reading trade papers, Wayne off somewhere resting, napping, or playing chess during a long break. (I can eyewitness report this: during breaks he shed his boots and slipped into a chartreuse pair of those fluffy marabou slippers more associated with women. Ludicrosity rampant. Probably a custom-made joke gift from a colleague. Or taken off a very large lady.)

A lone horse was at the hitching post. A huge horse. I had a sudden semi-rational urge. "Is that Dollar?" I asked. And I got onto John Wayne's horse. When I sat on Dollar, his back was so broad that my painfully separated legs stuck out closer to horizontal than to the customary vertical. It felt like trying to straddle a card table.

By the time Dollar's spine-punishing trot had escalated into something more hazardous, then de-accelerated from there, and I was returned, trembling, to terra firma, there'd been a great deal of yelling from the crew and scattering of sun-bonneted extras (one clarion voice sounded above the rest: "Who the——is that on Duke's horse?") and I was in a position to state for the record that an eternity lasts about forty-five seconds.

I had one more glorious day with Wayne. He had agreed to appear on my special, and as I sat beside him—he in full costume—on a buckboard, with me holding the reins, in one hand, he said, "Are we rollin'?" At "Yes," he took my hand mike and said into it, "Hi, this is John Wayne interviewing Dick Cavett." (Don't let me awaken, I thought.)

When we finished, the sun was up and the sky still bright, but it had gotten to the time in the afternoon when the light changes undesirably for color film. I asked if they had finished shooting for the day.

"Yeah, it's gettin' a little yella," he replied. (I won't force the symbolic poignancy of those words.)

When we parted, I told him as best I could what a good time we had had together and what it meant to me. I said I felt kind of foolish, asking for an autographed photo.

"That shouldn't be any trouble," he said.

He called for one, wrote on it, and without showing it to me put it in an envelope.

We talked for a while more, mostly about the current prices of Indian artifacts, which I had seen swoop suddenly upward. I asked him if he owned the beautiful beaded and long-fringed plains rifle case—probably Sioux or Cheyenne—that he had carried in John Ford's *The Searchers*.

"I wish you hadn't said that," he said, grinning. "I bet I've thought about it a hundred times. I can't watch the picture because of it. I tried later to find it, but somebody smarter than I am must've gotten it."

"Didn't it occur to you, maybe on the last day, to just slip it into your duffel bag?"

"It does now." (Laughter.)

Having said good-bye and still aglow, while driving on the freeway, I remembered the picture. Pulling over like a responsible citizen, I slipped it out of the envelope, hoping there might be more than just the traditional "Best wishes" and a signature.

It read: "To Dick Cavett from John Wayne."

This, of course, was enough. But below it there was another line.

"We should have started sooner."

You bet I cried.

APRIL 9, 2010

Acknowledgments

Several people deserve thanks:

George Kalogerakis, my faithful *New York Times* editor, for sharpening my copy and curbing my excesses.

Paul Golob, my astute editor at the Times Books imprint of Henry Holt and Company, who uncomplainingly treats me with undeserved patience.

Judy Englander, who, among other vital things, arranged the lunch that got this whole thing started.

And, at that lunch, Alex Ward at the *Times*, without whose promotional skills you might be holding some other book right now.

A blanket thank-you to the Henry Holt and Company employees, each of whom deserves a raise.

Kate Griffiths, for facilitating countless matters.

Emily DeHuff, copy editor *par excellence*, who misses not a comma.

Martha Rogers (the mysterious "M."), for aid beyond description.

(Sorry if I've made serious omissions. Maybe we can get you into the paperback.)

Index

About the Author

DICK CAVETT was the host of *The Dick Cavett Show*, which aired on ABC from 1968 to 1975 and on PBS from 1977 to 1982. He also hosted talk shows on the USA, HBO, and CNBC cable networks. He is the coauthor of *Cavett* and *Eye on Cavett*, and since 2007 he has written an online opinion column for *The New York Times*. He lives in New York City and Montauk, New York.